Unlocking the Scriptures for You

ACTS

John W. Wade

**STANDARD
BIBLE STUDIES**

STANDARD PUBLISHING
Cincinnati, Ohio   11-40105

I would be ungrateful if I did not express appreciation for a few of those whose contributions of one kind or another have made this book possible. I thank the editors of the Standard Publishing Company who planned the series and invited me to share in it. I am also indebted to a number of teachers and writers who have left their marks on my mind. I must also acknowledge my dependence upon my wife, Barbara, who caught my grammatical errors and made sense out of my garbled syntax.

Unless otherwise noted, all Scripture quotations are from the *Holy Bible: New International Version,* ©1973, 1978, 1984 by the International Bible Society. Used by permission of Zondervan Bible Publishers and the International Bible Society.

Sharing the thoughts of his own heart, the author may express views not entirely consistent with those of the publisher.

Second Printing, 1991

Library of Congress Cataloging in Publication Data:

Wade, John William, 1924-
  Acts.

  (Standard Bible studies)
  1. Bible.   N.T. Acts—Commentaries.   I. Title.
II. Series.
BS2625.3.W33 1987   226'.607   86-30152
ISBN 0-87403-165-6

CONTENTS

Preface 7
Introduction 9
Chapter 1: Beginning in Jerusalem 13
Chapter 2: When Pentecost Came 21
Chapter 3: A Lame Man Leaps 35
Chapter 4: In Trouble With the Establishment 43
Chapter 5: Trouble Inside and Outside the Church 53
Chapter 6: A Deacon Becomes a Preacher 63
Chapter 7: The First Christian Martyr 69
Chapter 8: Persecution Leads to Evangelism 79
Chapter 9: A Persecutor Becomes a Christian 89
Chapter 10: A Gentile Becomes a Christian 103
Chapter 11: Meeting Problems in a Growing Church 113
Chapter 12: The Church Faces New Threats 123
Chapter 13: A Great Missionary Effort Begun 131
Chapter 14: A Successful Missionary Journey Completed... 145
Chapter 15: The Jerusalem Conference 155
Chapter 16: Paul's Second Missionary Journey 165
Chapter 17: Through Macedonia and Into Greece 177
Chapter 18: Completing the Second Missionary Journey ... 189
Chapter 19: Paul's Ministry in Ephesus 199
Chapter 20: The Third Missionary Journey 209
Chapter 21: Jerusalem at Last 221
Chapter 22: Paul's Defense Before the Temple Mob 231
Chapter 23: In Jeopardy in Jerusalem 237
Chapter 24: On Trial in Caesarea 247
Chapter 25: On Trial Before Festus 257
Chapter 26: Paul's Defense Before Agrippa 261
Chapter 27: Heading for Rome 269
Chapter 28: Rome at Last 279

Maps

Temple Area 40
First Missionary Journey 144
Second Missionary Journey 176
Third Missionary Journey 210
Journey to Rome 278

PREFACE

On the shelves of my study are perhaps two dozen or more commentaries and Bible studies on the book of Acts. Some of them are quite scholarly—the five-volume work Foakes-Jackson and Lake, for example. Others are written on a very popular level, Barclay's volume in "The Daily Study Bible Series" being a good example of this approach. Some of them have been around for a long time. Barnes' Notes on Acts was first published nearly 150 years ago. Although it is obviously dated in places, it still stands as a monument to solid, common-sense exegesis. Many of us were brought up on J. W. McGarvey's Commentary, now over a century old but still valuable.

With all of these studies available, one is inclined to ask, "Why another one?" One might answer that archaeology and linguistics have brought new light to bear on the text, giving new insights to certain passages. But the truth is that these advances are relatively few in number and do little to affect our total understanding of the book.

We might offer, as another reason, the fact that in scholarly circles in recent years there has been a renewed interest in the beginnings and early years of the church. This may be a new intellectual pursuit for some, but a few groups have always emphasized the importance of going back to the roots of the church to find true doctrine and examples of how that true doctrine impacted the lives of those who believed it. Many commentaries on Acts have been written with the explicit purpose of finding the church of the New Testament in order to restore it in this age; so we cannot claim that this Bible study is unique in meeting this new need, nor that this need has only recently arisen.

This series has been described as a set of devotional commentaries. The term *devotional* has several different meanings. We sometimes understand a devotion to mean a short talk designed to bring exhortation, encouragement, or direction for Christian living to its hearers. We would not be disappointed if some readers did use this study to prepare devotional talks.

The word *devotion* also leads us to think of that substantial body of literature that has accumulated over nearly two thousand years of the history of the church. In his *Confessions,* Augustine shares with his readers his struggle against sin. Thomas a'Kempis stirs our emotions and challenges our wills in his *On the Imitation of Christ.* In his sweeping allegory, *Pilgrim's Progress,* John Bunyan sketches on a broad canvas the struggles of every Christian pilgrim. If this volume could, even in a very small way, do what these great classics of Christian devotion have done, we would be amply repaid for our efforts.

When we think of devotions, we also think of personal or family devotions. Many persons find spiritual strength in reading a passage of Scripture, discussing it or meditating about it, and then praying. The editors certainly had this use in mind when they planned this series of Bible studies. Such devotions should arouse emotions and lead to a deeper sense of commitment. To do this, a Bible study must provide intellectual as well as emotional stimulation. A good Bible study should stir one's imagination, cause one to raise questions, provide some keys to lock important passages in one's memory, and suggest application of the Scriptures to contemporary situations.

We have tried to design this study to do these things. We have deliberately sought to avoid the novel or unusual just for the sake of novelty. Nor have we resorted to tricks or gimmicks to gain or hold attention. Instead we have sought to present straightforward, common-sense interpretations of each chapter.

In some cases, the chapter and verse divisions as we have them in our English translations have been artificially imposed upon the text and do not coincide with the thought patterns. However, to avoid confusion, we have chosen to follow the chapters as they stand.

We pray that this volume, as well as others in the series, will lead the reader to a better understanding of the Word of God and to a more faithful commitment to our Lord.

John W. Wade
Atlanta, Georgia

INTRODUCTION

The book we usually refer to as Acts or Acts of the Apostles is unique in the New Testament. It does not deal with the life of Christ, and thus it is not one of the Gospels. And even though it was written to a certain Theophilus, it bears little resemblance to the writings we know as letters or epistles. Nor does it contain the prophetic and apocalyptic elements found in Revelation.

We sometimes refer to it as a book of early church history. This is not a bad designation if we understand that it is a highly selective history of a few of the events that occurred in the early years of the church. In fact, it is about the only information we have concerning the growth and spread of the first-century church. We might be able to piece together a sketchy framework of the early church from the epistles, but it would be only a framework with many gaps in it. One can scarcely overestimate the importance of Acts in helping us find the roots of the first-century church.

The Author

The author of Acts does not identify himself, perhaps out of a sense of modesty. However, we can conclude without any serious reservations that the author was Luke. The best evidence for this is the so-called "we" passages (Acts 16:10-17; 20:5-16; 21:1-18; 27:1—28:16) in which the author was an eyewitness to the events he recorded. By correlating these passages with Paul's letters in which he mentions some of his companions, the logical conclusion is that Luke is the author.

It is generally agreed that the third Gospel and the book of Acts flow from the pen of the same person. The writer of the third Gospel, when describing illnesses, often uses medical terms that are more precise than do the other three Gospel writers. When we add to this Paul's reference to Luke as the "beloved physician"

(Col... —he Gospel
that ...

The ... ts is quite
stron... book to
Luke. ... we can
safely ...

But ... Acts, we
know ... ed Paul
on som... Paul in
his epis... y 4:11).
Some b... ho had
become ... rother
of Titus ... ust be
recogniz... t them.

Some s... putting
it in the s... ity of the
book of A... ology of
the book ...

Certain ... s for dat-
ing events ... Agrippa I
(Acts 12:2... in Cyprus
(Acts 13:4-... 7), and the
procurators ... 4, 25).

We thus ... isonment in
Caesarea a... nment there
places the be... .D. 60 or 61.
The abrupt ... us to believe that Luke had
nothing further to write. In other words, Luke wrote Acts after
Paul had been in prison (actually, under house arrest) in Rome for
two years but before he had been released. This brings us to a date
of A.D. 62 or 63 for the writing of the book.

Purpose

In his introduction, Luke addresses Acts to Theophilus.
Theophilus may have been a government official or a pagan to
whom Luke was trying to present the gospel. Or he may have been
a convert who wanted to know more about his new faith. In any
event, these two volumes—Luke and Acts—would certainly serve
such a purpose.

10

Whatever Luke's immediate motive for writing may have been, the Holy Spirit has used his efforts to give us a trustworthy record of what one must do to be saved and the results that followed when men and women pursued this plan of salvation.

Acts provides us a history of the beginnings and growth of the church. Admittedly, it is a very selective history. Luke made no effort to chronicle everything that had happened in the three decades from Pentecost to the time he wrote. Guided by the Holy Spirit, he selected those details that typified both the troubles and the triumphs of the church.

Several things become obvious as the Acts narrative unfolds. First, Christianity did not at first break decisively with Judaism. Both Peter and Paul stressed the fact that Christianity was the fulfillment of numerous Old Testament prophecies. Although most Jews never accepted this view, Paul continued to present it even during the early days of his Roman imprisonment.

We also learn from Acts that the gospel is for all races and all nations. Jesus had made this abundantly clear in the Great Commission (Matthew 28:18-20), but God needed to intervene miraculously in order to convince Peter (Acts 10:9-18, 34). And Peter had his troubles convincing others (Acts 11:1-18). But that should not shock us, for even after two thousand years, many of us still retain some feelings (often subtly disguised, to be sure) that somehow Christianity ought to be reserved for our tribe or our class.

In recounting the early history of the church, Luke tells it as it is, giving us an accurate portrait of the church, "warts and all." In so doing, we learn how the church faced and solved problems. It met persecution, fraud within the church, racism, and narrow legalism. From the example set by the early church, we can learn how to meet similar problems in our own day.

The book of Acts serves one other important purpose: it encourages us. On Pentecost, twelve men took on the Jewish religious establishment and eventually the entire Roman Empire. Against such overwhelming odds, the chances for their success seemed ridiculous. Yet buoyed by the Holy Spirit, the apostles seemed completely oblivious to the possibility of defeat. Indeed, in the whole book of Acts, there is not a single note of despair. Even in the most threatening circumstances, we see optimism— even rejoicing. If our study of Acts infects us with some of that optimism, perhaps the church of the twentieth century will grow as did the church of the first century.

11

CHAPTER ONE

Beginning in Jerusalem

Acts 1

Introduction (1:1-3)

The Addressee (1)

Who was this Theophilus (whose name means "beloved of God" or "friend of God")? Some have suggested that he was an important government official whom Luke was attempting to impress with the claims of the gospel. Others suppose that he was a prominent Christian being tutored by Luke. We can only guess about his identity—whether he was Jew or Gentile, where he lived, and whether or not he was a believer. But we can be thankful for him, for his existence was the occasion for two important books of the New Testament.

Summary of Jesus' Ministry (2, 3)

In two brief verses, Luke summarized his first letter to Theophilus (the Gospel of Luke). Jesus' ministry was two-fold—action and teaching. Christians today should ponder this. Action must be preceded by teaching or the action might be inadequate or inappropriate. On the other hand, teaching that does not lead to action is sterile. "Faith without deeds is dead" (James 2:26).

Some scholars call attention to the word *began*. They suggest that He began His ministry in His earthly life, and that He continues His ministry from Heaven today through the church.

In his Gospel, Luke had already mentioned the resurrection, setting forth several appearances of Jesus (Luke 24:13-49). Here he reiterates the resurrection—and for good reason. If Jesus had not come forth from the tomb alive, the writing of the book of Acts would have been an exercise in futility. Christianity would be a religion based on "cleverly invented stories" (2 Peter 1:16), not one firmly grounded in history.

The proofs were "convincing," but convincing to whom? Obviously not to everyone, for many continued to reject Him. The proofs were convincing to those who approached the evidence with an open mind, but no amount of evidence is likely to bring conviction to one who is determined not to believe. We need to keep this knowledge ever before us as we witness to unbelievers.

Jesus' Final Meeting with the Apostles (1:4-11)

The Final Instructions (4, 5)

During the forty-day period following His resurrection, Jesus taught about the "kingdom of God," or the rule of God on earth. This period, brief though it was, gave Jesus an opportunity to review with the apostles His teachings of the past three years.

Jesus' ministry after His resurrection followed a definite timetable, just as it had before. Jesus resisted every pressure to run ahead of that schedule. For this reason, the apostles were told to wait in Jerusalem for a special gift from the Father. The intense excitement of those days must have made waiting a real test of their patience. Modern Christians need also to cultivate patience, learning to be still and know that He is God (Psalm 46:10).

The promised gift was a special outpouring of the Holy Spirit. John had spoken of this as he prepared his listeners for the coming of Jesus: "I baptize you with water, but he will baptize you with the Holy Spirit" (Mark 1:8). The word *baptize* means to immerse, and John immersed his disciples in the Jordan River. When used in relation to the giving of the Holy Spirit, the word has a figurative meaning, indicating that the apostles would be totally immersed in the Spirit.

This special outpouring of the Holy Spirit was promised only to the apostles. It is not to be confused with the gift of the Holy Spirit, which is promised to all believers when they are baptized (Acts 2:38).

The Final Questions Concerning the Kingdom (6-8)

During His ministry, Jesus had frequently referred to the kingdom, often describing its nature through parables. Yet in using this expression, our Lord labored under one serious disadvantage. Any reference to the kingdom immediately conjured up in the minds of patriotic Jews a vision of an earthly kingdom such as the Jews had enjoyed in the days of David and Solomon. In this vision, the Jews would throw off the hated yoke of foreign oppressors and once more become independent and powerful.

The three years the apostles had studied under Jesus looked forward to the time He would leave them. Now that moment was at hand, and the apostles were taking their final examination before their commencement. They took the test and failed miserably. They completely misunderstood the nature of the kingdom that Jesus had been preparing them to lead. But we need to look carefully at our own lives and our own failures before we become too critical about their failure. Our cultural biases are just as likely to blind us to the real nature of His kingdom as did theirs.

We can't help wondering how Jesus must have felt. In spite of all His efforts, the apostles had failed to grasp the central meaning of the kingdom. Any teacher who has ever given a final examination has some basis for understanding how our Lord must have felt. Yet with infinite patience, He continued to teach them.

Jesus quickly made it clear to them that their question revealed their misunderstanding of the kingdom. What God had planned for Israel and the kingdom was really none of their business. Their mission at the moment, the evangelization of the world, was more important than anything else. They had best get on with that mission rather than concern themselves with matters that really belonged to God. We today would do well to follow Jesus' advice. Rather than get ourselves involved in idle speculation about the time and conditions of His return, we should give ourselves to the great unfinished task, the evangelization of the world.

Jesus then assured them that they would not face this task alone. Through the Holy Spirit, they would receive power that would enable them to face this momentous mission. That mission was to carry the gospel to the "ends of the earth" (Acts 1:8).

We can't help wondering how the apostles perceived their mission. Being witnesses in Jerusalem and Judea would not have posed a problem. But Samaria? Perhaps in their excitement they never even heard Him mention Samaria. Or perhaps they interpreted His remarks so that they saw that their job was to take the gospel only to the few Jews who might have been living in Samaria. Even though Jesus had carried on a limited ministry in Samaria, it is not likely that these few contacts completely removed their long-standing prejudices. Our own struggles with prejudices should help us realize that deep-seated attitudes do not change overnight.

Jesus had stated this "Great Commission" to the apostles on other occasions. It is not likely that on any of these occasions did they fully grasp the magnitude of their marching orders. For them, a scant dozen Galileans, unlearned and inexperienced in the larger world beyond their limited little sphere, this had to be a "mission impossible." For them to have heard Jesus' words and not to have been panicked by them clearly indicates that they didn't understand them or that they possessed an unbelievable self-confidence.

The Final Farewell (9-11)

Perhaps the reason the apostles didn't ask questions about Jesus' commission or raise a hundred objections to it was that He immediately left them. We are told that even as they watched, He was taken up and a cloud hid Him from them. Some have problems with such a dramatic and miraculous departure. But if Jesus' entrance into this world in a physical body required a miracle, why should it trouble us that His departure required a miracle?

Theologically, it also seems that Jesus' return to Heaven should require a miracle. The Scriptures tell us that "flesh and blood cannot inherit the kingdom of God" (1 Corinthians 15:50). Thus we conclude that Jesus' physical body, in some fashion and at some point in the ascension, underwent a transformation.

The apostles continued to stare into the sky. Perhaps they thought that the cloud might evaporate and once more they would be able to see Jesus. But instead, they saw two men in white (Acts 1:10). Most take these to be angels. Their message served to shatter the apostles' trance-like gaze and bring them back to reality. Any temptation they may have had to linger there and engage in speculation about what had happened to the Lord was dispelled by the angels' words. The apostles were not to stay on the Mount of Olives but were to go back into Jerusalem and wait. They were assured that Jesus would return. Armed with this kind of assurance, they could prepare themselves for their missionary task.

Our Lord has not yet returned; so we too still await the fulfillment of this promise. Because Jesus is coming back, we ought also to await His return with the same enthusiasm.

Waiting in Jerusalem (1:12-26)

Waiting is never easy. Many of us can remember the growing anticipation we had as we waited for Christmas or the last day of school. It seemed as if the anticipated day would never come. But how much more difficult to wait for something that is unknown and whose time of arrival is also unknown. That is what the apostles faced.

We can imagine the animated conversation that must have taken place as these men made their way back to Jerusalem, which was a Sabbath day's journey (about five-eighths of a mile).

The Apostles Named (12, 13)

We are told that they returned to the upper room, which we assume was the same room where they had eaten the Last Supper. Luke then gives us a list of the Eleven. This is the last time that the apostles are named as a group. In fact, it is the last time that most of the apostles are named in the Scriptures. They are mentioned as a group in Acts 2. Then, in a few of the early chapters, we are told about the activities of Peter and John. Chapter 12 tells of Herod's having James, the brother of John, beheaded. Beginning with chapter 9, the message of the book of Acts shifts to the apostle Paul and those who worked with him.

In the early centuries, stories arose about where the other apostles labored and where they died. For example, according to some accounts, Thomas made his way to India, where he proclaimed the gospel and was eventually martyred. One group of Christians in India today claims to be spiritual descendants of Thomas' efforts there. Matthew is said to have carried the gospel to the Ethiopians, Macedonians, Parthians, and Medes. Some accounts have Philip laboring and being martyred in Phrygia.

While none of these accounts is based on solid historical evidence, we can understand the mentality of those circulating these stories. To them, it seemed entirely reasonable that those who had been so close to Christ would go to distant parts of the known world to carry out His marching orders to them.

Constantly in Prayer (13, 14)

All of us have found ourselves in situations in which we felt helpless. What can one do when he can't do anything? He can always pray! And that is exactly what the apostles did when they returned to Jerusalem to await the power from on high.

We are told that they prayed with "one accord" (King James Version), or literally, "with one mind." Whatever may have divided the apostles in the past had been resolved. The exciting

17

events of the past few weeks had made their differences seem petty indeed. Because they were united in their prayers, their prayers were effective.

Joining the apostles were three groups or individuals: "the women," "Mary the mother of Jesus," and "his brothers" (Acts 1:14). The women were probably the ones who had stood by Jesus faithfully throughout His ministry, even through the horrors of the cross—Mary Magdalene, Joanna, Mary the mother of James, Susanna, and others (Luke 8:2, 3; 23:49, 55; 24:10).

Mary the mother of Jesus was there. This is the last time she is mentioned in the Scriptures. It is obvious that the dogmas that later grew up around her have no basis in fact. Yet even as we reject these dogmas, let us take care that we not denigrate her. She was the noblest woman in the world, else God would not have chosen her to bear His Son.

Jesus' brothers also joined in the prayer meeting in the upper room. Previously these men—James, Joses, Judas, and Simon—had not been believers (John 7:5). But the resurrection had changed their minds. James later became a leader in the church at Jerusalem and the author of the book of James. Judas later wrote the brief epistle of Jude.

The Fate of the Traitor (1:15-19)

The Scriptures Fulfilled (15-17)

At some point in the ten-day period between the ascension and Pentecost, Peter took the lead in choosing a replacement for Judas. The group addressed by Peter now numbered 120, leading some to suggest that the upper room would have hardly been large enough to accommodate the group.

Peter addressed the believers as "brothers" (Acts 1:16), the first time the Scriptures mention this term to designate followers of Christ. It later became and still remains an appropriate term for Christians. Peter, who had often been a spokesman for the apostles, once more took the lead, this time indicating that he spoke with authority, basing his remarks on the Old Testament (possibly Psalm 41:9).

The Consequence of Judas' Sin (18, 19)

At this point, Luke, for the benefit of his Gentile readers, inserted information about the death of Judas. Luke supplies information not provided by Matthew 27:5-10. There is no discrepancy between the two accounts. Apparently Judas hanged himself. Then the rope broke, allowing his body to fall to the earth. Putrefaction had already set in, causing the body to burst open in a horrible fashion.

Judas, according to Peter, was "one of our number" and "shared in his ministry" (Acts 1:17). In other words, he had received an appointment to the high office of apostleship with all of the privileges and blessings that it conveyed. Yet for reasons that we find difficult to understand, he threw it all away for a paltry thirty pieces of silver. Still, are his actions all that difficult to understand? Have we not on occasion been guilty of betraying our Lord—and often for considerably less than thirty pieces of silver? The Gospel accounts make it evident that Judas' actions were not the result of some spur-of-the-moment whim, but the result of a steady deterioration of character. His fate stands as a solemn warning to all of us that every day we need to take heed lest we also fall (1 Corinthians 10:12). His tragic end came after spending three years with Jesus, which reminds us that a good environment will not insure sainthood. We certainly should provide the most spiritual surroundings we can in our homes and churches; yet we must recognize that some, for reasons we don't understand, only become worse under the best of conditions.

A Replacement for Judas (1:20-26)

After giving the report of Judas' tragic end, Luke turns again to Peter's speech. Peter quoted first from Psalm 69:25 and then from Psalm 109:8, although his quotations do not literally follow either the Hebrew or Septuagint versions. The number *twelve* had symbolic significance among the Hebrews, and this significance apparently carried over into the Christian era. For this reason, it was necessary to replace Judas.

His Qualifications (20-22)

Peter set forth two qualifications. Judas' successor must have been a follower of Jesus during His entire ministry, beginning with His baptism by John. The second qualification was that he should have seen the resurrected Christ so that he could be a witness of this event. We know that there were disciples of Jesus who are not named in the Gospel accounts. The seventy-two immediately come to mind (Luke 10:1, 17). There may have been others. Witnesses to Jesus' resurrection numbered several hundred (1 Corinthians 15:6).

As it turned out, only two men were proposed or nominated. It would seem reasonable to suppose that several others met the basic requirements, but these two were selected because of their outstanding virtues, both mental and spiritual.

Matthias Selected (23-26)

The apostles had a problem. Only one man was needed to take the place of Judas, but two men were especially qualified. (We might wish that our churches today had two qualified men for every office open.) How were the apostles to select the right one? Neither of the men, Justus (called Barsabbas) or Matthias, was mentioned in the Gospel accounts. Interestingly, neither is mentioned again by name after this.

The apostles continued the process of selection by praying to the Lord for guidance. Scholars have debated whether they were referring to God or Christ in their prayer. Since the designation *Lord* came increasingly to be applied to Christ, it is reasonable to suppose that that was the case here. It also seems appropriate because the one selected was to be an officer in Christ's church.

Their prayer was that the Lord would show them which one He had already selected. The apostles had no doubt that He had already made the decision. Their only concern was that He communicate His decision to them. The Lord might have given them this information in any of several ways. He could have spoken in an audible voice, used some visible symbol like the tongues of fire at Pentecost, or sent an angel to bring the information. Instead, He made His choice evident through the drawing of lots.

The casting or drawing of lots as a means of ascertaining God's will was often used among the Jews. The partition of Palestine, for example, was made by casting lots (Numbers 26:55). On occasion, this method was used to determine who was guilty of committing a crime. On the Day of Atonement, it was used to select the scapegoat that was to be released (Leviticus 16:8-10). This is the last time that the casting of lots is mentioned in the Bible. We conclude that this was a unique situation and that the apostolic church did not commonly use this method to make decisions. We may further conclude that this one example did not establish a divinely approved precedent for the casting of lots in the later history of the church.

CHAPTER TWO

When Pentecost Came

Acts 2

The Coming of the Holy Spirit (2:1-21)

The Eleven had been told to go back to Jerusalem and wait—for how long they did not know. A week? A month? A year? This uncertainty must have intensified their anxiety. But within ten days, their problem was resolved. We often find ourselves in similar situations. We become anxious and begin to fret when with just a short wait our problems would be settled.

His Appearance (1-4) *Birthday of the Church?*

We often speak of the coming of the Holy Spirit, a statement that may be misleading. Such a statement might lead one to suppose that the Holy Spirit appeared for the first time at Pentecost. Of course, this is not the case. All through the Old Testament are references to the activities of the Holy Spirit. For example, in the time of Noah, God indicated that His Spirit would not always contend with man (Genesis 6:3). Several of the Psalms mention the work of the Spirit (104:30; 106:33; 139:7). Isaiah mentioned the coming of the Spirit (Isaiah 61:1), a prophecy that Jesus declared was fulfilled in Him (Luke 4:18). The prophet Joel looked forward to the work of the Spirit (Joel 2:28, 29), a prophecy that Peter later quoted on Pentecost (Acts 2:16-18).

Pentecost was one of the three major holy days in the Jewish religious calendar. It came fifty days after Passover, making it fall in May. Pentecost, also known as the Feast of Weeks, had agricultural significance. On that day, the people offered the firstfruits of the wheat harvest (Numbers 28:26). In Jesus' day, Jewish tradition held that Moses received the law on the fiftieth day after the Passover, thus giving this day added significance.

Acts 2:1 leaves two questions unanswered. First, who were the "they" who were all together? Some say it included both the apostles and the one hundred twenty that had been meeting with them. Others argue that only the apostles were assembled, since the logical antecedent of the pronoun is the "eleven apostles" in Acts 1:26.

The second question deals with where they met. Some feel that they were meeting in the upper room. If this were the case, then we can see some problems with having more than a dozen men in the room together, because the upper room was in all probability a relatively small room, hardly able to accommodate the one hundred twenty.

Some argue that they met in the temple area, perhaps in Solomon's Porch, for prayer. This is entirely possible because the church had not yet been founded; thus, these people's presence would not have aroused the bitter opposition from the religious leaders that it later did. Some scholars believe that they might have met on some broad steps that archaeologists have only recently uncovered immediately to the south of the temple area. These wide steps would have provided plenty of room for the crowd that soon gathered, and would also have been within easy walking distance of the Pool of Siloam, which may have been used for the baptisms that were soon to follow.

The first evidence of the presence of the Holy Spirit was the sound "like the blowing of a violent wind" (Acts 2:2). The Spirit is associated with the idea of wind in other Biblical passages (1 Kings 19:11; Ezekiel 37:9; John 3:8), and the Greek word *pneuma* that is here translated "Spirit" may also be translated "breath" or "wind."

The second evidence of the presence of the Spirit was "what seemed to be tongues of fire," that came to rest upon the apostles (Acts 2:3). Fire was also a well-recognized symbol for the presence of God. This phenomenon may very well have been a fulfillment of the prophecy by John, who was speaking of Christ: "He will baptize you with the Holy Spirit and with fire" (Luke 3:16).

The third evidence of the presence of the Holy Spirit came as the apostles "were filled with the Holy Spirit and began to speak in other tongues" (Acts 2:4). The practice of speaking in tongues (also known as *glossalalia)* has become a controversial one in the contemporary church. It centers around the activities described in Acts 2, Acts 10, and 1 Corinthians 14. In view of the importance this practice has assumed, we would do well to look at it more carefully.

22

First of all, it would seem that at Pentecost, only the apostles were baptized in, or filled with, the Holy Spirit. In the house of Cornelius, however, others had this experience (Acts 10:44-46; 11:15). In Corinth, it is evident that the gift of speaking in tongues was rather widespread, so much so that it was creating a problem for the church there.

At Pentecost, it would appear that the apostles were enabled by the Spirit to speak in other languages that they had not consciously learned. That they did not speak in some strange or esoteric languages is evident from the response of the crowd: "Each of us hears them [speaking] in his own native language" (Acts 2:8). It is rather likely that most of the people visiting Jerusalem could speak either Greek or Aramaic in addition to his own language. Thus, the apostles could have communicated with them without the benefit of a miracle. The purpose of this miracle seems to have been to serve as credentials for the message they were about to bring.

The miracle in the house of Cornelius served a similar purpose. It convinced Cornelius and his household that the message brought by Peter was indeed from God. But, more importantly, it convinced Peter and his Jewish companions that the gospel should also be made available to the Gentiles (Acts 10:47; 11:17, 18).

The gift of tongues exhibited in the Corinthian church, while it did serve to convince the unbelievers, was also used as a means of edifying the saints. Further, the experience of tongues at Corinth was in a language unknown to the Christians there since an interpreter was needed to make it intelligible to them (1 Corinthians 14:1-17). In view of this, it would appear that the modern tongues movement might be more appropriately called Corinthians than Pentecostals.

The Audience (5-12)

On Pentecost, Jews from all over the Roman Empire and even from beyond the Empire (the Parthians, Medes, Elamites, residents of Mesopotamia, and perhaps the Arabs), were gathered for the occasion. This catalog of Jews and converts to Judaism illustrates how widely they had been scattered both by war and persecution and in the pursuit of business interests. It also gives us an insight into the faithfulness of the Jewish people, who would undertake such an arduous pilgrimage on behalf of their faith.

How many modern Christians would make such a sacrifice for their faith?

Criticisms (13-21)

While some were amazed by the phenomenon of tongues, others were critical. "They have had too much wine," they sneered (Acts 2:13). Peter brushed aside this remark by reminding them that it was only nine o'clock in the morning (Acts 2:15). The critics were aware that Jews did not ordinarily drink in the morning. Further, even a biased observer would have no difficulty realizing that these men were certainly not drunk.

The unusual phenomena they had witnessed were not due to drunkenness, but were the fulfillment of prophecy. Peter reminded them of this by quoting 2:28-32. This outpouring of the Spirit was to come "in the last days" (Acts 2:17), that is, in the final age of the world. This did not mean that the end of the world was imminent; two thousand years of history since then demonstrate that was not the case. It does affirm, however, that we are in the final era of God's dealing with man and that we are approaching the end.

God's Spirit was to be poured out on all people. While this does not necessarily mean that every person would be so blessed, it does mean that all classes and ages would be touched—sons and daughters, old men, and servants (Acts 2:17, 18).

Peter Preaches Jesus (2:22-36)

Once Peter had disposed of the charge that he and his companions were drunk, he could turn to the heart of his message.

Jesus Crucified (22, 23)

Jesus had been accredited by God by miracles, wonders, and signs. Only the stubbornness of the people, especially the leaders, had kept them from believing on Him. Yet the historical irony of the situation was that their very rejection of Jesus had made it possible for God to accomplish His purpose.

In their angry rejection of Him, they had turned Him over to "wicked men"—the Romans. They had subjected Him to the painful and degrading death on the cross. In the first century, the cross was not an ornament to decorate jewelry or a symbol to grace church buildings. It was a cruel, inhumane method of disposing of criminals and other undesirables.

Jesus Raised Again (24-33)

The judgment of the Jewish leaders, which had been carried out by the Romans, was reversed by the power of God. Thrust into the tomb by brutal hands, Jesus had been stirred by the touch of God's hand. Since it was a part of God's plan to raise Him up, there was no way that death could keep Him bound in the grave.

Peter found evidence of God's purpose in Psalm 16. In this psalm, David wrote that God would not abandon His holy one to the grave nor allow Him to see decay. By divine inspiration, David had been led to speak of the resurrection of the Messiah as if it were his own. Yet, as Peter quickly pointed out, David could not have been referring to himself, for his body still remained in the tomb. The people knew that Peter was telling them the truth because they could still point out where David's tomb was in that day. David knew of God's promise to place one of his descendants on his throne. By prophetic insight, he was also able to see the day of Christ and that God would not abandon Him in the grave.

[Handwritten margin note: Example of Smart Thinking People Knew where David was.]

Jesus Exalted (33-35)

Peter, having established the truth of Jesus' resurrection both through the testimony of witnesses and by the fulfillment of prophecy, next turned to His exaltation. Not only had Jesus been raised, He had ascended to Heaven. There He took His place at the right hand of God, a place that all would recognize as a place of honor. There, in some special way, Christ received the Holy Spirit, who in turn had that day been imparted to them. Peter's point was further affirmed by another psalm attributed to David. In this quotation (Psalm 110:1), the Lord (God, in this case) speaks to my Lord (Christ), assuring Him that He will be at God's right hand until all of His enemies have been subdued.

Peter's Conclusion (36)

Peter had marshalled the evidence from fulfilled prophecies, from the testimony of witnesses, and from the events of that day. He was ready to drive home his conclusion with precision and force. "Therefore," he began, "let all Israel be assured" (Acts 2:36). Assured of what? Assured that they were guilty of the cruel murder of Jesus—a terrible indictment! But Peter also assured them that this Jesus whom they had crucified had been made both Lord and Christ; he offered a glimmer of hope.

Two or three things should be noted in Peter's remarks. First of all, he addressed them to all Israel (literally, all the house of Israel). Did this mean that all Israelites were responsible for the crucifixion of Jesus? Not directly, of course, but the whole nation would have to bear the consequences of what their leaders had done. Some would escape this judgment by repenting, but that required a decision on the part of every person who would set himself free from it.

The second point worth noting is that Peter refers to Christ as Lord. This is a clear reference to Christ's deity, since the word that is translated "Lord" is the same word that is used in the Greek Old Testament to designate God.

Jesus was also the long-awaited Christ. Christ, which means the "anointed one," is the Greek equivalent of the Hebrew term *Messiah*. For centuries, the Jewish people had longed for the coming of the Messiah, who would be their invincible champion against all their enemies. Under His leadership they would throw off the yoke of foreign domination and once again know the glory that had been theirs in the time of David and Solomon. But instead of welcoming the Messiah when He came, they had rejected Him and allowed Him to be crucified.

We stand aghast at the perversity of a people who could so reject the greatest blessing God could ever send. Yet, do we not at times treat with similar neglect, and even contempt, the blessings God has sent us? Americans have been blessed more than any nation in the history of the world, yet they often demonstrate the same neglect and contempt toward God as did the Jews in first-century Palestine. If God dealt sternly with the ancient Hebrews who rejected Him, how will He deal with us?

Response to Peter's Sermon (2:37-40)

When a person is confronted with God's truth, he may respond in one of three ways. He may angrily reject it and even attack the messenger who brought it. He may consider it meaningless or irrelevant and show his lack of concern with a yawn. Or he may hear and believe, allowing the message to melt his hardened heart.

Their Hearts Were Melted (37-40)

Those who heard Peter responded in this latter fashion. The combination of the powerful presence of the Holy Spirit, the testimony about Jesus' resurrection, and Peter's forceful

26

presentation of the claims of the gospel had touched their hearts to the quick—"they were cut to the heart," the Scriptures say (Acts 2:37). As one man, they cried out, "What shall we do?" In one short sentence, they posed the most important question that human lips can pronounce. What must we—all of us—do to escape the wrath that should justly fall upon us because we have crucified the holy one of God? Their question was motivated by the deepest of human concerns—survival. It was an emotional question! Yet it was also an intellectual question that required an intellectual answer. They did not ask what they must feel in order to be saved, but what they must do.

Peter's reply seems clear enough. Yet across the centuries, it has generated an abundance of theological heat as well as even some theological light. The first part of his answer—*repent*—has not posed many serious problems. The Greek word that we here translate "repent" means to change one's mind. But from its use in this and other passages, we know that this change or *turning* involves much more than the intellect. It involves the total person. This turning has both its negative and its positive sides. Negatively, when one repents, he turns away from sin and the world. Positively, he turns to Christ and God.

Although faith in Christ and God is not mentioned by Peter, it is quite obvious that faith logically must precede repentance. What Peter's hearers had come to believe led them to seek an escape from their sin of crucifying our Lord. Without this belief that Jesus was the Christ, they would have had no rational basis to repent.

It seems clear from this passage that repentance must precede baptism. In fact, if it does not, then baptism becomes either a meaningless symbol or it must be invested with some magical power that imparts its saving blessing upon a person irrespective of what he believes or whether he has turned to God and Christ.

This raises another question. What about infants or very young children? When we look at the inspired record, we find no mention of infants being present at Pentecost; so we cannot base our answer upon a precedent set by an inspired apostle. If we attempt to justify infant baptism by the logical inferences we may draw from this passage, we face another problem. It is clear that Peter makes repentance a prerequisite for baptism. Yet one cannot seriously argue that infants are emotionally and intellectually developed enough to repent. We are forced to conclude, then, that the only proper candidate for baptism is a penitent believer in Jesus Christ.

Many of Peter's hearers would be familiar with baptism, having learned of it through John's baptism. In some ways, John's baptism and Christian baptism were similar. Both required repentance as a prerequisite, and in both cases, the action was by immersion in water. John's baptism offered forgiveness of sins and prepared people for the coming of the Messiah. But Christian baptism involved much more than John's baptism. Christian baptism offered the gift of the Holy Spirit, which John's baptism did not (Acts 19:1-6).

We are not to suppose that the waters of baptism have some special magical qualities that in and of themselves are able to impart forgiveness from sin and the gift of the Holy Spirit. This can occur only because God has so decreed that baptism should have this power. It also is possible only when the candidate has met God's prerequisites—faith in Christ and repentance. If these prerequisites are not met, one enters the baptismal waters a dry sinner and emerges a wet and still unforgiven sinner. Nothing else has changed.

In addition to the forgiveness of sins, Peter declared that baptism also brought the gift of the Holy Spirit. It is important that we distinguish between the *gift* and the *gifts* of the Holy Spirit. The gifts of the Holy Spirit are those qualities that the Spirit imparts to each Christian to a greater or lesser degree. Some of these are prophecy, serving, teaching, encouraging, contributing to the needs of others, leadership, and showing mercy (Romans 12:6-8; 1 Corinthians 12:1ff). The gift that Peter promised at Pentecost, however, was not these spiritual faculties, but the Holy Spirit himself—the indwelling of the Holy Spirit.

While Peter informed his hearers that they would receive the Spirit at baptism, he did not give any detailed explanation of what this involved. We know the Spirit ministers to our weaknesses, quickens our minds, leads us as we study the Scriptures, and aids us in our prayers and supplications. We do not know how He accomplishes these things, but we know that He does.

In extending these promises, Peter explained that they were not limited just to those who heard his voice but to their children. But, further, God's grace under the New Covenant was to extend beyond the Jews. Just as the good news was not confined to just one generation, so neither was it limited to one nation. Peter's invitation included those "who are far off"—Gentiles as well as Jews. It seems likely that neither Peter nor the others who heard these words understood their full implication. At least it later took a miracle to convince Peter that Gentiles ought to be accepted into the church. And it took much more to convince some of his Jewish countrymen. Prejudice blinded them to the full import of Peter's words. But we dare not be too critical of them, for we are often equally blind and deaf to the words of the Scripture.

They Accepted His Word and Were Baptized (41)

Peter's offer of salvation was accompanied by further words of warning and pleadings that the offer be accepted. The blessings of the gospel ought to be presented in a logical, rational manner. Yet man is more than just a thinking machine. He also has feelings and emotions. When one presents the gospel to a sinner, he certainly has a right to appeal to the sinner's heart as well as to his head. Peter urged them to save themselves from "this corrupt generation" (Acts 2:40). The word here translated "corrupt" was sometimes applied to a piece of timber that was so warped that the carpenter had to throw it aside. He did not mean that they could actually save themselves by their own efforts, but that they could believe, repent, and be baptized, thus accepting God's grace in the manner He had determined for those seeking salvation.

We have no way of knowing how many were present and heard Peter and the other apostles proclaim the gospel message. But we are told that three thousand received the word and were baptized. In one day, more people responded to the invitation than Jesus had attracted as loyal followers in three and a half years. This gives us some understanding of what He meant when He said that His disciples would do greater works than He had done (John 14:12).

Baptizing three thousand people in one day was no small task. Some, in fact, even question whether it would have been possible to immerse that many people in one day in the city that was crowded by pilgrims who had come to observe Pentecost. We need to observe, first of all, that the physical means for immersion were available. First-century Jerusalem had several pools and reservoirs that could have served this purpose. Since it was in the spring of the year, these would be full from the "latter" rains, the heavier rain that fell in late winter and early spring.

Others question whether it would be physically possible for the apostles to immerse so many people in one day. The Scriptures do not tell us who actually performed the baptisms. There was no need for the apostles to have baptized the entire three thousand, for the validity of one's baptism does not depend upon who baptized him. It is entirely possible that those who were first baptized would then in turn baptize others. If this was the situation, then the ceremonies could easily have been completed in a few hours.

We cannot help wondering what effect these baptisms had on others who witnessed them. No doubt those who had not heard the sermon would be inquisitive about what was going on. Their questions would afford the new Christians an opportunity to witness to their faith. It is no accident that both the Lord's Supper and baptism provide visual lessons to the central facts of the gospel. The Lord's Supper points to His suffering and death; baptism depicts His death, burial, and resurrection.

We often speak of people "joining the church" as if it were some kind of a club in which we can take membership. But the Scriptures tell us that those who were baptized "were added to their number" (Acts 2:41), indicating a quite different situation. Luke tells us later that the "Lord added to their number" (Acts 2:47). While one must take certain action if he is to become a part of the church, yet it is the Lord who does the adding.

The Aftermath of Pentecost (2:41-47)

A successful evangelistic meeting is a high point in the life of a congregation, but what happens after the last amen is said? All too often, a church returns to its old comfortable rut. But not the Jerusalem church. It had no ruts to return to. What an exciting future this church had! How often does a new church begin with three thousand charter members? And with no traditions to live up to and no sacred cows to feed?

The Believers Continued Together (41, 42)

How did the apostles cope with such a large group of people without any kind of an organization? No doubt, they soon developed some kind of an organization to handle the situation, but the organization was not nearly as important as what they did.

First of all, the apostles devoted themselves to teaching. These first converts, since they all came from Jewish backgrounds, had a clear understanding of the God revealed in the Old Testament.

But they needed to build a Christian faith on top of this Jewish foundation, and that's exactly what the apostles began to help them do.

The need for sound teaching in modern churches is much greater because most people do not come into the church today with anything resembling a clear understanding of God and His purposes as revealed in the Old Testament. We could only wish that churches today put as much emphasis upon teaching as did the apostles. Is there any wonder then that the church today is filled with Biblical illiterates who have only the vaguest notion about what Christianity really is and what is required of them as Christians?

These new Christians also devoted themselves to the "fellowship." The word translated "fellowship" is a rich one. It is sometimes rendered "communion," or "sharing," or "participation." It suggests having things in common, whether these be goods, service to others, a love of the Lord, or their hope of Heaven. It is used, for example, in 1 Corinthians 10:16 to refer to the Lord's Supper and is in some versions translated "participation." In 2 Corinthians 8:4, Paul compliments the churches of Macedonia for sharing ("fellowship" in the King James Version) in his ministry in Corinth. Their sharing took the form of providing financial support, which allowed Paul to pursue his preaching and teaching full time. In Galatians 2:9, the same word is used to indicate the approval of James, Peter, and John ("the right hand of fellowship") to Barnabas and Paul to preach among the Gentiles.

One way this new body of believers had fellowship was in the "breaking of bread." Some commentators seem to think that this refers only to the sharing of a common meal together. Although this practice is mentioned in Acts 2:46, it seems much more likely that the "breaking of bread" in Acts 2:42 has reference to the Lord's Supper. In the first century, the Lord's Supper was often referred to as "the breaking of bread." It came to be a regular weekly observance (Acts 20:7), although in those early days of the church it may have been observed daily.

One wonders where such a large group of people could have assembled all in one place. The temple area would afford such a place, but it seems likely that they also met in several places, such as homes and businesses, to observe the Lord's Supper. Before long, the church came under persecution, making it necessary to meet in homes rather than in public places.

Prayer was another activity that characterized the Jerusalem church. Since these people came from Jewish backgrounds, frequent prayer was a part of their religious heritage. They had before them the example of the Pharisees, who were notorious for their long, elaborate prayers. While they engaged in private and family prayers, here the reference seems to be to their prayers in public worship.

Peter's sermon on Pentecost had filled the hearts of his hearers with a conviction of their sins. This sense of awe was sustained in their hearts by the miracles that were performed by the apostles (Acts 2:43). This "fear," as the King James Version expresses it, was not necessarily confined to the believers. Since many of these miracles were probably done in public, and the results of even the private miracles would become a matter of public knowledge, others outside the body of believers must have become aware of them. Some undoubtedly were moved by these signs to become believers, as the evidence of a growing church indicates. Others, however, only hardened their hearts and began to seek ways to stop the miracles and silence the apostles.

Benevolent Believers (44, 45)

Yet another mark of the Jerusalem church was its concern for the needy. We wish that Luke had given us more details about how they accomplished this. Certainly, those who had food shared it with those who hungered, and those with homes provided shelter for the homeless. But clearly their benevolence went beyond this. They even sold their possessions and gave to those in need. It would appear that at first, the apostles were responsible for administering this benevolence. But soon this became such a task that they had little time for their teaching and preaching. As a result, others were appointed to look after the tables (Acts 6:2-4).

Unified Believers (46)

Another characteristic of this church was its unity. The New International Version omits the expression of unity found in most translations of Acts 2:46 ("with one accord," KJV; "by common consent," Phillips; "with one mind," NASB and NEB). Satan had not yet found a way to arouse the divisive spirit that has proved so devastating to the church across the centuries. Day by day, they met in the temple for worship. Since Christians had not yet felt the wrath of the authorities, they were free to use the temple.

Because the temple was not a convenient place for meals, they took their meals together from house to house.

Joyous Believers (47)

Yet another feature marked this church—its joyous praise of God. This was apparent to everyone, Christians and non-Christians alike. Perhaps this feature is more likely to be missing from the modern church than any other. At least, outsiders do not get the immediate impression that Christians are a joyous lot.

All of these qualities found in the early church at Jerusalem had one important consequence—it was a growing church. Christian leaders today are greatly concerned about church growth, and rightly so. Many formulas have been suggested to achieve this growth. Every one of these formulas may have some value, but the church at Jerusalem, without any scientific studies or volumes of statistics, had a successful formula. Their total commitment led to a joyous and winsome life-style that proved irresistible to those outside its ranks.

CHAPTER THREE

A Lame Man Leaps

Acts 3

In Acts 2:43 we are told that the apostles worked many miracles. Acts 2:46 informs us that the Christians continued to meet in the temple courts. In the healing recorded in chapter 3, Luke may be giving us a specific example of one of these miracles performed on one of these visits to the temple. Luke apparently mentions this miracle because of the reaction it stirred among the religious leaders.

The apostles continued to remain faithful to many of their Jewish religious customs until they were forced to abandon them. This may come as a surprise to us since we recognize that the coming of Christ did away with the Old Covenant that embodied these customs. But their visits to the temple did not violate any commandments of the New Covenant. This situation should help us to realize that becoming a Christian does not mean that one will instantly abandon everything he has believed or practiced in the past. Missionaries dealing with non-Christian cultures are often faced with situations like this.

The text literally states that Peter and John went up to the temple at the ninth hour. Since the Jews began their day at 6 A.M., the ninth hour would be 3 P.M. as we count time. It was the Jewish practice to observe 9 A.M. and 3 P.M. as special hours of prayer.

As they entered the temple, they saw a man being carried to the Beautiful Gate. The location of this gate is disputed by scholars, but many believe it to be the gate that separated the Court of the Gentiles from the Court of the Women in the temple area. This would have been a strategic place for the beggar to have been stationed because most of the people entering the temple would pass by him. Luke notes that the man was crippled from birth, thus removing any doubt that the miracle that followed was genuine.

When the apostles approached, the beggar raised his voice, crying out for alms. He must have done this scores of times every day just to eke out a meager existence. Little did he realize what was in store for him! Both Peter and John looked at him, and then Peter asked the man to look at them. This certainly must have aroused his hopes, because most people who gave him anything tossed him a coin or two in a perfunctory gesture of charity, scarcely looking at him as they passed.

But just as quickly as his hopes were aroused, they were dashed. "Silver or gold I do not have." As he heard the first words of Peter's sentence, the poor beggar knew that he was going to suffer disappointment and humiliation again. How many times in the past had people raised his hopes of a gift only to disappoint him sadistically.

Then the rest of Peter's words fell on his ears: "What I have I give you. In the name of Jesus Christ of Nazareth, walk" (Acts 3:6). What could this mean? Surely Peter didn't mean that he would be able to walk. How cruel even to suggest it. The two men offered him no money, and now they further taunted him with hopeless promises. But suppose Peter really meant it?

These thoughts must have tumbled about in the poor man's mind, leaving him uncertain about what might come next. As we read this account, we already know how it will turn out, and so we feel none of his pent-up emotions. Further, most of us have never been in the beggar's situation; so we don't know how he really felt. It is entirely possible that he may have had some reservations about being healed. Poverty-stricken though he was, he had some security in his situation as a beggar. At least he knew what his problems were and how he could cope with them. Being made whole would expose him to a variety of new situations that could pose all kinds of threats to his security.

But the man had only an instant to ponder these thoughts. Peter's actions eliminated any reservations he might have had about the decision. When Peter took him by the hand, his feet and ankles were immediately strengthened (Acts 3:7). The man must have felt the surge of strength flow through his crippled limbs, for he jumped up at once and began to walk without any hesitation. The miraculous element in this healing is all the more obvious when we realize that the man had never walked before. Yet he was able to walk and even leap without having to go through the hesitating, step-by-step process of learning to walk.

36

How often in our own lives we have gone through situations similar to that of the lame beggar. He asked for a few paltry coins. We in like manner sometimes hold up a tiny thimble for God to fill with blessings. The beggar, in spite of his meager request, received a blessing that far exceeded his fondest hope. And doesn't God sometimes deal with us in the same way? Instead of a thimble, we ought to be using a fifty-five gallon drum to hold His blessings.

The Consequences (8-10)

With a joy that made him throw aside normal restraints, the beggar went leaping and shouting across the temple court. The pious priests might have thought this behavior quite inappropriate in the temple, but, of course, they had never been lame and then enjoyed healing. His behavior quickly attracted the attention of other worshipers, who at once recognized him. Luke uses two strong words to emphasize their response (Acts 3:10). The first, translated "wonder," conveys the idea of astonishment or fear. The second, translated "amazement," is the word from which the English word *ecstasy* comes. It means to stand outside or away from oneself, with the idea that one has been driven out of his senses. As we would say, he is "beside himself."

Peter Speaks to the Crowd (3:11-26)

Peter, who was never one to miss an opportunity to proclaim his faith, saw his chance as the amazed crowd assembled. This event resembles Pentecost in that an unusual occurrence attracted a crowd and gave Peter an opportunity to preach the good news.

Peter Gives God the Credit (11-16)

The grateful beggar did not abandon his benefactors as did the nine lepers whom Jesus healed (Luke 17:12-19). Instead, he clung closely to Peter and John. Seeing the three together, the crowd quite correctly supposed that the miracle they had seen was in some way connected with the apostles, and so they quickly surrounded them in Solomon's Colonnade (or Solomon's Porch). This covered area was probably located east of the temple and provided a convenient place for the group to assemble. Although it was built during Herod's reconstruction of the temple, it takes its name from the fact that its foundation stones were quite possibly a part of Solomon's temple.

The crowd seemed ready to give Peter and John credit for this miracle. Peter's question immediately shocked them out of this notion: "Why do you stare at us as if by our own power or godliness we had made this man walk?" (Acts 3:12). It is likely that some of these people had witnessed the miracle of Pentecost, and others may have seen some of Jesus' miracles, and so they should have known better than to have thought that the apostles were responsible for this miracle. There is not the slightest inclination on the part of the apostles to take credit for this miracle. Would that all church leaders would be as modest about the wonders God works today!

Peter immediately identified the source of his miracle in terms with which his audience would be familiar—the God of Abraham, Isaac, and Jacob. With this brief introduction, Peter came immediately to the main point of his message. God had glorified Jesus through whom the crippled man had been healed. But, and this was the painful point Peter made, they had handed Jesus over to Pilate to be killed. Even though Pilate sought to free Him, they had disowned Him and asked for a murderer instead. Peter made his accusation direct and pointed, leaving no doubt about their guilt. (Is it possible that modern preaching has lost much of its power because in its efforts to be polite it leaves no one feeling guilty?)

Peter accentuated his charge with striking paradox: They had killed the "author of life" (Acts 3:15; the King James Version has "Prince of life"). How was it possible that they had killed the very giver of life? Yet they had. Rejecting the giver of life, they had chosen the taker of life, Barabbas, a murderer. They had killed, but God had made alive. Now it was through faith in the name of this risen Jesus that the man had been healed.

A Call to Repentance (17-20)

At this point, Peter injected a new note into his message, one that he had not sounded in his sermon at Pentecost. As vile as their crime had been in killing Jesus, they had acted in ignorance. Even their leaders had so acted. They had not been totally ignorant of the fact that they had executed an innocent person. Certainly the leaders knew that Jesus was not guilty of any crime worthy of death. Yet, in a fuller sense, they were ignorant of what they were doing. In His petition on the cross, Jesus prayed, "Father, forgive them, for they do not know what they are doing"

(Luke 23:34). While these words were specifically directed toward the Roman soldiers at His crucifixion, yet they certainly applied to others involved in His death. In what sense were they ignorant? They were ignorant of God's ultimate purpose in sending His Son into the world to die. Somehow, they had misread all the prophecies that pointed to God's great plan for human redemption.

But ignorance and innocence are not the same thing. In part, their ignorance had been willful, for which they had to assume guilt. Certainly their religious leaders had greater guilt, but the people could not escape their responsibilities. Many today blindly follow religious leaders who are leading them down the wrong path. Their ignorance will not excuse them before God.

But at least their ignorance provided mitigating circumstances. Because they had acted in ignorance, they were more likely to respond to that offer. On the other hand, had they acted knowingly and deliberately, they would be much less likely to repent.

In reporting this sermon, Luke probably has summarized the content of Peter's message. It is rather unlikely that Peter could convey the gospel message to such a crowd in a few brief sentences. The climax of the message came when Peter demanded a response on their part. To those on Pentecost and to those here who were guilty of Jesus' blood, the command was the same: "Repent!"

The word here used for repentance means a change of mind, a dramatic change of direction for a particular action or series of actions or even for one's entire life. In this text, the action is emphasized by the verb that follows, which means "to turn." (The King James Version translates this "be converted," leaving the unfortunate impression that conversion is a rather passive activity, something that happens to one, rather than something that comes about because of one's conscious, intelligent action.)

Repentance leads to the forgiveness of sins—"that your sins may be wiped out" (Acts 3:19). This promise applied to their sin in helping crucify Jesus, but it certainly extended further. Their repentance and turning to God would wipe the slate clean, allowing them to start afresh.

Acts 3:19 contains a phrase that offers some interesting possibilities. The King James has "when the times of refreshing shall come from the presence of the Lord," tying it to the first part of verse 19. This leads to the conclusion that the "times of refreshing" come as the result of repenting and turning to God. The New

TEMPLE AREA

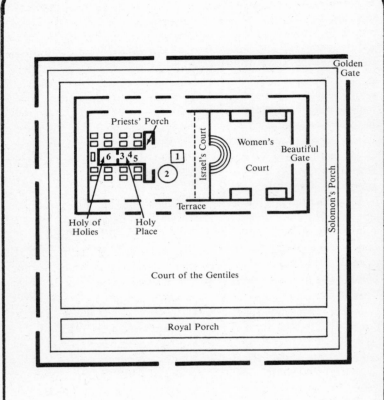

1. Altar of Burnt Offering
2. Laver
3. Incense Altar
4. Table of Showbread
5. Candlestick
6. Ark of the Covenant

International Version, on the other hand, translates it "that times of refreshing may come from the Lord," and connects it with verse 20. This leads to the conclusion that the people's repentance and turning to God would help bring about the return of the Lord and with His return, "times of refreshing."

This latter view has some breathtaking possibilities. It suggests that people's repentance and turning to God can have an influence on our Lord's return. To acknowledge this possibility is to attempt to fathom the depths of God's wisdom in establishing times and events in His eternal plan for the human race. Our finite minds cannot begin to comprehend the mystery of God's foreknowledge, on the one hand, and our free will on the other. But even if we cannot understand it, we can rejoice that we have been invited to become partners with God in this great cosmic venture. To put the matter simply, our success in winning others to repentance will help determine when our Lord returns. Here is another compelling reason for us to be actively engaged in evangelistic activities.

Prophecy Fulfilled (21-26)

In the meantime, Jesus is in Heaven, awaiting the time of His return. When Jesus does come again, God will restore all things just as He had promised through His holy prophets. Although Peter did not cite a specific Old Testament prophecy to support his statement, many such prophecies look forward to the time that the Messiah will reign triumphant in His kingdom.

At this point in his sermon, Peter takes a different direction. To document the authority of the Messiah, he quotes Moses (Deuteronomy 18:15, 18, 19). In this passage, Moses was attempting to keep the people from following after diviners and other false teachers. Through the law, Moses provided divinely inspired leadership to guide the people. At the same time, he looked forward to the time when God would raise up another prophet like himself who would similarly provide divinely inspired leadership. Moses instructed the people to obey this new prophet when he arrived.

In Peter's day, the people gave the highest respect to the teachings of Moses. If Peter could demonstrate that Jesus was the Messiah prophesied by Moses, they would accept His authority. The penalty if one refused to listen to the Messiah was dire—that one would be cut off from his people.

Peter did not conclude his presentation by quoting Moses alone. He showed his listeners that "all the prophets from Samuel

41

on" (Acts 3:24) had also foretold these days. The Jewish people were heirs not only of the prophets, but also of the covenant God had made with their fathers. God had promised Abraham that He would bless him and then bless all the peoples of the world through his offspring. It is rather interesting that Peter himself did not understand the full implications of this prophecy. It took a vision and a miracle later on to convince Peter that God did indeed intend to bless all nations (Acts 10). Peter concluded his message by pointing out that God sent the resurrected Christ first to the Jewish people. They could receive God's promised blessing by turning from their wicked ways. Peter reminded his hearers that God had promised to bless all the nations through Abraham (Acts 3:25). Several modern translations state that this blessing would come through Abraham's "posterity" (Revised Standard Version), "offspring" (New English Bible, New International Version), and "children" (Phillips). This indicates that the blessing will come from many of Abraham's descendants. The Greek word here is literally *seed* (as in the New American Standard Bible), and Paul takes it to be singular (Galatians 3:16) and makes the point that the blessing that comes to the whole world comes through Christ, not through all the Jewish people. It is reasonable to suppose that Peter had the same thing in mind since his purpose in this sermon was to exalt Christ.

Peter climaxed his sermon with an affirmation of Christ's resurrection (Acts 3:26). This sermon in that respect exactly parallels Peter's sermon on Pentecost, and rightly so, for the resurrection of Jesus is the foundation stone of the Christian faith. Once He was raised from the tomb, Christ was sent to bless the people by turning them away from their sins. Though Christ had ascended to His Heavenly home, He was continuing His ministry of redemption through Peter and other faithful Christians. That ministry still continues today through the preaching and teaching of Christians.

CHAPTER FOUR

In Trouble With the Establishment

Acts 4

Trouble in the Temple (4:1-4)

Peter's sermon attracted a sizable crowd, which in turn attracted the attention of the temple guards. Whether Peter's sermon was finished by the time they arrived or whether they actually interrupted him is not clear. It seems that he had made his main points, but apparently the people had not had an opportunity to raise questions or respond to the message.

The Authorities Intervene (1-3)

Three groups intervened to bring the meeting to a halt. The priests who are mentioned were probably those priests who had been serving in the temple that day. The captain of the temple guard was in charge of the guards who maintained order in the temple and surrounding courts. The Sadducees were the political and religious party who controlled the temple. In their teachings, they gave greater authority to the five books of Moses than to the rest of the Old Testament. In contrast to the Pharisees, they did not believe in the resurrection. Since their positions of power depended upon keeping the Roman government happy, they were greatly concerned about any commotion that might attract the attention of the Romans. This explains their interest in the crowd that had assembled to hear Peter preach following the healing of the cripple. Such a gathering could get out of hand and lead to a riot. They remembered all too well what had happened a short time before when similar crowds had gathered about Jesus.

The thing that especially seemed to upset the Sadducees was Peter's preaching about the resurrection. Since they did not believe in the resurrection, they felt threatened by Peter's affirmation of it. Further, Peter's sermon contained an indictment of those who had killed Jesus. It is not likely that they felt any guilt about this, but they would have some concern lest others begin to point the finger of guilt at them. Clearly, Peter and John were too dangerous to be left loose to continue their preaching.

And so the two apostles were seized and, because it was late in the day, they were thrown into jail. By jailing them overnight the authorities would keep them away from other church members and perhaps also cool some of their enthusiasm. It would also give the officials time to plot their strategy against the two. As in the case of Jesus' trial, they needed to trump up charges against them. In addition, they had to make sure that they did not arouse the people.

The Church Continues to Grow (4)

At this point, Luke inserted some rather surprising data about the growth of the church. From the three thousand at Pentecost, the number had grown to five thousand. We are not told how long after Pentecost this incident occurred. Perhaps only a few weeks had elapsed. During that period, the church had been busy carrying out the first step in Christ's marching orders (Acts 1:8). These converts were probably added day by day as Christians witnessed of their faith to family and friends. The love they showed in their care for the needy along with the miracles they saw certainly were factors in bringing these nonbelievers to Christ. It is likely that some surrendered to Christ as the result of the healing of the lame man and Peter's ensuing sermon. Even seeing Peter and John cast into jail would not be a serious deterrant to those who had seen this great miracle and heard Peter's explanation of it. Tyrants have not yet learned the truth of the statement made by Tertullian, an early Christian: "The blood of the martyrs is the seed of the church."

Peter and John on Trial (4:5-23)

The Sanhedrin Assembles (5, 6)

When morning came, the religious leaders were ready to make their case against Peter and John. The hours that followed their arrest had allowed time for the Sanhedrin to assemble. Three groups made up this august assembly: "rulers, elders and teachers of the law" (Acts 4:5). The "rulers" were the chief priests, some of whom are named in Acts 4:6. The "elders" were prominent men in the community who were drawn from the leading

44

families. The "teachers of the law" were specialists in the Scriptures and the Jewish traditions. Most of these were Pharisees, whereas the rulers were Sadducees. The Pharisees believed in life after death; so at least on that issue Peter and John had a chance to get a fair hearing.

Annas had been high priest in A.D. 6-14, but he had been deposed by the Romans. Several other members of his family had succeeded him at this high post, including his son-in-law, Caiphas, who at that time was recognized by the Romans as the high priest. Even though Annas was not officially the high priest, he was given this title out of deference to his prestige and out of recognition of the influence he continued to have with others who held the office. Caiaphas we know from his involvement in the trial of Jesus, but we cannot identify for certain either John or Alexander.

The Inquisition Begins (7)

One wonders what thoughts must have gone through the minds of Peter and John. Only a short time before, Jesus had stood on the same spot surrounded by most of the same accusers. The two apostles had good reason to be afraid, for they knew they were not likely to get a fair hearing. But there is not the slightest trace of fear either in their words or their conduct.

Peter and John had been arrested because they had preached about the resurrection. But the inquest began with a question about the power by which the lame man had been healed. The leaders of the Sanhedrin were clever enough not to raise the question of the resurrection because this would immediately divide the council, since the Pharisees believed in the resurrection. Interestingly, they did not raise a question about whether a miracle had really taken place. Apparently, the lame man had been so well known and his instantaneous cure so obvious and so well-witnessed that the leaders knew it was futile to challenge these facts. In asking about the power or authority by which the miracle had been performed, the leaders were unwittingly playing right into the hands of Peter, for he was most eager to tell everyone about the authority by which the miracle had been worked.

Peter Makes His Defense (8-12)

The Lord promised that in times just like these, when His disciples faced hostile tribunals, they need not worry about what to say. The Father would send His Spirit to guide them (Matthew 10:19, 20; Luke 12:11, 12; 21:12-15). For the first time in the Christian era, Peter and John were in a position where they needed to claim this promise. Their faith was not in vain, for Peter was "filled with the Holy Spirit" (Acts 4:8). Although we may never face persecution as the apostles did, do we have the faith to claim this promise when our beliefs are challenged?

Peter addressed the members of the Sanhedrin with respect. A respect for all duly constituted authority, whether civil or religious, is both demonstrated and taught in the New Testament. Peter made no attempt to avoid the question put to him. There was no hemming or hawing and no quibbling about the meaning of words. His answer was straightforward and to the point. The cripple was healed "by the name of Jesus Christ of Nazareth" (Acts 4:10). Peter added "of Nazareth" so that there would be no question about his answer. He certainly knew that to connect Jesus with the designation Christ, the Messiah, would infuriate the Sanhedrin members, yet he did not shrink from making that identity. This was precisely the reason that the religious leaders crucified Jesus in the first place. His claim to be the Messiah, with all its implications for deity, cut across the grain of all of their theological beliefs. Now, to have this thrown up to them, the intellectual elite of Israel, by an uneducated Galilean fisherman must have been especially galling.

Consider Peter's situation, too. Only a few weeks before, he had been questioned about Jesus and his relationship with Him. At that occasion, he had cravenly denied Him—not once but three times. Now he was standing before the highest tribunal in the land, a tribunal that might very well bring dire punishment upon him, and yet he did not hesitate a moment to make this bold affirmation. What accounted for this change? Two things. First of all, he had seen the risen Christ, the ultimate transforming power. In the second place, he was filled with the Holy Spirit.

But Peter did not stop with simply identifying Jesus. He went on to point the accusing finger at these leaders for the part they played in Jesus' crucifixion. But their cruel act was nullified by the power of God, who raised Him up alive. Here, as in his sermons on Pentecost and in the temple after healing the cripple, Peter joined the crucifixion and the resurrection (Acts 2:23, 24; 3:15). The two belong together and can never appropriately be separated.

46

Peter's indictment was not finished yet. Quoting from Psalm 118:22, he showed that their actions in rejecting the Messiah had been anticipated in the Old Testament. Jesus himself quoted this psalm to point up the nature of His rejection (Luke 20:17). Peter's final verbal blow was the most devastating. Jesus had saved the crippled man, but more importantly, He offers the same spiritual salvation for every soul under Heaven. It is amazing that the Sanhedrin remained so restrained at this bold declaration. To their ears, it certainly would have seemed blasphemous. Perhaps they were so amazed by the audacity of Peter's statement that they couldn't believe their ears.

The Response of the Court (13-18)

A moment of stunned silence must have followed Peter's bold announcement. Then the court must have begun to buzz as its members gave vent to their feelings. Then discussion and deliberation followed before a conclusion was reached.

The first response was amazement. They were astonished at the courage of Peter and John, and they could clearly see that they were commoners, unschooled in technical matters of the law. How could members of the high court account for their forceful argumentation? The simple answer was that they had been with Jesus (Acts 4:13). Some of them must have remembered with embarrassment their efforts to win an argument with Jesus. These simple Galileans had learned their tactics from Him.

The Sanhedrin might have been tempted to brush Peter's arguments aside with an arrogant wave of the hand. But standing in their midst was the former cripple, who was now whole (Acts 4:14), a living refutation of any objections they might have attempted to raise.

Needing time to discuss the matter among themselves, they had Peter and John and probably the beggar removed. The Sanhedrin, faced with the clear evidence of a miracle that was already known all over Jerusalem, had two options. They could recognize the validity of what Peter had said and also become disciples of Jesus. This would have meant surrendering their prestigious posts and taking their place among the persecuted. For most, this was too great a price to pay. Lest we be too critical of these men, we need to place ourselves in their position. An honest appraisal of our own motives might very well reveal what a grip power and position have on our lives.

The Sanhedrin's other option was to try to silence these men and hope that this movement would go away. It is a bit surprising that they thought such a tactic would work. But they had seen other movements come and go, and so they convinced themselves that the followers of the Nazarene would soon disappear if only the leaders of the movement could be muzzled.

Peter and John's Response (19-21)

Once they had made their decision to try to silence Peter and John, they called them back and issued an order to the two apostles that they were not to speak or teach again in the name of Jesus (Acts 4:18). The Sanhedrin did not cite any law they had broken, but instead gave this order with the expectation that their prestige would intimidate the apostles into silence.

If this was their hope, it proved vain, for Peter and John were not in the mood to be intimidated by anyone. Without a moment's hesitation, they made it clear that while they respected the Sanhedrin, they were under orders to a higher authority (Acts 4:19, 20). The choice was between obeying the Sanhedrin or obeying God, options that were clearly opposed. That left no room for compromise. Christians have an obligation to obey the civil authorities (Romans 13:1-7). But when civil authorities make demands that violate the will of God, Christians must obey God no matter what it may cost. Such a decision may lead to martyrdom, but how often the cause of Christ has been glorified by the precious blood of martyrs!

Peter and John had been commissioned to be witnesses of Jesus (Acts 1:8). Thus, they were under divine compulsion to carry out that commission: "We cannot help speaking about what we have seen and heard" (Acts 4:20). Once men surrender their hearts to Christ, this divine mandate leaves them no room to compromise with the powers of this world no matter what the cost may be, whether in position, wealth, or physical suffering. Across the centuries, men have faced similar threats and have stood unflinching before the power of Godless men. It was said of John Knox, the champion of the Scottish Reformation, that "he feared God so much that he feared the face of no man."

The Apostles Released (22, 23)

Confronted by such immovable loyalty, the religious leaders could do little but huff and puff. Without any legal basis on which to punish Peter and John, they had no choice but to let them go. And so, with further threats, they released them, knowing that the mood of the people who were aware of the miracle would not permit any other action.

Once they were released, Peter and John quickly made their way back to their Christian brothers, who must have been anxiously awaiting the outcome of their hearing. We are not told what happened to the man they had healed. No doubt, he was released also, for there was no legal basis for holding him. It is reasonable to suppose that he accompanied Peter and John, seeking to learn more about this power that had made him whole.

The Church Responds (4:24-37)

A Praying Church (24-31)

Once the church learned what had happened, they did what comes naturally to Christians—they raised their voices in prayer. With one accord, they lifted up their voices in praise and honor of God in language that reflected their familiarity with the Old Testament. After recognizing God as maker of heaven, earth, and the sea, they quoted the second psalm. In so doing, they attributed the words to David, who spoke by the Holy Spirit.

We do not know the exact circumstance under which David composed this psalm, but apparently it was written at a time when he was beset by powerful enemies beyond the borders of Israel. But beyond the situation in David's day, it looked forward to a similar situation in the life of Christ and His church. The "nations" that rage against David and the "people" who plotted against him were representative of the "Gentiles and the people of Israel" in the present situation. The "kings" and "rulers" were in similar fashion represented by Herod and Pontius Pilate (Acts 4:27).

As awesome as these powers may appear, they need not disturb the disciples. Everything that had happened had occurred according to God's power, and God in his infinite wisdom had already decided beforehand what would happen. What a source of strength it is to know that when we are in the will of God, we are also under His sheltering hand!

In their prayer, the Christians did not ask to be relieved of their dangers. They asked only that God would strengthen them to speak with boldness. To support their words as messengers of

God, they further asked God to continue to undergird their ministry with miraculous healings and signs (Acts 4:30).

They did not have to wait long for an answer to their prayers. As soon as their prayers were concluded, the place in which they were meeting was shaken as if by an earthquake. Although such an indication of God's special presence was not frequent, it had occurred in the past (Exodus 19:18; Isaiah 6:4). They were also filled with the Holy Spirit. Whether this was a renewing of their experience at Pentecost or a different experience, we are not told. Perhaps it was a special filling of the Spirit designed to prepare them to meet the threats of persecution that were soon to come upon them.

Some, noting the parallels between this situation and Pentecost, have referred to this as a "second Pentecost." While there are parallels, there are also differences. At Pentecost, for example, the apostles spoke in tongues; here they "spoke the word of God boldly" (Acts 4:31). Bolstered by the special activity of the Holy Spirit, they disregarded the threats of the Sanhedrin and continued to preach the good news.

A Generous Church (32-37)

The proclamation of the Word to non-Christians resulted in the winning of converts and the continued numerical growth of the church. At the same time, the Christians were growing spiritually and in concern for others.

This growing band of believers had one quality that is so rare in the modern church—they were "one in heart and mind" (Acts 4:32). Many things hamper the church today, but nothing is more damaging to its growth than its many divisions. Though we have often disregarded Jesus' prayer for unity (John 17:20-23), the early church experienced its fulfillment. Its unity was not that of visible organization, but of its heart and mind. They held a common faith united in a common love.

This unity led to specific action, action that is possible only when believers have a common mind and spirit. We have already read in Acts 2:44, 45 about the attitude that the first converts began to take toward their property. What may have seemed a temporary practice to meet a temporary situation seems to have been extended beyond the first few days. Luke here seems to be reporting events that happened weeks or even months after Pentecost. Thus it would appear that the sharing of possessions was more than just a temporary practice. These early Christians had the proper attitude toward possessions. They looked upon themselves as stewards whom God had entrusted with possessions. As good stewards, they were to use their possessions in such a way as to glorify God. In this particular situation, they believed that God was most honored when their possessions were used to care for the needy.

This generous practice of the church at Jerusalem, while most commendable, did not become the general practice of the churches. In fact, the New Testament mentions no other church that followed the example of the Jerusalem church. Though times have changed, the principle that Christians have an obligation to use their possessions to glorify God still remains. In some situations, this may mean helping the poor, the elderly, and the orphans. In others, it may mean supporting missions. In still others, it may mean supporting educational institutions that are preparing people for Christian leadership.

Even as the church's ministry of benevolence was being carried out, its ministry of preaching was not being neglected. The apostles continued to give witness to the resurrection. This was foundational in their preaching, for if the resurrection could be established as a historic event, then the other claims about Christ would become compelling.

As a result of their preaching, "much grace was upon them all" (Acts 4:33). This may mean that God's grace was upon the apostles to bless their preaching. It may, on the other hand, refer to the hearers. When they heard and responded to the gospel, God's blessings came upon them. A third possibility is that God's grace came upon the church because of their generous care for the needy.

In Acts 4:34, 35, we are told the details of how the church cared for its members. It would appear that all the members who owned houses or lands did not immediately sell them. To have tried to sell everything all at once would have flooded the market and depressed prices. Rather, they sold their possessions only as the need arose. The money from the sales was then brought to the apostles, who distributed the funds to the needy.

In leading the people to rid themselves of their possessions, God was providentially preparing them for the persecutions that would shortly come upon them. When persecutions did come, many Christians were forced to flee Jerusalem. In such an event,

51

it is likely that they would have lost their property anyway because it would have been confiscated by the Jewish authorities. Had they still owned this property, the temptation would have been strong for them to have compromised their faith in order to save their property.

Barnabas Introduced (36, 37)

The unselfishness of Joseph, whom the apostles had named Barnabas, is specifically mentioned by Luke. This leads us to believe that his contribution was especially generous. His name Barnabas means "son of consolation" or "son of encouragement" (Acts 4:36). We are given other information about him: he was a Levite and he was from Cyprus. When the Israelites invaded the promised land, the Levites were not given any land. The impression is left that Levites were not to own land. But apparently, this provision had long since been abandoned, because Barnabas did own land.

Luke's mention of Barnabas in this situation illustrates a literary technique he uses at other places in the book of Acts. This technique is to introduce a person in some minor or incidental role before he is brought into the narrative as a major character. This same technique is later used to introduce Stephen, Philip, and Saul of Tarsus.

CHAPTER FIVE

Trouble Inside and Outside
the Church

Acts 5

Trouble in the Church (5:1-10)

Luke's honesty as a historian is put to the test in the case of Ananias and Sapphira. He might very well have omitted this incident and kept intact the idea that the church was perfect. But guided by the Holy Spirit, he told it as it was, warts and all. Some, obsessed by the idea that the early church was perfect, might be shocked that not everyone in that church was a perfect saint. Assuredly, our experience in the church today should prepare us for the fact that there have always been sinners in the church.

Ananias and Sapphira's Scheme (1, 2)

The good, the valuable, the precious always invite the counterfeits. Counterfeiters do not copy play money, but real currency, because only real currency has value. Those who counterfeit art works mimic the masterpieces, not the works one might buy at a rummage sale. And so it was that Barnabas' great act of generosity soon attracted a counterfeit.

We know nothing of this couple except what we are told in these few verses of Acts 5. We are not told when they had become members of the congregation, but they had been members long enough to understand how people were giving their possessions to care for the needy. People who gave their possessions were not seeking the praise of men. Generous actions, however, even if done secretly, cannot long be hidden. The normal response is for others to praise such acts.

Ananias and Sapphira saw what happened when Barnabas and others gave their possessions, and they wanted some of the same praise and attention. And so they hatched this clever little scheme to gain the plaudits of men without paying the full price for them. In many a marriage, one partner has been dissuaded from a vile deed by the other. But neither partner had any reservation about carrying out this plot. Tragic indeed is the household in which there is no restraining voice of decency or honesty.

The scheme was simple enough. They would sell a piece of property, turn part of the proceeds over to the apostles, while keeping back part of the price and pretending all the while that they had donated it all. Why did they think they could get away with it? Did it not occur to them that someone might learn the selling price, especially if it was a piece of land? Did they stop to consider that Peter, who had the power to perform miracles, might also have the power to read their hearts? If these considerations ever occurred to them, they must have readily brushed them aside. Satan was involved in this whole affair, and we know how persuasive he can be. He can lead us to believe that we will never get caught or even if caught, the consequences will not be serious. From the Garden of Eden on, he has enjoyed a successful career of convincing men that black is white and white is black.

The Fate of Ananias (3-6)

It is likely that Ananias sought to carry out his plan at a public worship service, or at least when many others were around. After all, his purpose was to gain attention, and so the bigger the crowd the better. He probably expected words of praise from Peter, but instead, he suffered a shocking thunderbolt. He hadn't fooled Peter for a minute. While the Scriptures do not indicate it, it seems evident that Peter was informed of the plot by revelation. Without a bit of hesitation, he challenged Ananias. Ananias thought his scheme was foolproof, but he didn't get to enjoy the fruits of it for even a few moments.

Peter's words make several things clear. Satan was behind the whole plot. The devil had sought to hinder the church through the threats of the Sanhedrin, but when this failed, he turned to subtler methods, using the weakness of Ananias and Sapphira to attack from within. Through the centuries, Satan has used threats and persecution to hamper the church. In many situations, these have worked very well. But his attacks from within that have divided the church and compromised its witness have, in the long run, proved far more devastating.

Peter also pointed out another important truth. Ananias may have thought his actions involved only the apostles and other members of the church, but even as he lied to them, he was also lying to the Holy Spirit. That important fact should never escape our attention. It is possible to sin against God without sinning against our fellow men, but it is impossible to sin against our fellow men without also sinning against God. (Acts 5:3 states that the sin was against the Holy Spirit, while in verse 4, it was said to have been against God. This is not a contradiction but rather an indication of the unity of God and the Holy Spirit.)

Peter made yet another important point. Ananias was not compelled to donate the money. He owned the land before the sale and was free to use the money as he chose after he had sold it (Acts 5:4). Across the centuries, groups have claimed to find in the practice of the Jerusalem church a model for communism or community of property. Regardless of what term we may apply to the practice of the apostolic church, it differed markedly from most contemporary forms of communism, which are both atheistic and coercive.

Judgment upon Ananias was swift and certain. Even as Peter concluded his condemnation, Ananias fell down and died (Acts 5:5). Commentators have written many pages in an effort to explain exactly what happened. Some feel that Ananias, aware that he had been caught violating a serious taboo, was so frightened that he died of shock. Others feel that God miraculously struck him dead. Luke gives us only the barest details, and thus it is tempting to engage in lengthy speculation about what actually happened. Regardless of what was the physical cause of Ananias' death, Luke leaves no doubt that his death was an act of divine judgment. Those who witnessed this event were immediately overwhelmed with fear. It is not difficult to realize the cause of this fear. They recognized Ananias' death as an act of God's judgment. They may very well have felt, "There but for the grace of God go I."

Some of the young men present acted quickly to take care of the body, wrapping it for burial as the custom was. We find it difficult to understand why Sapphira was not notified of her husband's death. An effort may have been made to inform her, but it is possible that she returned before she could be found and told what had happened.

The Fate of Sapphira (7-10)

Three hours later, Sapphira arrived, completely unaware of what had happened (Acts 5:7). We find it difficult to understand how this was possible, but we have to take Luke's word for it. Peter knew that she was involved along with her husband; so she, too, was questioned. She was given an opportunity to tell the truth, but she brazenly tried to carry the scheme through. When Peter spoke to Ananias, he may not have known what the outcome was going to be. But as he questioned her, he knew what awaited her. What a fearful declaration of judgment his words were! As soon as he spoke, she fell stricken to the ground. The young men once more had to carry out their grim task. It would seem that Ananias and Sapphira had no close family members to survive them, because the family ordinarily took care of burials in that day.

Once more, the church reacted with fear, but not the church alone. Even those outside who heard of the deaths were fearful. It is worth noting that no one blamed Peter for the deaths. If there had been any possibility of bringing any kind of criminal charges against him, the Sanhedrin certainly would have seized upon the opportunity. Everyone either accepted what happened as an act of God or had become afraid to challenge Peter.

We would do well to examine closely the nature of Ananias and Sapphira's sin. Actually, we should say sins, for they committed several sins in carrying out their plot. Our understanding of their downward steps and their becoming enmeshed in the devil's trap should help us avoid such an entrapment.

Their first mistake was to listen to Satan. He is a clever, smooth-talking, persuasive liar. He began by creating envy in their hearts for the praise others were receiving for their generosity. This envy opened the door to everything that followed. Greed entered next. They not only wanted to gain the praise of men; they wanted to gain this praise and still keep back some of the money. Next they lied, not only to their fellow Christians, but to God.

This incident should make it clear to us that temptation and the sin that results from it are not a simple process. We can also see that the process is easier to halt in the earlier stages, while it exists in the heart and mind only. Envy, dangerous though it is, can be handled easier than lying. Once the overt act is committed, a person is likely to find it almost impossible to turn back.

The Church Continues to Attract People (5:12-16)

Activity attracts people. Persons who find themselves in a sick or dying church need to keep that in mind. Of course, not all

activity is appropriate for a church to be involved in. Someone has observed that it is easier to get people to a dog fight than to a prayer meeting, but we can hardly encourage churches to hold dog fights just to gain an increase in attendance. The Jerusalem church did not suffer from a lack of activity, and most of it was the wholesome variety that drew people to it.

The Apostolic Ministry Grows (12, 13)

In Acts 5:12, 13, Luke provides us a summary of the activities of the church, just as he did in Acts 2:43-47 and 4:32-35. The signs and wonders—that is, miracles of healing—were performed openly among the people. The believers met in Solomon's Colonnade, a covered space in the temple area. This was one of the few places large enough to accommodate the growing church, which now numbered several thousand. By meeting in such a public place, the apostles signaled their defiance of the Sanhedrin's order to cease preaching in the name of Jesus. This site also afforded them an opportunity to reach with the gospel the thousands of non-Christians who came to the temple to worship.

The Response of the People (14-16)

Non-Christians had mixed emotions about the apostles. They were afraid to join them, perhaps because of what had happened to Ananias and Sapphira, and yet they held the apostles in high esteem. But many lost their fears of the church as they watched the miracles of healing being performed. Good works have the power to melt hardened hearts and sweep away fears and suspicions, a lesson that the modern church would do well to heed.

The healing ministry of the apostles and especially that of Peter became so widely acclaimed that the city streets were turned into virtual hospital wards, lined with the sick hoping to be healed. Commentators differ about the healing power of Peter's shadow (Acts 5:15). Some feel that even his shadow had the power to heal much as Jesus' touch did (Mark 5:27-29) or as handkerchiefs touched by Paul did (Acts 19:12). We are not actually told here that Peter's shadow had such curative powers. It may have been that the sick were brought into such close proximity to Peter in order that he might be sure to see them and thus heal them.

Word of this healing ministry quickly spread beyond the confines of Jerusalem, and the sick were brought in from the surrounding towns. Even some vexed by evil spirits were cleansed.

Although the casting out of demons or evil spirits is mentioned several times in the Gospels, this is the first time that it is mentioned in the book of Acts (Acts 5:16).

The Apostles Face Renewed Persecution (5:17-42)

The religious leaders could not for long ignore the great evangelistic and healing meeting going on right under their noses. It should not surprise us that they soon took action to put a stop to it.

The high priest and his associates might have pretended that their attitudes toward the apostles was the result of their concern for doctrinal orthodoxy. But Luke unmasks their real motives—they were "filled with jealousy" (Acts 5:17). The hypocrisy of these religious leaders is obvious to us today, but do we sometimes fall into the same sin? We may be tempted to set up ourselves as righteous defenders of the faith when actually we are using this as a mask for our jealousy.

The Apostles Jailed and Freed (17-21)

The first effort to suppress the gospel was directed against Peter and John. But the growing influence of the apostles required sterner measures. This time all of the apostles were arrested and lodged in the public jail. We do not know where the public jail was located, but since it was a place where common criminals were kept, we can be certain that it did not afford the comforts of a Hilton hotel. The authorities must have arrested them when no crowd was present. Acts 5:26 tells us that when they arrested them the second time, they carefully avoided using violence because they feared the people.

They did not remain long in the jail. In the middle of the night, an angel of the Lord opened the doors and released them. In the Old Testament, the term *angel of the Lord* seems to designate a special presence of Jehovah God. If that is the case here, then this may indicate God's special involvement in the imprisonment of the apostles, the first time that Christians faced physical persecution. Their release was quite plainly a miracle, for the next day, the doors were locked and the guards had seen nothing. We have no explanation about how this happened, but since it was a miracle, no explanation is either possible or necessary.

The angel of the Lord gave the men explicit instructions as they were being released. They were to go to the temple and give the

message of life to the people. At daybreak, the apostles were found in the temple carrying out their orders. Faced with the choice of obeying God or men, they didn't hesitate a moment in carrying out their divine orders.

The Religious Leaders Bewildered (22-25)

Later, the high priest and his associates arrived and began to make preparations to try the apostles. The whole assembly of the elders—the Sanhedrin—was called together to hear their case, and as they were gathering, the high priest sent for the prisoners. One can imagine the surprise of the officers when they discovered that the prisoners were missing. The most obvious explanation would have been that the guards had been bribed to release them. But in reporting back to the Sanhedrin, the officers reported only what they had observed, not their conclusions about how it happened. The doors were securely locked, the guards were in place, but the prisoners were gone. One can imagine the response the officers' report brought among the members of the Sanhedrin. Some may have suspected a plot, but most of them were puzzled (Acts 5:24), having no adequate explanation for what had happened.

But before the religious leaders had much time to speculate about the situation, word came that the missing prisoners were in the temple preaching. The captain of the guard went with his officers to check out the report. When they found the report to be true, they cautiously and without the use of force arrested the apostles again. Had the apostles chosen to do so, they might very easily have resisted the officers. The mood of the crowd was such that they could have overpowered the officers and protected the apostles. The Twelve, like their Master before them, chose to face their accusers rather than flee from them.

The Response of the Sanhedrin (26-28)

When the apostles were finally returned to the court, it is surprising that no inquiry was made into how they had escaped from the prison. Perhaps the leaders feared that an inquiry might turn up too many embarrassing answers. They may have concluded that some stones are best left unturned.

Instead of asking about their release, the high priest immediately began to scold them for teaching in violation of his strict orders to the contrary. The high priest was concerned because they were teaching what he believed to be false doctrine. But he had a more pressing concern. He was fearful lest their teaching arouse the people against him and the other religious leaders for conspiring to murder Jesus.

Of course, the apostles in their preaching had no intention of arousing the people to do violence against the high priest. But at Pentecost and after the healing of the cripple, Peter had insisted that the Jewish leaders, including the religious leaders, were responsible for Jesus' death. Most of the hearers acknowledged their guilt and repented. The religious leaders, no doubt, felt a sense of guilt too, but their response was to attempt to silence the critics rather than to repent.

The Apostles' Defense (29-32)

In most circumstances, a Christian is under divine command to obey the civil officials (Romans 13:1-7). Yet when the authorities exceed their authority and demand what they have no right to require, then the Christian must look to a higher authority. A decision to disobey the civil authorities must be made only after careful and prayerful consideration. It must be made humbly and with a willingness to accept the consequences. This is the attitude the disciples took as they made their defense (Acts 5:29ff).

Peter began by stating his authority to preach. He spoke out of obedience to God. In his earlier hearing, when he and John had been brought before the Sanhedrin, Peter had given a similar answer (Acts 4:19). But the religious leaders had rejected it then, and they rejected it here.

Once Peter stated his authority, he went right to the heart of the issue. They had been guilty of crucifying Jesus, but God had raised Him up. The first statement they could not deny. Of course, they justified their actions by telling themselves that Jesus deserved it because He was guilty of blasphemy. But Peter's second affirmation—that God raised Jesus up—the Sanhedrin would vehemently deny. Peter's next statement aroused even greater opposition. He claimed that God had exalted Jesus as "Prince and Savior" in order that He might give repentance and remission of sin to the people (Acts 5:31).

Nothing that Peter could have said would have infuriated the Sanhedrin more than did these words. They certainly considered these words blasphemous. And well they might, for in saying that Jesus would bring forgiveness of sins, he was saying that Jesus was divine. Only God can forgive sin!

Immediately, the hearts of the members of the Sanhedrin were filled with intense anger. Those who had murdered Jesus were ready to kill again (Acts 5:33). Perhaps the only thing that restrained them was the knowledge that the apostles were popular with the people.

Gamaliel's Advice (33-40)

Fortunately, wiser heads prevailed. Gamaliel, a Pharisee who was widely respected, counseled caution. (Saul of Tarsus was one of his students [Acts 22:3].) His reputation gained a hearing for his words. But the fact that he was a Pharisee was also a matter of some significance. The other major party among the Jews, the Sadducees, were often at odds with the Pharisees. The two parties had collaborated in Jesus' death, but they differed on several major points of doctrine, including belief in life after death. While the Sadducees probably formed a majority of the Sanhedrin, they really needed the support of the Pharisees if they were to take violent action against the apostles.

Once the apostles had been led from the court, Gamaliel began his argument. He cited two examples of leaders who had arisen in the past, gathered a few followers, and then been crushed by the authorities when they rebelled. Although these two men, Theudas (Acts 5:36) and Judas the Galilean (Acts 5:37), must have been well known to Gamaliel's audience, we know nothing about them today except what we read here. In the face of the disastrous failure of these two rebellious groups, Gamaliel urged the Sanhedrin to be cautious, to wait and see. If the apostles were espousing a cause that was not of God, it would die of its own accord. On the other hand, argued Gamaliel, it if should turn out that Christianity was of God, then the Sanhedrin, if they opposed it, would be fighting against God.

We don't know for certain whether Gamaliel was acting on the basis of political expediency or from deep religious conviction. And it really doesn't matter, because his policy spared the apostles serious persecution at this time. The rest of the Sanhedrin, perhaps realizing that their legal case against the apostles rested on rather shaky grounds, might have welcomed Gamaliel's advice as a way out of a rather difficult situation.

There are times when Gamaliel's advice makes good sense today. Many of the problems that we fret about will often just disappear, given enough time. But it is not always sound advice.

Some problems, when we hesitate to take steps to solve them, can become even more serious.

"You will only find yourselves fighting against God" (Acts 5:39). How prophetic Gamaliel's words turned out to be. In what ways can one fight against God? A person fights against God when he opposes the spread of the gospel. He fights against God when he teaches false doctrine. One fights against God when he lives a worldly life. A person fights against God when he goes through the motions of being righteous but follows his own will rather than God's will.

The religious leaders were guilty of fighting against God in every one of these ways. The most flagrant example of their fighting against God is seen in their opposition to the spread of the gospel. They had already threatened Peter and John for preaching. Shortly after Gamaliel delivered his speech, they ordered the disciples beaten and further threatened. Later, they resorted to even more violent efforts to hinder the preaching of the gospel.

Gamaliel's speech persuaded the Sanhedrin not to imprison the apostles. But before they released them, they had them beaten. This beating was no trifling thing. The men were stripped and given thirty-nine blows across the back with rods. Such treatment would leave them painfully bruised, bleeding, and sore for days to come. The Sanhedrin may have so treated the men because they had ignored the decree to refrain from preaching the gospel. They, no doubt, also believed that a severe beating would intimidate the apostles into silence.

Rejoicing in Suffering (41, 42)

The Sanhedrin's expectation that they could frighten the apostles into silence by a beating was in vain. The religious leaders expected the apostles to creep from the court in pain and disgrace. Instead, they left in triumph, rejoicing as they went. They were not masochists who derived a distorted sense of pleasure from physical suffering. They rejoiced because they were counted worthy of suffering for the name of Jesus.

Nor did the beating they received keep them from preaching. Daily they continued to teach and preach in the temple and from house to house (Acts 5:42). The Sanhedrin members must have seethed with anger when they realized that their threats had gone unheeded. But for the time being, at least, they did not raise a hand to stop them.

CHAPTER SIX

A Deacon Becomes a Preacher

Acts 6

The First Church Officers Are Chosen (6:1-7)

Satan had a way of keeping trouble stirred up in the church at Jerusalem. When he did not use forces of persecution from outside the church, he used sinful members such as Ananias and Sapphira within the church. Now a new threat arose from within the church.

A Problem in the Church (1)

When a church grows, especially when it breaks out of its little socio-economic cocoon, it is likely to have some growing pains. The church at Jerusalem was no exception. Most of those who first responded to the gospel were Aramaic-speaking Jews. (The King James Version calls them "Hebrews," but the difference was in language and not in race. Even Jews living in Palestine no longer spoke Hebrew but Aramaic.) These were natives of Palestine. But as the evangelistic outreach of the church grew, it began to baptize Greek-speaking Jews. These Jews were part of the Dispersion who lived beyond the borders of Palestine. Some of them may even have been Gentile proselytes to the Jewish faith.

The church did not actually create the problem, for tensions had developed between the Aramaic-speaking and Greek-speaking Jews long before Pentecost. It is quite likely that the Aramaic-speaking Jews, whose language was closer to the ancient Hebrew, took a condescending attitude toward those who spoke only Greek. The people who became Christians simply carried their prejudices over into the church with them. We probably don't need a reminder that the church today still has this problem.

When the tensions between the two groups finally came to a head, it was over a relatively minor matter. The church almost from Pentecost on had been supplying food for the needy among

63

them through the contributions of wealthy members. No doubt, may of those receiving help were widows, usually the most needy in every society. The problem arose when the Grecian Jews complained that their widows were being neglected in the daily distribution of food. Their complaints may have been justified. On the other hand, the tensions between the two groups might have led them to exaggerate the extent of their neglect.

That this problem arose at all points up another weakness in the Jerusalem church. Other than the apostles, there were no other officers in the church. In the first few weeks of its existence, the church could get along without any organization, meeting needs as they arose. Yet by this time, the church must have numbered several thousand members, and to try to maintain such an operation without any organization was an invitation to chaos. Even today in a society that thrives because of efficient organization, many fail to see the need to carry this administrative efficiency over into the church. It is entirely possible that many needs are neglected in the church today because it is not effectively organized.

The Solution to the Problem (2-7)

The apostles quite wisely chose not to ignore this problem and called a congregational meeting to deal with it. The church had so grown that it would have been difficult, if not impossible, for all the Christians to have met together. Thus, it seems reasonable to suppose that the "whole group" of Acts 6:5 included only those who had a special interest in the matter.

We are not told the exact manner that the church used to collect the contributions and distribute the money or food to needy members. At first, the money had been brought to the apostles and laid at their feet (Acts 4:34-37). As the church grew, it probably became increasingly difficult for them to oversee directly the dispensing of benevolence, and it is likely that others were increasingly involved in the actual distribution of the money and goods. The fact that the apostles were less involved may have led to the feeling by the Grecians that they were being neglected.

Some may have suggested that the apostles themselves once again handle the distribution. But the apostles vetoed this suggestion. They did not refuse to take on this task because they felt themselves too good to do it. At one time, they may have been tempted to lord it over others, but that temptation had been left behind in the upper room when Jesus washed their feet in a lesson on humility. Their objection was based on the special ministry to which they had been called. The ministry of the Word of God was not superior to the ministry of waiting on tables. But they alone at this point in the history of the church had been especially called and endowed to preach and teach. To do anything else would have been to neglect their unique ministry.

The solution was for the congregation to choose seven from their number to handle the benevolence program of the church. Certain qualifications for these men were mentioned. The King James Version and several other translations indicate that these men must have a good reputation among the church members. The New International Version translates this somewhat differently. The second qualification was that they had to be filled with the Spirit (Acts 6:3). There is nothing to indicate that this filling of the Spirit involved the possession of miraculous gifts. Rather, this office required men whose lives demonstrated the fruit of the Spirit. They were also to be filled with wisdom, that is, the common sense needed to carry out the specific assignment at hand. Once the men were selected, the apostles would turn the task over to them and give themselves to prayer and the ministry of the Word.

This suggestion satisfied the whole group, and seven men were chosen for the task. We are not given the details of how these men were selected, but it seems evident that in some manner the congregation was allowed to indicate its choice.

Of the seven chosen, Stephen was mentioned first, along with the fact that he was full of faith and the Holy Spirit, perhaps indicating that he was especially blessed in both of these qualities. Next came Philip, whom we later meet as an effective evangelist in Samaria and with the Ethiopian eunuch. We know nothing for certain about the other five men. The last of the group, Nicolas, was a proselyte, or a convert to Judaism, from Antioch. It is significant that all of these men bore Greek names. This does not conclusively prove that these men were Hellenistic Jews (after all, two of the apostles, Philip and Andrew, had Greek names), but at least this remains a possibility. If such is the case, their selection shows a most generous attitude by the Aramaic-speaking Jews in this matter. Would our church disagreements today be more easily settled if the parties involved would show similar generosity toward their opponents?

Once the men had been selected, they were presented to the apostles, who prayed and laid their hands upon them. There is no evidence that this laying on of hands was for the purpose of imparting to them any special powers. Its intent was to indicate to all present that to these men was delegated the responsibility of caring for the tables. These seven men are commonly referred to as "deacons." They are not specifically called this in this passage, but our English word *deacon* is derived from the Greek verb that is used to indicate the service they rendered.

At this point, Luke once more gives us a summary of the status of the church. This brief note assures us that neither the persecution of the Sanhedrin nor the problems within the church seriously hampered its growth. The Word of God grew and the number of Christians in Jerusalem increased. He adds another interesting note. Many priests also became Christians. This must have brought special joy to the church, but it certainly must have brought consternation to the religious leaders.

Stephen's Ministry (6:8-15)

Luke now turns his attention to Stephen, who has just been mentioned. He did not for long confine himself to serving tables, but soon turned to proclaiming the Word publicly. Not only did he preach, but he also did wonders and great signs, terms that are generally used in the New Testament to indicate miracles. How Stephen gained the power to work miracles is not clear. Some hold that he received this power at the laying on of the apostles' hands (Acts 6:6), but the Scriptures do not clearly state this.

Opposition soon arose. The opposition obviously was to his teaching, not his miracles. This opposition came from the Synagogue of Freedmen, made up of Jews from Cyrene, Alexandria, Cilicia, and Asia. It is not clear why these people took such strong exception to Stephen's teaching. The text does not state that he actually entered their synagogue; the confrontation may very well have occurred in the temple. Stephen became the center of opposition, in part because he was a Hellenistic Jew and in part because he was so eloquent in his espousal of his faith.

The men from the Synagogue of the Freedmen made the mistake of trying to refute Stephen's arguments. They had two problems: first, they were trying to defend a false position, and second, they had to face a man who was under the guidance of the Holy Spirit.

We don't know the exact nature of these arguments, but from verses 13 and 14 we can infer their content. It is evident that Stephen preached the Messiahship of Jesus as the fulfillment of the law. To the Jews, this would seem like a blasphemous attack on everything that they held sacred. Though both Stephen and his opponents accepted the authority of the Scriptures, they drew radically different conclusions from them.

Stephen Before the Sanhedrin (12-15)

Once these men realized that they could not best Stephen in argument, they did what men in such circumstances often resort to—falsehoods and violence. If you can't beat your opponent with logic, beat him with lies or attack his character or his person.

Of course, these men were not yet to the place where they would physically attack Stephen. They were far too clever for that. Instead, they used the courts to bring false charges against him. Little did they realize that their actions would simply give him a bigger pulpit. Instead of silencing him, they succeeded in putting him in such a situation that his words still speak to us. Blasphemy in first-century Judea was a serious charge, one that could lead even to the death penalty. Such a charge was serious enough that it was immediately brought to the attention of the Sanhedrin.

This was the same body that only a few weeks ago had commanded the apostles not to preach in the name of Jesus. Now they were to hear a case that arose because their gag order had not been obeyed. Thus, these religious leaders were more than slightly motivated to hear this case.

The Sanhedrin had been afraid to take more severe action against the apostles because the apostles had the support of the people. In bringing charges against Stephen, his enemies sought to change this and turn the people against him by charging that his preaching threatened the temple. Not only did all Jews look upon the temple as sacred, but many derived their livelihood directly or indirectly from the temple. Thus, they had twin motives for becoming alarmed at anything that seemed to threaten it.

Stephen's opponents wanted to make sure that there would be no slipups in the trial, and so they undoubtedly coached the witnesses in their false testimony. It is interesting that one charge brought against him, that Jesus would destroy the temple (Acts 6:14), was similar to the charge that had been brought against Jesus himself (Mark 14:58). The Gospel of John informs us that

Jesus had spoken about the destruction of the temple but actually meant the destruction of His own body through His crucifixion (John 2:19-21). Jesus' words had been twisted to make it appear that He was threatening the physical temple.

Stephen's sermon before the Sanhedrin gives us some insight into the basis for these charges. It is clear that Stephen understood the fuller implications of the gospel. Jesus, in fulfilling the law, was the perfect sacrifice. This meant that the temple sacrifices and all their attendant services were no longer necessary and would gradually be phased out. Stephen's opponents were able to twist this teaching into a threat to the physical temple.

As these charges were brought against Stephen, it was natural for the whole court to watch him carefully. As they did, they could not help noting his countenance. It was like the "face of an angel" (Acts 6:15). We cannot be sure exactly what this expression implied, but probably it indicated that his fate revealed a calm assurance, a serenity that was extraordinary even though he was the target of false and threatening accusations. Such an appearance can come only to one who has placed his life completely in the hands of God.

In reporting this unusual phenomenon, Luke is undoubtedly reporting the testimony of an eyewitness, for Luke's close friend and companion, Saul of Tarsus, was there. That Luke reports this seems to indicate that Stephen's appearance, along with his words, had a far-reaching impact upon Saul.

CHAPTER SEVEN

The First Christian Martyr

Acts 7

Stephen's Defense Before the Sanhedrin (7:1-43)

We often speak of Stephen's speech before the Sanhedrin as his "defense." In so doing, we are likely to think of his presentation as a lawyer's attempt to get his client freed of the charges against him. In the first part of his defense, he did take steps to show that the charge of blasphemy was false. But as his speech developed, it became increasingly clear that his main concern was not in gaining his freedom but in indicting the Jewish leadership. He showed that in every age, the Hebrew people were rebellious against God and His messengers. This leads to his conclusion, a stinging indictment of his accusers. His defense is much like that of the apologists of the second and third centuries, who wrote to set forth the claims of Christianity rather than to defend themselves. Like Stephen before them, many paid for their defense with their lives.

God's Promise to Abraham (1-8)

The charges had been leveled against Stephen that he had said that Jesus of Nazareth would destroy the temple and that He would change the customs of Moses (Acts 6:13, 14). Apparently, the high priest presided over the proceedings. Having heard the charges, he asked him if they were true. Then he gave Stephen a chance to respond.

Stephen addressed the council in a respectful manner, calling them "Brothers and fathers" (Acts 7:2). Immediately, then, he turned to a review of a part of their history that was dear to the heart of every Hebrew. The Jewish people never forgot their origins and their unwavering conviction that they were chosen of God for a special mission. Stephen's reference to their beginnings certainly would have softened some of their antagonism and

69

would have made them more receptive to what he was about to say.

He first mentioned God's call of Abraham while he still lived in Ur of Mesopotamia. Genesis 11:31—12:1 indicates that God's call came to Abraham while he was in Haran rather than in Ur. As a result, some critics charge that Stephen made a mistake and got it wrong. However, Genesis 15:7 and Nehemiah 9:7 make it evident that Abraham was called while still at Ur. Clearly, God extended more than one call to Abraham. As a result of the first call, he moved with his father from Ur to Haran. Later, at Haran, after the death of his father, Abraham received a second call from God. If Stephen had got his history wrong, the scholars of the Sanhedrin would certainly have stopped him and corrected him.

The expression "God of glory" (Acts 7:2) describes God's majesty and splendor. It may also indicate some special manifestation of His presence in this very significant revelation to Abraham. After the revelation, Abraham, along with his father, Terah, moved to Haran. He remained there until the death of Terah. At that point, God sent him out to seek the land of his promised inheritance, the land where the Jews were then living.

But this required a tremendous act of faith on the part of Abraham. He had to leave the comforts of a settled community and become a wanderer in a difficult land surrounded by people who were often hostile. Though a land was promised to him and his descendants, Abraham himself never gained a square foot of ground. True, he did later purchase the cave of Machpelah as a burial place for Sarah, yet a cemetery can hardly be called a place of inhabitance. But some people, even though they will never know great blessings for themselves, are willing to labor on in the hope that their children will some day realize this great blessing. However, Abraham seemed to have been denied even this remote hope because he had no children, and Sarah was well past the age of childbearing.

God's next words added an additional test of Abraham's faith. His children would not be able to possess the land until they had served four hundred years in bondage in a strange land. This is a reference to the time they spent in Egypt. Some see a problem in Stephen's assertion that they would be in Egypt 400 years, whereas Exodus 12:40 states that the sojourn was 430 years. But only a person seeking to find a contradiction in these two statements would see a problem here. Obviously Stephen was speaking in round numbers and not attempting to give a precise chronology. All of us occasionally speak in this way without anyone's supposing that we have committed a blunder.

Stephen then injected a significant observation into his speech. God would punish the nation that enslaved the Israelites. Stephen and his audience knew, and we today know, how God did punish Egypt through the plagues for the way it mistreated Israel. Is there a veiled hint in Stephen's words that God would deal in similar fashion with those in his day who mistreated God's people? Once the Israelites had been delivered from bondage, they would eventually enter and inhabit the promised land.

In his survey of Jewish history, Stephen next mentioned God's covenant with Abraham. He referred to it as the covenant of circumcision because circumcision was its outward physical mark or seal. A covenant should not be understood as a contract between two equals. Rather, a covenant is a promise made by God to a man, the fulfillment of which depends upon that person's carrying out certain requirements. God's promises were never absolute. They could be, and often were, withdrawn when man proved unfaithful in obeying His commands.

Israel's Stay in Egypt (9-22)

Abraham had fathered Isaac, who in turn fathered Jacob. Jacob had twelve sons who became the progenitors of the twelve tribes of Israel. In his survey of history, Stephen carefully selected the items that would lead up to his final conclusion. He showed how through jealousy, the other brothers sold Joseph into slavery. "But God"—how significant were those words (Acts 7:9). How often man has exercised his freedom to act contrary to the will of God only to find God using that rebellion to accomplish His own purpose.

"But God was with him." Few Old Testament stories are more familiar to us than that of Joseph and the difficulties he faced. Yet through faith and God's grace, he was able to persevere and rise above them to become second only to the pharaoh himself.

When a famine came upon Canaan and Egypt, God had already made preparations for the children of Israel through Joseph. Jacob sent his sons to Egypt to buy grain. On their first visit to Egypt, they had not recognized Joseph. (Was Stephen suggesting a parallel between Joseph and Jesus, both of whom brought salvation to their people? Just as Joseph was not recognized by his brothers, so God's own Son was not recognized by the Jews.) On the second visit, Joseph revealed his identity to them. They were made known to the pharaoh, who invited Jacob and his whole family to settle in Egypt.

Stephen stated that the family of Jacob numbered seventy-five in all (Acts 7:14). However, Genesis 46:27 states that the number is only seventy. Apparently Stephen was quoting the Septuagint (a Greek translation of the Old Testament widely used in Stephen's day), which places the number at seventy-five by including some additional sons of Joseph that are not mentioned in the Hebrew version of the Old Testament.

Eventually, Jacob and all of his sons died in Egypt. Jacob's body was carried back to Canaan, where he was buried in the cave of Machpelah purchased by Abraham (Genesis 23:16-20). Joseph and his brothers were later buried at Shechem in a plot that had been purchased by Jacob (Joshua 24:32). Apparently Stephen in his abbreviated speech telescoped the two accounts of the purchase of two separate burial plots. It must have been rather galling to the Jews to be reminded that their fathers had been buried in land that now was claimed by the despised Samaritans.

The Israelites prospered in Egypt and their number increased greatly—to the point that a new pharaoh, "who knew nothing about Joseph" (Acts 7:18), began to consider them a threat. This may have been the member of a new dynasty. Several views exist as to the identity of this new king, but he cannot be positively identified. His rule became increasingly oppressive, but still the Israelites increased. Finally, in desperation, he decreed that all male babies born to the Israelites were to be exposed and left to die. We shudder at such cruelty, yet we who have lived in the twentieth century are no strangers to this kind of brutality. We immediately think of Hitler's Holocaust, the Russian blood purges, and our own laws that permit abortion. The anguished cries of the Israelites went up to God. They did not go unheard, but God knew that the people were not yet ready to accept His leadership, and so the burden of their sufferings had to increase before they were ready to surrender themselves to His will.

Moses' Preparation for Leadership (23-34)

Finally, God was ready to send a deliverer in the person of Moses. The parallels between his life and that of Jesus are quite obvious, and it seems likely that Stephen had these parallels in mind. Both were born under difficult conditions and both faced the threat of death by a wicked ruler. For a time, the parents of Moses were unwilling to follow the king's decree and secretly kept the baby hidden for three months. They realized, however, that as the child grew, it would be impossible to keep him hidden, and they finally were forced to leave him on the banks of the Nile.

Stephen's hearers would be quite aware of the story of Moses' rescue. But it was a story they never tired of hearing again. Stephen's use of it in his defense may very well have been designed to prove to the Sanhedrin that he shared this in common with them. Certainly his inclusion of this account could not have hurt his case. Moses was God's chosen instrument for the deliverance of his people. But to become useful, he had to be prepared. It is both ironic and a tribute to God's power and wisdom that He chose to allow the Egyptians to help prepare Moses for his future task. Reared in the house of Pharaoh's daughter as her own son, he received the best education possible in that day.

It seems evident that Moses had gained an understanding of who he was and that he had a mission in life to perform. When he was forty years old, those feelings came to a dramatic climax. Moses visited his Israelite brothers and became their champion by attacking an Egyptian who was mistreating an Israelite. But he acted rashly and soon was involved in a situation that did not go as he had planned. He wrongly supposed that this one act would cause the Israelites to turn to him for leadership.

The next day, he sought to settle a dispute between two Israelites. The aggressor, unwilling to allow Moses to interfere, taunted him about the murder of the Egyptian. Moses had taken steps to cover his crime, but obviously there had been witnesses. Word about Moses' action had spread quickly in the slave community, and soon the Egyptians would know, too. Moses learned the hard way that murder will out. To save his life, he had little choice but to get out of town in a hurry. Fleeing Egypt, he traveled into the Sinai Peninsula, a sparsely settled desert area where he would be safe from the Egyptians.

Moses paid a heavy price for presumptuously supposing that he was ready to lead the Israelites from their bondage. God certainly intended to free them, but in His own time and in His own way. Moses' mistake was in supposing that he could accomplish the job on his own without the help or guidance of God. He needed to learn patience, which took him forty years in the desert to learn.

Finally, God was ready to act. Near Mount Sinai, Moses saw the burning bush and heard the voice of the Lord: "I am the God of your fathers" (Acts 7:32). Moses' response, a very normal one for a human being in that situation, was to tremble and cover his face. At this point, he was commanded to remove his shoes as a mark of reverence for the holy spot upon which he stood. Then God reassured him that He had not forgotten the Israelites who were suffering in Egypt. God had heard their groaning, was preparing to free them, and Moses was to be the instrument He would use to accomplish His purpose.

Moses the Deliverer (35-43)

Stephen reminded his audience that this was the same Moses that the Israelites had earlier rejected. Of course, we cannot read Stephen's mind and know his motives for certain, but it seems that in his recounting of Jewish history, he selected those elements that supported one of his major theses: the Jewish people had always been a stiff-necked and rebellious people.

When Moses returned to Egypt, he went armed with the assurance that God would go with him. The people in turn were assured that God was leading Moses by the miraculous works that accompanied him in Egypt, at the crossing of the Red Sea, and in the wilderness.

At this point in his defense, Stephen, quoting from Deuteronomy 18:15, reminded them of Moses' prophecy that God would eventually send a prophet like himself. It certainly would not have been obvious to Stephen's listeners, but it is clear to us that this prophet was Christ himself.

One of the charges lodged against Stephen was that he had blasphemed against Moses. In relating this account of Moses, Stephen had completely exonerated himself of this charge. It is difficult to imagine how he could have been more respectful of the great lawgiver. It was the Israelites who had rejected him, and their sons, the very group before whom Stephen stood, continued this rejection.

In the wilderness, the people rejected him by demanding that Aaron fashion them gods who would then lead them. They did this even while Moses was on the holy mount receiving the "living words." They proceeded to bring sacrifices to the golden calf "in honor of what their hands had made" (Acts 7:37-41). Stephen had been charged with saying that Jesus would destroy the temple.

74

Just as the Israelites in the wilderness had worshiped an idol built with their hands, so their descendants had, for all practical purposes, become guilty of worshiping the temple also built by human hands. Thus, the Jewish leaders were the ones who were guilty, not Stephen.

Once the Israelites had started down the road to apostasy, one thing led to another. God punished them by turning away from them and allowing them to suffer the consequences of their sins. As a result, they turned to worship the heavenly bodies. Stephen quoted Amos 5:25-27 as evidence that what was started in the wilderness developed and came to dismal fruition in the time of the eighth-century prophet. The end result of their seeking strange gods was that they ended in exile in Babylon.

Stephen's Criticism of the Jewish Leaders (7:44-60)

In these verses, Stephen further defended himself against the charge that he had blasphemed against the temple. He did this by showing that the Jews had exalted the temple as a holy place far beyond what God had intended.

Worship in the Tabernacle and Temple (44-50)

In the wilderness God had given the Israelites a pattern for the tabernacle. Once it was constructed, this tabernacle or tent became a continuous witness or testimony of God's presence in their midst. It was carried with them as they invaded the land of Canaan. During the conquest and the time of the Judges, up until the time of David, the tabernacle continued to be the center of worship. David desired to build a more permanent dwelling place for God, but because his hands had been stained by the blood of his wars, God refused to permit him to build it (1 Chronicles 22:8). He was, however, permitted to begin to assemble the materials that were later used by Solomon to build the temple.

Then Stephen dropped the bombshell that he had been building up to. God *"does not live in houses made by men"* (Acts 7:48). This was not just a personal conclusion that he had come to. It was an idea that had been affirmed by the prophet Isaiah (66:1, 2). Stephen had been accused of speaking against the temple. His enemies were probably prepared to bring some petty charges against him. But in one short sentence, he had made their trumped-up charges unnecessary. Pagan gods might live in houses built by human hands, but not Jehovah God, the God of

Abraham, Isaac, and Jacob. Stephen's assertion, backed by Scripture, was far more radical than any charges his enemies might bring against him. His statement undercut the temple cult and all of the religious establishment that drew its existence from the temple. His sin, in the eyes of the religious leaders, was twofold. Not only had he spoken against the temple, he had also threatened the livelihood of the priests, both grievous sins indeed.

Charges Against the Jewish Leaders (51-53)

Stephen started out by using Israelite history to defend himself. Now he was using his brief survey of history to bring the most serious accusations against the Jewish leaders. The suddenness of his outburst has led some to suppose that his prior statements had caused his accusers, perceiving where his logic was leading them, to interrupt him in anger. Once they had quieted down enough that he could speak, he brought his indictment against them.

Stephen made no effort to tone down his charges. He knew what the Sanhedrin had done to Jesus and to the apostles; so he certainly must have known that his charges would further ignite their anger against him. Yet, like an Old Testament prophet, he thundered out his accusations without fear or favor. This was certainly no way to win friends, but Stephen was not at the moment seeking to become the most popular man in Jerusalem.

"You stiff-necked people!" (Acts 7:51). The allusion is to a stubborn ox that bowed his neck to resist the yoke. "With uncircumcised hearts and ears!" The Jews prided themselves on their circumcision as a mark of their faithfulness. Stephen pointed out that while they may have been circumcised physically, they remained uncircumcised in their hearts. They were uncircumcised in their ears because they refused to accept the truth when it was proclaimed to them. Their rebellious attitude had never been cut away, leaving them spiritual Gentiles. Old Testament prophets had on occasion used similar language to describe their fathers, and now the same language was turned against them.

"You always resist the Holy Spirit!" They resisted the Holy Spirit by refusing to heed those whom the Holy Spirit had sent as His messengers—Moses and the prophets. Individually, their fathers (and Stephen was careful not to say "our fathers") had resisted the Holy Spirit, turned Him off, until it had become a habit ingrained more deeply in each succeeding generation. We do not understand all the ways that the Holy Spirit works in our lives, but we do know (as Stephen charged here) it is possible for us to resist Him and refuse to accept His invitation of grace.

Their fathers had resisted the Holy Spirit, and they had also persecuted the prophets who served as messengers of the Holy Spirit. Stephen did not necessarily mean to imply that every prophet was persecuted, but enough of them had suffered that no one would challenge his point. Tradition (perhaps founded on Hebrews 11:37) has it that Isaiah was sawn asunder and that Jeremiah was stoned to death. Others suffered imprisonment and other cruelties. Their fathers had even killed those who prophesied the coming of the Righteous One, that is, the Messiah.

But Stephen reserved his most serious charge for his hearers, not their fathers. They had actually betrayed and murdered the Promised One! Stephen was not the first to level such a charge against them. On Pentecost, in his sermon reported in Acts 3, and before this same body, Peter had made a similar charge. In the first two sermons, those who heard Peter were moved to repentance by the charge. But the Sanhedrin stubbornly refused to hear Peter's accusation, trying rather to silence him. They were soon to take even more violent action against Stephen.

Stephen entered the courtroom charged with blaspheming and breaking the law. Now the tables were completely turned. Stephen was accusing them of receiving the law but not obeying it.

Stephen's Martyrdom (54-60)

At this point, the pent-up anger of Stephen's accusers burst forth without restraint. The Greek here literally says that "their hearts were sawn in two" (Acts 7:54), a rather striking figure indicating just how intense their feeling was. They further indicated this by gnashing their teeth.

Stephen, filled by the Holy Spirit, and with a vision clearer than theirs, could see into the very courts of Heaven. There he beheld the glory of God, and Jesus standing at the right hand of God (Acts 7:56). Stephen could expect no mercy from the Sanhedrin, but looking Heavenward, he could find strength there.

His joy at seeing Jesus at the right hand of God so overwhelmed him that he could not keep the scene to himself. He had to share his vision with those about, even though he knew that it would further enrage them. When Stephen told of his vision, he spoke of Jesus as the Son of Man, a title that Jesus often applied to himself. It was a title that had Messianic overtones. Jesus himself was

77

accused of blasphemy because He claimed to be the Messiah. Stephen could expect the same for confirming what Jesus had claimed. To allow Stephen to get away with this statement would have been an admission that they had erred in condemning Jesus.

The Sanhedrin chamber was already lacking in judicial decorum, but now it became a virtual mob scene. To show their rejection of Stephen's words they considered blasphemous, they began to shout at the top of their voices and to cover their ears. Then they rushed upon him with one accord. Stephen made no attempt to flee or resist the mob, but there was little he could have done to save himself at this point. The mob brutally dragged him out of the city where they proceeded to stone him to death. Tradition has it that they left the city through a gate in the eastern wall of Jerusalem, north of the temple area. To this date, it bears the name St. Stephen's Gate. Stoning was the method of execution prescribed by the Mosaic law for blasphemy.

From the description that Luke gives us, it is quite evident that the stoning of Stephen was not an execution as the result of the due process of law. The Romans had forbidden the Jews to execute capital punishment without permission. There is no evidence that the Sanhedrin sought such permission; so the Jewish leaders were acting in an illegal manner.

At this point, Luke injects a most interesting note. Observing these activities but apparently not actually involved in them was Saul of Tarsus. As he stood by watching, the participants, in order to be better able to throw the stones, removed their outer garments and laid them at his feet. Some suggest that Saul was acting in some official capacity as he watched over the garments of the participants, but we have no clear proof of this. This is another example of Luke's narrative style of introducing a character in a minor way before bringing him to the center of the drama.

In spite of the violence of the crowd, Stephen was able to get in the last word. With his final breath, he prayed for the Lord to receive his spirit and for forgiveness for those who were persecuting him (Acts 7:59, 60). His words remind us of Jesus' words on the cross: "Father, forgive them, for they do not know what they are doing" (Luke 23:34). There is no greater testimony to the power of the Christian faith than this example of a dying man praying for those who are murdering him. But Stephen's example does not stand alone. He is but the first in a long line of martyrs whose blood has stained the pages of history.

78

CHAPTER EIGHT

Persecution Leads to Evangelism

Acts 8

The Aftermath of the Martyrdom of Stephen (8:1-25)

The murder of Stephen began a whole new phase for the church, introducing a time of more violent and more widespread persecution. It seems evident that this persecution was not aimed just at restricting the church, but at destroying it. Saul of Tarsus came on the scene as the grand inquisitor, determined to root out every trace of what he considered to be heresy.

Great Persecution of the Church (1-3)

At the death of Stephen, Saul had stood by holding the coats of the executioners as a sign of his approval of their actions. The calm and saintly way that Stephen met his death might have melted the heart of a less determined man, but in Saul's case, it seemed only to incite him to increased frenzy against Christians. Like a vicious animal, the taste of blood made him all the more vicious. The bitterness that had been directed at Stephen did not disappear at his death but was transferred to all Christians.

Godly men buried Stephen. These men may not have been Christians, but pious men from among the Jews who felt that Stephen had not had a fair trial. Like Joseph of Arimathaea and Nicodemus, who cared for the body of Jesus, these men properly interred the body of Stephen. In taking such action, they exposed themselves to strong criticism.

As a result of this persecution of the church, many Christians fled Jerusalem, seeking refuge in Judea and Samaria. Even though going to Samaria meant that they would have contact with the outcast Samaritans, this was far less dangerous than remaining in Jerusalem and facing the wrath of Saul. They undoubtedly had reason to believe that such an orthodox Jew as he would not pursue them there.

The apostles, however, remained in Jerusalem. How they were able to escape Saul's inquisition is hard to understand, for certainly they would have been prime targets for persecution. It is likely that they were hidden by other church members. They did not leave Jerusalem because they were needed to counsel and comfort the young church in its affliction. Had they fled, many would have taken their actions for cowardice and lost faith in the church. Their courage, on the other hand, served to bolster the weakening faith of many. Apparently, members of the Sanhedrin were not directly involved in this persecution. Instead, it seems they put Saul in charge and gave him the authority and the manpower needed to get the job done.

It is likely that the Sanhedrin supplied him members of the temple guard to assist him as he arrested persons suspected of being Christians. We are left to wonder whether the persecution would have been pursued so vigorously had Saul not been involved. It seems evident that he was the driving force behind it.

"Saul began to destroy the church" (Acts 8:3). The Greek verb here was often used to describe the devastation a wild animal would wreak in its fury. Not content to arrest church members as they appeared in public, Saul, assisted by the temple officers, went from house to house in search of his victims. He seized men suspected of being Christian and put them in jail. Nor did he spare Christian women, who suffered along with the men.

God in His providence can use even the anger of His enemies to accomplish His purpose. Many Christians had found the fellowship with other Christians so fulfilling that they preferred to remain in Jerusalem. As edifying as this was, it was not carrying out the Great Commission. God thus used persecution to send Christians first into Judea and then into Samaria. (See Acts 1:8.)

How frustrated Saul would have been had he only known what his persecution was accomplishing. Like a person trying to put out a campfire by beating on it with a stick, his efforts only succeeded in scattering sparks far and wide. Each spark started a new fire.

Philip Begins a Ministry in Samaria (4-8)

Those who had been scattered by the persecutions instigated by Saul "preached the word wherever they went" (Acts 8:4). The Greek literally says, they were "announcing the good news of the word." These were not ordained ministers, professional evangelists, or specially commissioned missionaries. They were just ordinary Christians doing what should come naturally to a Christian. If the church had had to depend on a handful of specialists to evangelize the world, it would have taken a century for the message to have got out of Judea.

After this brief statement, Luke then called special attention to the work of Philip, one of the seven chosen to serve tables. Leaving Jerusalem, he traveled to Samaria, where he began a ministry that proved most fruitful. We are not quite certain where Philip actually carried on his ministry. Some texts say he went to "the city of Samaria" (Acts 8:5). The ancient city of Samaria had been destroyed. Herod rebuilt it and named it Sebaste. Some texts say "a city of Samaria," which might have been any of several cities.

It may come as a surprise that his message was so warmly received there because of the long-standing antagonism between Jews and Samaritans. But we need to remember that Philip was probably a Hellenistic Jew who did not share the feelings of his Judean brethren against the Samaritans. We need also to remember that Jesus had been well received in Samaria (John 4:39-42; Luke 17:11-19). This certainly helped pave the way for the coming of Philip. In addition, the word he preached was verified by the miracles he worked. The casting out of unclean spirits and the healing of paralytics and cripples are especially mentioned. The result was great joy (Acts 8:8), both because of the physical healings and the blessing of salvation that had come to them.

Simon the Sorcerer (9-25)

It soon developed that Philip had a rival in the city—Simon the sorcerer. Through his sorcery, he had amazed the people, and he had made great claims about himself that the people had believed. In fact, they said he had divine power and they called him the "Great Power" (Acts 8:10).

Early Christian literature has many references to Simon. In some sources, he is considered a great heretic and a leader of the gnostic heresy. One account states that he was accompanied in his travels by a woman assistant, who he claimed was an incarnation of the divine mind. Another account tells how he had himself buried alive with the promise that he would rise on the third day. But when the miracle did not occur, his nefarious career came to an abrupt end.

Although Simon had misled these people for some time, many of his followers accepted the good news brought by Philip and

81

were baptized. Finally, Simon himself, witnessing the miracles worked by Philip, realized that he was confronting a power greater than his own. As a result, he believed and was baptized.

Whether Simon was truly converted to Christianity or not has been long debated by theologians. Some have held Simon only went through the motions of becoming a Christian in the hopes that he could acquire the power to work miracles as Philip had. His efforts later to purchase this power from Peter and John give credence to this view. Yet there is nothing in Luke's words to indicate that Simon's conversion was sham and pretense. In fact, the words that Luke used—"believed and was baptized" (Acts 8:13)—are the same words he used to tell of conversions that undoubtedly were sincere (Acts 2:41; 16:15, 31-33; 18:8). Since we do not have the power to look into the heart of Simon, it would be wise for us to accept the words of the inspired historian that he was truly a believer. That he later was guilty of a very serious sin does not alter this fact. Faith and baptism have never given absolute assurance against one's falling into sin, even into apostasy.

Before long, word of Philip's work in Samaria got back to Jerusalem, and Peter and John were sent to investigate the report. The two apostles may have been sent because some in Jerusalem may have entertained some doubts about whether the gospel invitation was properly open to Samaritans. Later, some had questions about the conversion of Cornelius and about the large number of Gentiles who had become Christians at Antioch. But sending Peter and John to Samaria may not really have been aroused by suspicions at all. They may have been sent to assist Philip, who in the midst of a great revival certainly needed some extra help.

When Peter and John arrived, one of the first things they did was to pray that the Samaritan Christians might receive the Holy Spirit. Luke makes it clear that even though the Samaritans had been baptized, the Holy Spirit had not come on them (Acts 8:16). The Greek says "fallen on them," apparently a reference to some dramatic manifestation of the Spirit's presence. They actually received the Spirit when Peter and John placed their hands on them.

All of this raises an interesting theological question. At Pentecost, the Holy Spirit came upon the apostles in a highly visible way. Then, when many responded to the gospel invitation, Peter assured them that if they repented and were baptized, they would receive the "gift of the Holy Spirit" (Acts 2:38). However, after their baptism, there was no outward evidence that the Holy Spirit came upon them as He had upon the apostles. It seems reasonable to conclude that there is a difference between the indwelling "gift of the Holy Spirit," which is promised to all believers at baptism, and the charismatic gifts of the Spirit that come only under special circumstances.

It is significant that Philip, while he could perform certain miracles of healing, could not pass the gift of healing on to others. Thus we conclude that the apostles imparted this special power to these Samaritan Christians who already had received the indwelling gift of the Spirit at baptism. It seems evident that Simon was not offering to buy the gift of the Spirit, which presumably he had received at baptism. The receipt of this gift does not have any immediately visible consequences. What Simon wanted was something he saw happening when Peter and John laid their hands upon the Christians. He wanted for himself the ability to pass on to others the power to work miracles, an ability that, so far as the New Testament teaches, only Jesus and the apostles possessed.

We are appalled at the crassness of his offer of money for this power. It is quite evident that he completely misunderstood the nature of Christianity. His previous background may have conditioned him to think of Christianity in such materialistic terms. But even this does not excuse the seriousness of his sin. As a result of his act, his very name has been given to the practice of buying and selling religious powers and offices—simony. Unfortunately, Simon's offer was not the last time this sin appeared within the church. This practice became so frequent and accepted in the corrupt church of the later Middle Ages that few voices were raised against it until the Protestant Reformation. Simony may not be an obvious sin of the modern church, yet we see evidence of it in more subtle forms. Do we not today see examples of persons currying favor with the church or attempting to soothe an irritating conscience by their gifts?

Peter minced no words in his rejection of Simon's offer. In a stinging denunciation as strong as any found in the New Testament, Peter consigned both him and his silver to perdition (Acts 8:20). Simon had no part in "this ministry" (the Greek says "in this word"—Acts 8:21). This might be narrowly understood to mean only the special power of the Spirit that Simon wanted to buy. But from Peter's words that followed, it is obvious that Simon's very salvation was in doubt.

The reason for Simon's tragic condition was that his heart was not right before God. Solomon pointed out the necessity of guarding the heart, "for it is the wellspring of life" (Proverbs 4:23). There was but one solution to Simon's problem. He must repent and pray for forgiveness. Then, perhaps, God would see fit to forgive him. The "perhaps" does not apply to God's willingness to forgive. He always stands as a loving Father to receive the penitent prodigal. The question Peter injects concerns the sincerity of Simon's repentance. Could a man with a heart so corrupt that he thought he could buy spiritual blessings ever come to true repentance? Peter did not reject the possibility that Simon could truly repent. Under the circumstances, however, it would be a difficult thing for him to do, and Peter did not want to create any illusions that it would be easy. In evaluating the condition of Simon's heart, Peter was not necessarily exercising any special spiritual insight. We ordinarily judge a person on the basis of several acts rather than just one act. But this one evil act that Simon proposed revealed that his heart was "full of bitterness and captive to sin" (Acts 8:23).

Simon had hardly expected this kind of response from Peter, and he was panic-stricken as a result. Peter had directed him to pray for himself, but Simon instead asked that Peter pray for him. Apparently, Simon was too frightened or too proud to offer the appropriate prayers on his own behalf. He had yet to learn that it is never inappropriate for a penitent sinner to offer up a prayer for forgiveness. His problem seems to have been that he was more concerned about escaping the punishment for his sin than he was about his guilt. With these words of Simon, Luke drops him from the narrative, never to mention him again. We would like to know what happened to him, whether he did repent and gain acceptance back into the fellowship of the church. The fact that we are told nothing further about him is probably the reason that so many accounts about his alleged later evil activities are recorded among early Christian writers.

At the conclusion of this episode, Peter and John started back to Jerusalem. But they did not return directly. Instead, they traveled from village to village preaching as they went, using this opportunity to undergird the work of Philip in Samaria. Even though returning to Jerusalem may have entailed some danger for the two apostles, they were needed there to give stability to the church during those trying times.

An Ethiopian Eunuch Becomes a Christian (8:26-40)

With the problem created by Simon's attitude now removed, Philip was prepared to continue the successful evangelistic efforts he had begun. But God in His infinite wisdom chose to call him away from this work to undertake a quite different mission. Instead of witnessing to large numbers, he was called to present the claims of the gospel to one man.

Philip Sent to Witness to the Eunuch (26-29)

Philip received very explicit orders from the angel of the Lord (Acts 8:26). He was to go south to the desert road that went from Jerusalem to Gaza. We are not told exactly how the angel made his revelation known, merely that he did so.

We might reasonably ask why God did not send an angel to preach to the eunuch. We can't really say for certain. All we can affirm is that all of the conversions recorded in the New Testament come as a result of a human being, not an angel, delivering the message of salvation. God has always used human beings as His evangelists from Pentecost to the present.

We cannot determine for certain the road that Philip was sent to. One ancient route went from Jerusalem to Hebron and then to Gaza. Along this road a few miles north of Hebron is a spring, called St. Philip Spring, reputed to be the place where Philip baptized the Ethiopian. The more likely road was one that ran directly from Jerusalem to Gaza. This was the shorter route and one that a traveler would be more likely to take. This route was called a desert road, not because it ran through a dry, arid place, but because the area was only sparcely inhabited. Actually, this area receives more rain than does much of Palestine.

As Philip made his way along this road, he saw a chariot bearing an Ethiopian eunuch. This man had a very responsible position (in charge of the treasury) in the government of Candace, queen of Ethiopia. This was the country we now call Sudan, directly south of Egypt, not the area we now call Ethiopia.

The race of the eunuch has been debated by scholars. Some think he was a Jew serving in this high office of a foreign government much as did Joseph, Daniel, or Nehemiah. Others hold that he was a native Ethiopian who had embraced the Jewish faith. If he was, then he was a proselyte, and because he was a eunuch, he was considered a "proselyte of the gate" and would not have been permitted to enter the inner courts of the temple.

In that period, many Gentiles were attracted to Judaism because of its high ethical standards and its belief in one God. Archaeologists have discovered records of a Jewish settlement in southern Egypt; so it would have been quite possible for Ethiopians to have had contacts with Jews. This man certainly had made a serious commitment to Judaism, for he had made a trip of several hundred miles to visit the temple in Jerusalem, probably for one of the important annual feasts. Devout proselytes such as this Ethiopian were often ready converts to Christianity, seemingly more responsive to the gospel than other Jews.

As the eunuch rode along, he was reading from the book of Isaiah. This would have been in scroll form and was probably the Septuagint, a Greek translation of the Old Testament. Reading from a Greek scroll would not have been easy, for these manuscripts had no word divisions, punctuation, or accent marks. Bumping along in a chariot on a road that was not exactly a superhighway did not make his task any easier. It certainly seems providential that he was reading at that time from Isaiah 53, one of the richly Messianic passages from that book.

It was just at that moment that the Spirit directed Philip to approach the chariot. Previously he had been sent on this mission by the angel of the Lord; now it is the Spirit. (Whether these were two distinct entities or whether simply two ways of indicating that Philip was under divine direction, we cannot say for certain.) We are not told how the Spirit communicated with Philip, but this prompting was apparently necessary for him to know to approach this particular chariot.

The Eunuch's Problem (30-35)

When Philip came near, he heard the man reading aloud, a common practice in that day. The chariot was probably traveling slowly enough that Philip could walk alongside of it. It may have seemed a bit presumptuous for Philip to have approached a man of the Ethiopian's rank and spoken to him as he did. But it is safe to assume that Philip was still acting under the direction of the Spirit.

"Do you understand what you are reading?" (Acts 8:30). How appropriate a question! How often we need others to ask this same question of us. The Bible contains much figurative language and references that are no longer meaningful to us today. Even though God intends us to understand the Scriptures, we often need help to comprehend the meaning of many passages. At times, we are led to believe that God intends to make us work and struggle to find that meaning.

The Ethiopian was a humble man, and he did not hesitate to admit that he needed help. How many times have we missed opportunities to learn because our pride kept us from asking for help? Acknowledging his need, the eunuch immediately invited Philip to join him in the chariot and share his understanding of the Scriptures with him. There was something about Philip, perhaps his clothes or his conduct, that led him to believe that Philip could help him.

The passage he was reading was Isaiah 53:7 and 8, a part of the moving "Suffering Servant" poem. It should not surprise us that the Ethiopian did not understand it, for the Jewish scholars from Isaiah to the time of Christ did not consider these verses Messianic. Their concept of the Messiah saw Him as majestic and triumphant, not rejected and humiliated. What they could not see is obvious to us because we have the advantage of historic hindsight. It is quite likely that Isaiah himself did not understand the full import of the words he wrote.

As the eunuch pondered these verses, the question that puzzled him was the identity of the sheep that was led to the slaughter. He mentioned two possibilities: the prophet himself or some other person. And if another person, who?

The eunuch's question was exactly the opportunity that Philip needed, and beginning with that passage, he told him the good news about Jesus. One would be hard pressed to think of a better text from the Old Testament upon which to base a gospel sermon. The Gospels give accounts of Jesus' suffering and death, but none of the New Testament accounts describe any more vividly the real meaning of Jesus' passion than this passage from Isaiah. How could one more accurately describe Jesus' death than as an innocent lamb silently and meekly dying for others?

As they traveled along, the Ethiopian, seeing some water, asked to be baptized. His request indicates that Philip's message, like that of Peter's on Pentecost, led men to repentance and baptism. The words of Acts 8:37 are not found in many Greek manuscripts, and so most modern translations have omitted the verse or included it only as a footnote. Many scholars believe that the inclusion of these words reflects the practice of a later time when candidates for baptism were required to make such a statement of faith. Even if Philip did not ask the eunuch about his faith, such a question and such an answer would not have been out of place. It reminds us of Peter's good confession at Caesarea Philippi (Matthew 16:16).

Once the chariot stopped, both Philip and the eunuch went down into the water. Whether this was a pool or a stream, we have no way of knowing for certain. The fact that both men went down into the water indicates that it was large enough for both of them to enter the pool or stream. This was necessary, since baptism in the first century was by immersion. There in a ceremony that was both simple and profound, the eunuch died to the old man of sin and arose to walk in the new life (Romans 6:1-10).

As soon as they came up out of the water, the Spirit of the Lord suddenly took Philip away. We are not explicitly told that this was a miracle, yet the language strongly suggests that it was. Something similar was suggested in the case of Elijah (1 Kings 18:12; 2 Kings 2:16). The eunuch must have been mystified by the sudden disappearance of the man who had brought him the word of salvation. But he apparently was not upset by it but went on his way rejoicing.

This is the last we hear of the Ethiopian eunuch. A second-century Christian writer, Irenaeus, informs us that the eunuch returned to Ethiopia, where he evangelized among the people. While this was certainly the response to be expected from a Christian, we have no clear historic evidence that this is what actually happened. We do know that missionaries arrived in Ethiopia at a later date and a church was established there. If the eunuch did win converts in Ethiopia, most of them would have been Gentiles. But they were so isolated from Jerusalem that news of this activity would not readily have reached Jerusalem.

Philip, in the meantime, next appeared at Azotus, known in the Old Testament as Ashdod, one of the five great Philistine cities. It is located about ten miles north of Ashkelon and two or three miles inland from the Mediterranean. Philip evangelized in the area and then made his way up to Caesarea, preaching as he went. It is likely that he preached in Lydda and Joppa. Whether he was responsible for evangelizing those two cities or not, we know that Peter found saints there only a short time later (Acts 9:32-37). Philip later made his home in Caesarea, and Paul and his companions visited with him there. We are told that he had four daughters who prophesied (Acts 21:8, 9).

CHAPTER NINE

A Persecutor Becomes a Christian

Acts 9

The Conversion of Saul (9:1-19)

Chapter 9 begins a dramatic change in the book of Acts. The first eight chapters are concerned mostly with the activities of the apostles and their immediate converts. Now Saul of Tarsus, who had been mentioned briefly at the stoning of Stephen, comes to occupy the center of the stage. Most of the remaining twenty chapters will be devoted to the story of Saul's conversion and his subsequent missionary journeys.

Saul's Mission to Damascus (1, 2)

Saul had been largely successful in driving Christians from Jerusalem. Yet he was not satisfied. In persecuting Christians, he demonstrated an unflagging zeal—just as he later did in preaching Christ. It is entirely possible that the calm and forgiving way that Stephen died only intensified Saul's rage. Nothing enrages a zealot more than to have his attempts to enforce orthodoxy thwarted by the people he is attempting to convert.

Obsessed with the idea of stamping out Christianity wherever it appeared, he went to the high priest and asked permission for authority to move his inquisition to Damascus. The high priest at the time may have been Caiaphas, who was involved in the trials of Jesus and the apostles (Acts 4:6). However, we cannot be certain of his identity, for Caiaphas was deposed in A.D. 36, and some would date Saul's conversion later than this.

Saul wanted letters to the synagogues in Damascus that would give him the right to bring Christians back to Jerusalem for trial. Apparently the break between Christians and Jews had not yet developed in Damascus, for Saul expected to find Christians still worshiping in the synagogues. We know that earlier the Romans had granted Jews extradition rights to bring Jewish lawbreakers back to Jerusalem. This leads us to believe that the Christians whom Saul sought were refugees from Jerusalem rather than natives of Damascus.

Christians in Damascus were said to belong to the "Way" (Acts 9:2), a designation that is used several times later in the book of Acts (19:9, 23; 22:4; 24:14, 22). It may suggest that they were followers in the way of God or in the way of salvation. A similar use of this term has been found among some of the writings of the Essenes found at Qumran. Anyone found in Damascus who belonged to the Way, man or woman, was subject to being arrested and brought back to Jerusalem.

Damascus is located about a 150 miles north and east of Jerusalem. It is one of the oldest continuously occupied cities in the world. It lies in a plain east of the Anti-Lebanon Mountains and was on the major trade routes that went from Mesopotamia to Egypt and to Arabia. Damascus was watered by the Abana River, which made it a lush green spot in comparison to the desert areas to the east. Damascus is mentioned frequently in the Old Testament and was the capital of Syria, a bitter enemy of Israel. Later, Damascus was captured by the Romans, who placed a governor over the city. At the time of Saul's conversion, Aretas ruled over Damascus, or at least the area around it. At the time, it also had a sizable Jewish population and many synagogues.

Saul's Experience on the Road (3-9)

Saul was accompanied by temple guards (probably Levites), who came along to assist him in arresting Christians. By the time this band of men reached Damascus, they had been on the road a week or more. As they approached the city—the exact spot cannot be determined—a Heavenly light fell upon Saul. This light was brighter than the noonday sun (Acts 26:13).

Some have attempted to explain Saul's experience on the basis that he suffered an epileptic seizure. But an epileptic seizure hardly explains the subsequent turn of events in his life. A good deal more than epilepsy is needed to explain the complete change in the direction of his life and his complete dedication to a cause that he had once despised. Saul's own explanation was quite simple: he had met Christ face to face on the road outside Damascus. Just as Peter and the other apostles had met the risen Jesus face to face in the upper room, beside the sea, and on the Mount of Olives, so Paul had met Him on the Damascus road.

Suddenly a light flashed around Saul. Whether he was walking or riding a donkey, he fell to the ground, momentarily stunned. Those who accompanied Saul saw the light and heard the sound, but these phenomena could not mean the same to them that they did to him. Light has often accompanied God's revelation to man. He led the Israelites with a pillar of fire at night; on the mount of transfiguration, Jesus' face shone like the sun and His clothes were as white as light (Matthew 17:2); later, when an angel appeared to release Peter from prison, a light shone in the cell (Acts 12:7).

Then he heard a voice call out to him. "Saul! Saul!" came the salutation from the unknown and unseen speaker. By addressing Saul by name, there was no likelihood that he would suppose that the message was for someone else. But the question that followed, "Why do you persecute me?" must have left Saul bewildered. At this point, he had no idea who the speaker was, and he certainly did not believe that he was persecuting anyone unjustly.

Thus he asked, "Who are you, Lord?" In addressing the speaker as Lord, Saul was not ascribing deity to Him. The word *kurios,* here translated "Lord," may also be translated "master" or even "sir." It was a term of respect that did not necessarily convey deity. Since Saul at this point did not know who was speaking, it is obvious that he was using the word as a term of respect, not deity.

Then the speaker identified himself: "I am Jesus, whom you are persecuting" (Acts 9:5). Our Lord needed to make no further identification. All of Saul's time and energy had been committed to searching out and destroying those who had become followers of Jesus. We are not told what form Jesus took or exactly what Saul saw. But whether Jesus appeared in human form or as a manifestation of His glory, one thing is certain: He did appear to Saul in person. Just as the resurrected Lord appeared to the apostles, so He also appeared to Saul, "as one abnormally born" (1 Corinthians 15:8).

At this point, the King James Version inserts two sentences that are not in most modern translations. Once Jesus had identified himself, He went on to say, "It is hard for thee to kick against the pricks." Then verse 6 continues: "And he, trembling and astonished, said, Lord, what wilt thou have me to do?" The first statement is actually found in Acts 26:14. Perhaps a scribe wrote this in the margin of the ninth chapter and then accidentally it became incorporated into the text. The second statement, found in Acts 22:10, may have found its way into the text of the ninth chapter in a similar fashion.

Once Jesus established His identity, He then instructed Saul to go on into Damascus and await further instructions. It is significant that Jesus did not tell Saul directly what he needed to do to be saved. In every conversion recorded in the New Testament, a human being, not an angel or even Christ himself, was the agency by which the gospel was proclaimed. Thus it is incorrect to state that Saul was converted on the road to Damascus. It began there, but it was not completed until he had entered the city and responded to the message brought by Ananias.

Those who traveled with Saul were witnesses to this exciting drama. But they had no idea what was happening. They saw the light (Acts 22:9) and heard the sound, but they did not see anyone. We are not told how many were with Saul, but there may have been a dozen or more, at least enough to give him assistance in arresting Christians and transporting them back to Jerusalem. They may have been thrown to the ground as was Saul, and they were certainly every bit as perplexed as he by what had happened.

Acts 26:16-18 indicates that Jesus set before Saul the terms of his calling, that he was being sent as a special witness of what he had seen and what the Lord was yet to show him. After this, Saul arose to his feet, but as he did, he made another agonizing discovery. He was blind! When the brilliant light enveloped him, he must have closed his eyes against its brightness. He must have kept them closed until he arose to his feet. Only when he stood up to go into the city, did he discover that he was helpless. His companions then led him into Damascus.

Saul remained in this helpless state for three days. During that time, he was forced to make a painful reappraisal of his life. Everything that he had deemed important—his great learning, his proud position as a Pharisee, his leadership in defending Jewish orthodoxy—had been swept away. Whatever chance he might have had to make a name for himself was now gone. Only ashes remained. With these things gone, he had to find a way to give meaning to his life. But he had still another burden. Outside of Damascus, he learned for the first time that he had been persecuting Christ by persecuting His followers. He thus had to grapple with a guilty conscience, and none of his Jewish training could provide him a way of escape from that sense of guilt.

The Master, whom he had met outside the city, had told him that he would receive further instructions about what he was to do. He had dutifully followed these instructions, but no further word had come. One day stretched into two and two into three, and yet additional word had not come. At some point during this long wait, doubts must have arisen. Had he really heard a voice? Or had his mind, traumatized by the brilliant light, deceived him? No wonder he went three days without food or drink.

Ananias to the Rescue (10-19)

Even as Saul agonized, God was preparing to send him relief. In a vision, the Lord spoke to a certain Ananias, a disciple previously unmentioned in the Scriptures. Ananias was not shocked by this vision nor when he was summoned to service. He responded affirmatively to the Lord's call.

The Lord's instructions were quite explicit. He was to go to the house of Judas on Straight Street and ask for Saul of Tarsus. Saul, who was in serious prayer at the time, had already been informed in a vision that Ananias would be coming. But Ananias, who had been quite ready to do the Lord's bidding, recoiled in horror when he learned what his task would be. Do we not on occasion behave like Ananias? We are eager to obey the Lord until we learn that His will for us goes contrary to what we have expected.

Ananias may have had two reasons for hesitating about following the Lord's orders. He may have feared for his own personal safety—and for good reason. Saul's reputation had preceded him to Damascus. Ananias knew how he had persecuted Christians in Jerusalem, and he also knew that Saul had come to Damascus with the authority to wreak similar havoc on the church there. But Ananias' personal safety was probably not his major concern. It seems more likely that he was unwilling to lend any support to one that he knew was an enemy of the church. It is one thing to love one's enemies; it is another thing to lend assistance to an enemy who seems bent on one's destruction. In this case, to do so seemed a betrayal of his fellow believers.

The Lord understood Ananias' plight; so He gave him further information to reassure him. Saul had been selected by the Lord for a very special mission. He would carry the gospel to the Gentiles and to their rulers as well as to the sons of Israel. As Saul carried out the Lord's orders, he would suffer many things. This information must have shocked Ananias almost as much

93

as the initial call to go to Saul. As a faithful Jew who had become a Christian, there is no reason to suppose that Ananias understood at this time that God intended the blessings of the gospel to be made available to all people. Yet, in spite of whatever reservation he may still have had, Ananias went without any further objection. Obedience such as this receives our Lord's commendation: "Well done, thou good and faithful servant."

Ananias proceeded immediately to the house of Judas on Straight Street, where Saul agonized in prayer. Guides today point out Straight Street, which still remains an important street in Damascus. It is wider than most streets in this old city and is much straighter than streets ordinarily were in ancient cities.

Upon entering the house, Ananias did not upbraid Saul for his previous persecution of the church but spoke directly to his needs. We might learn a lesson from Ananias' behavior. All too often, we are tempted to condemn those agonizing souls who need instead to be encouraged. As soon as Ananias came into Saul's presence, he laid his hands upon him. It is interesting that Ananias addressed Saul as "Brother," a reassuring note that Saul needed at that moment. Some legalists might insist that Ananias had no right to address Saul in this fashion, since he had not yet been baptized. Such narrow legalism would have been strangely foreign to Ananias in this situation. He was, after all, on an errand of mercy for the Lord. He had no time for such trivial hairsplitting.

After addressing Saul, Ananias then told him the purpose of his mission. The same Jesus who had appeared to Saul outside of Damascus had sent Ananias to minister to Saul in his time of need. The mention of the name of Jesus must have immediately struck a responsive chord in Saul's heart, leaving him ready to hear Ananias' message. Ananias first mentioned two things that would result from his visit—Saul would receive his sight and he would be filled with the Holy Spirit.

At once Saul's sight was restored. The language suggests that it happened as if scales had been suddenly removed from his eyes. The suddenness of the recovery of his sight makes it clear that the action was miraculous. A natural healing process would have taken considerable time, whereas this recovery was instantaneous. We can imagine the joy and relief that came to Saul when he once more was able to see. His future, which had before been covered with a mantle of darkness, had suddenly been given new life and hope.

Luke has given us a very abbreviated account of what happened. We are told that Saul was baptized, but certainly Ananias must have given him some explanation about what was involved in his becoming a Christian. Otherwise, how would he have known that baptism was commanded as an act of obedience? In Acts 22:16 we learn some of Ananias' words to Saul: "Now what are you waiting for? Get up, be baptized and wash your sins away, calling on his name." But even these words must be only a brief summary of the dialogue between the two men.

We are not told where the baptism took place. It may have been in one of the two rivers in the area—the Abana or the Pharpar. It is more likely that it occurred in a nearby pool or reservoir, for we are told that after this, he took some food and regained his strength (Acts 9:18, 19).

Saul in Damascus and Jerusalem (9:20-31)

5/24/92

We wish that Luke had given us more information about what happened immediately after Saul's baptism. Even though he was a scholar and knew the Old Testament Scriptures quite well, he needed help and guidance in gaining a fuller understanding of them. We can be certain that Ananias led him in a crash course in understanding the Old Testament Scriptures in the light of the New Covenant. As a Pharisee, his spiritual eyes had been covered by the scales of legalism. Now these had been removed, and just as his physical eyes had been opened, so now his spiritual eyes were opened.

Saul's Preaching in Damascus (20-22)

After spending a brief time with the disciples in Damascus, Saul began to preach in the synagogues. It is not surprising that he would be allowed to do this, since it was a common practice to invite visiting teachers and scholars to speak. It is possible that the Christians were at this time still meeting in the synagogues. The break between Judaism and Christianity had not yet become complete and final.

Saul's message brought astonishment to his hearers for two reasons. First of all, they were amazed that he who had come to persecute Christians was now proclaiming the Christian message. The second thing that must have shocked them was his bold assertion that Jesus was the Son of God. Saul's great learning came to his aid as he engaged in argumentation with the Jews. Luke tells us that he baffled them by proving that Jesus is the Christ (Acts 9:22), accomplishing this, no doubt, by using the Old Testament Scriptures.

Luke has given us an abbreviated account of Saul's activities in Damascus. In writing to the Galatians several years later, Saul (by then known as Paul) related how he went into Arabia (Galatians 1:17). This area included only the area east and north of Palestine, not the whole peninsula that we now know as Saudi Arabia. A group of people known as the Nabataeans lived in this area in New Testament times. Their territory included the city of Petra and parts of the Sinai Peninsula. It seems likely that Saul sojourned in this area, where he had an opportunity to meditate about what had happened to him and how he could best use his life in the future. Knowing Saul's concern for the lost, it would be surprising indeed if he did not find many opportunities to preach the gospel.

Saul's Escape from Damascus (23-25)

After spending some time in Arabia, Saul returned to Damascus, where he began preaching again with renewed vigor. His preaching aroused bitter opposition, and his Jewish enemies began to plot to get rid of him. This provides eloquent testimony to the effectiveness of his preaching. In seeking to take his life, they were admitting that they could not refute his arguments. When Saul learned of their plot, he probably had to go into hiding or, at least, to curtail his public appearances. Determined not to let him escape, the Jews kept the city gates under close surveillance around the clock. By keeping him confined within the city, they no doubt hoped soon to ferret him out and carry out their violent plan. We are told that the Nabataeans under King Aretas cooperated in this effort to take Saul (2 Corinthians 11:32).

But their efforts came to naught. Saul was able to escape when some of the disciples lowered him over the wall in a basket. In ancient cities, it was a common practice to build houses on or very close to the wall. Thus, at night, Saul could have been lowered through a window in such a house without attracting any attention. It is likely that some friends waited outside the wall to escort him to Jerusalem or at least for a safe distance down the road from Damascus. Already, Saul was beginning to understand the meaning of the Lord's words warning him that he would suffer many things for His name (Acts 9:16).

96

Saul in Jerusalem (26-29)

Saul's return to Jerusalem was quite different from his departure. When he had left for Damascus some three years earlier (Galatians 1:16), he had been accompanied by an armed escort to seek out Christians. Now he returned, himself a Christian and a fugitive from the authorities. Persons today who become Christians are not likely to experience such a dramatic turn of events; yet even today there are circumstances under which becoming a Christian might lead to such a drastic change.

But escaping to Jerusalem did not immediately change Saul's situation. If he had expected the Christians there to welcome him with open arms, he suffered a severe disappointment. They harbored serious suspicions about him. After all, can a leopard change his spots? We who live in an age of spies and secret agents can readily appreciate the reservations of the Judean Christians about accepting Saul. The role of the double agent was certainly not unknown in the ancient world, and those who had suffered severe persecution were likely to be careful about whom they accepted into their ranks. Christians who live behind the iron curtain today regularly face this kind of threat. The sad part of such a situation is that their fears create crippling suspicions and cause them to withhold their fellowship from sincere converts. Let us pray that we never have to live under such a cloud.

But then there was Barnabas—generous, big-hearted Barnabas. Luke had mentioned him earlier (Acts 4:36, 37) as one who had given generously of his possessions. Here Barnabas demonstrated that his generosity was not limited to his possessions alone. He took Saul and presented his story to the apostles. It seems surprising that they were not familiar with his conversion and preaching in Damascus. We need to keep in mind two or three things. First of all, even if they had heard of his conversion, it surely must have seemed incredible—too good to be true. In the second place, Paul mentions in Galatians 1:18 that three years elapsed before he returned from Damascus to Jerusalem. Actually, as the Jews counted time, it may have been only parts of three years and thus a little over a year. We also need to understand that communications were not instantaneous or as certain as they are today. Further, Herod Antipas had been involved in a war with King Aretas of Arabia; so the flow of news that ordinarily was carried by travelers would have been greatly reduced.

We today ought to be thankful for the blessings of instantaneous communication and rapid transportation. By way of the printed media, radio, television, telephone, and the informal "grapevine," we have ready communication with fellow Christians around the world. Thus, we are kept aware of their needs and their victories for the Lord.

While Luke tells us that Barnabas took Saul to the apostles, Galatians 1:18, 19 states that he saw only Peter and James, the Lord's brother. There is no contradiction here if we understand that James was considered an apostle, not one of the twelve but in a more general sense. The rest of the twelve apparently were not in Jerusalem at the time, having left because of persecution or to carry out evangelistic work.

In presenting Saul to the church leaders in Jerusalem, Barnabas noted three things to verify Saul's conversion. First of all, Saul had seen the Lord. Not all of the Christians then living in Jerusalem had actually seen Jesus. Of course, Saul had not seen Jesus in the flesh, but seeing Him in a vision was even more impressive. In the second place, the Lord had spoken to Saul. The implication was that He had conveyed a special message to him. These first two points would have been difficult to prove since they relied upon the word of Saul for confirmation. But the third point that Barnabas made—that Saul had preached boldly in Damascus—could be confirmed by many witnesses.

Once he was accepted into the fellowship of the church, Saul immediately began to preach in the name of the Lord. He was soon drawn into discussion and debate with the Grecian Jews. It is a rather interesting irony that it was probably this same group that responded so violently to the preaching of Stephen. They wasted no time in rejecting Saul, whom they must have considered both a heretic and, even worse, a turncoat.

Saul wrote in Galatians 1:18 that he remained in Jerusalem only fifteen days, and so it apparently did not take long for the antagonism of the Jews to turn to violence. As they had done in Damascus, so in Jerusalem they plotted his death. Christian friends of Saul soon learned of this plot and arranged for him to leave Jerusalem. This was to become a regular pattern later in Saul's ministry. Whenever he entered a city, his preaching would first attract attention, then opposition, and then he would have to flee for his life. His effectiveness and faithfulness insured that he would never enjoy a permanent mailing address. Some modern ministers may experience frequent changes of address, but not always for the same reasons. In fact, their changes may be for the very opposite reasons.

Saul Sent to Tarsus (30, 31)

Saul's friends took him to Caesarea, the impressive seaport city built by Herod the Great. The Roman governor made his headquarters there. Years later, Saul would spend two years in prison there before he finally was sent to Rome. At this time, the disciples sent him back to his hometown of Tarsus. For some time, he dropped out of the picture as Luke turned his attention to other matters. We can only speculate what Saul did during these silent years, but knowing him, it is safe to assume that he busied himself preaching and teaching.

Luke concludes his account of Saul's conversion and brief visit to Jerusalem with a summary of the status of the church (Acts 9:31) just as he had done at other points in his narrative (Acts 2:42-47; 4:32-35; 5:12-16; and 6:7). Following Saul's departure from Jerusalem, the church enjoyed a period of peace. The death of Stephen and the conversion of his chief persecutor brought a time of relief. Persecution may on occasion purge the church and even cause it to grow. But under most circumstances, the church grows most rapidly in a time of peace. The church throughout Palestine—Judea, Galilee, and Samaria—enjoyed this prosperity. (This is the first time that any mention is made of a church in Galilee.) Two factors contributed to this. The members of the church walked in the fear of the Lord and in the comfort of the Holy Spirit. In most situations today when a church is growing, it happens that its members are walking in the fear of the Lord and enjoying the encouragement of the Holy Spirit.

Peter at Lydda and Joppa (9:32-43)

With this summary of the status of the church in Palestine and Saul's retirement to Tarsus, Luke turned back to the apostle Peter. The events at Lydda and Joppa serve as a prelude to the events of even greater significance at Caesarea.

Peter Heals a Paralytic at Lydda (32-35)

Apparently, Peter set out to visit several of the churches that had sprung up all over Palestine. His travels led him to Lydda, a town located about a dozen miles inland and southeast from

Joppa. It was near the route one would take on his way to Joppa and Caesarea. A body of believers lived there, including a man named Aeneas, who had been paralyzed and bedridden for eight years. The name Aeneas is Grecian in origin, leading many to believe that he was a Hellenist.

Peter came to him and immediately announced that he was healed by the power of Jesus. The miracle was instantaneous, and Aeneas immediately got up. Since his affliction was probably well known, the news of his healing created quite a stir in the town and in Sharon, the name of the plain that surrounded the town. This miracle and the excitement that followed it led to a successful period of evangelization, during which time many turned to the Lord.

Peter Heals Dorcas in Joppa (36-43)

Peter's stay in Lydda was cut short by an emergency call from Joppa. This ancient city was located on a promontory overlooking the Mediterranean. During much of its history, it served as the chief seaport of Palestine even though it had a poor harbor that offered little protection from the sea. By this time, Joppa had a church among whose members was a woman named Tabitha (or Dorcas when translated into Greek, or Gazelle in English). Dorcas had gained a good reputation because of her works of charity. Her efforts seemed especially praiseworthy because she had worked to help the poor.

However, Dorcas had become ill and had died. Her body had been washed and placed in an upper room in preparation for burial. The disciples at Joppa had heard that Peter was only a few miles away at Lydda. Two men were sent to bring him to Joppa quickly. We can understand the need for haste. In that climate, it was the usual practice to bury the dead the same day that death occurred, or early the next day if death occurred late in the evening. Since the round trip would take six or eight hours, Peter would have to make haste before Dorcas was buried.

What did the disciples in Joppa expect Peter to do when he arrived? Did they want him present to comfort the bereaved? Or did they hope for more, even that Dorcas would be raised from the dead? We can only guess about this, but the fact that the body was only washed rather than treated with spices or other embalming practices might lead us to conclude that they hoped for a miracle.

Peter recognized the urgency of the situation, and without any hesitation left his work in Lydda and accompanied the two men back to Joppa. When he arrived, he was immediately ushered into the upper room. There he found a number of widows, lamenting the loss of this dear sister and showing the robes and other clothing Dorcas had prepared for them. It seems likely that they were wearing some of the examples of her handiwork. These were not hired mourners, but persons who experienced in a very poignant way the great loss. What a wonderful example Dorcas has set for Christians in every age since. Though she was but a seamstress, she gave that talent to the Lord and used it in such a way that her good works lived after her. Have we so dedicated our talents to the Lord that His name will be glorified in our passing?

Peter then asked the mourners to leave the room. We are reminded of a similar incident in the ministry of Jesus—the raising of Jairus' daughter (Mark 5:35-43; Luke 8:49-56). In Mark's version of this miracle, Jesus put the mourners out, taking only the girl's parents and the disciples into the girl's room with Him. No doubt, Peter recalled that incident even as he prepared to duplicate it. Some observant students have pointed out still another striking similarity. Jesus spoke in Aramaic to Jairus' daughter the words "Talitha koum," which means "Little girl, get up." If Peter spoke in Aramaic, he would have said, "Tabitha koum," which means "Tabitha, get up." Only one letter in the two commands was different.

Prior to issuing his order, Peter had knelt beside the lifeless body and prayed. For what did he pray? Did he ask that the mourners have the faith and courage to face the future without their beloved benefactor? This would certainly have been an appropriate prayer. Or did he ask God for more—the resurrection of Dorcas? We can only speculate about the precise content of his prayer, because Luke gives us no clue about it. But from his command to her, it is clear that he prayed for her resurrection!

As soon as Peter called her name and told her to arise, she opened her eyes, looked at Peter, and sat up. Then Peter helped her to her feet, perhaps because she was wrapped in grave clothes, making it difficult for her to arise. After Dorcas had been called back from the grave, Peter summoned the widows and the believers ("saints" in the Greek) and presented her to them alive. We can only imagine the cries of joy that replaced the lamenting that had filled the room only a few minutes earlier.

It did not take long for word of this miracle to spread all over town. At this point, the account of Jesus' healing of Jairus' daughter and this miracle diverge. Jesus gave strict orders that the people present were not to let anyone know of the girl's resurrection. In contrast, Peter gave no such command to those who were in the house when Dorcas was raised. In fact, it would seem that the people were encouraged to spread this good news, for many came to believe on the Lord because of this miracle (Acts 9:42).

Peter remained in Joppa for a time, preaching and teaching, we can be sure. While there, he lived with Simon the tanner. Luke seems to have had a reason for giving us this bit of information. Earlier Peter, along with John, had gone to work among the Samaritans. His willingness to work among a people usually shunned by the Jews indicates that he was abandoning some of his prejudices. Living with Simon indicates another step in this direction, since a tanner was considered ceremonially unclean by the Jews because he had to deal with dead bodies. Tradition locates this house near the sea, which would provide adequate water needed for the tanning process. It is also likely that it was at the edge of town or even outside the town, since the odors emanating from a tannery are hardly pleasant. This was Peter's situation as God prepared to use him in the next great venture in carrying the gospel to all the world.

CHAPTER TEN

A Gentile Becomes a Christian

Acts 10

Cornelius Sends for Peter (10:1-8)

The tenth chapter of Acts relates one of the events that is a crucial turning point in the history of the early church. Up until this time, the gospel message had gone out to the Jews, the Samaritans, and perhaps to a proselyte—the Ethiopian eunuch. The spread of the gospel had followed the order given by Jesus— Jerusalem first, then Judea and Samaria (Acts 1:8). Finally the time had come for the message of salvation to break out of these narrow limits and reach out into the Gentile world, to "the ends of the earth." For this reason, Luke wrote a detailed account of the conversion of Cornelius and his house, including the two visions that led up to it.

Without any prior introduction, Luke brought Cornelius to the center of the stage. He did not give us much information about him, but the details are adequate for the purpose of his narrative. We learn that Cornelius was stationed at Caesarea. This city was relatively unimportant until Herod began a building program there. This included an artificial harbor that soon made Caesarea the major seaport for Palestine. During much of the first century, it served as the residence for the Roman governor of Judea.

We learn that Cornelius was a centurion, the commander of a hundred men in a Roman legion. He was a part of the Italian Regiment, actually a cohort, a body of some 400 to 600 men. He would be roughly equivalent in rank to a modern infantry captain. When we look at some of the centurions mentioned in the New Testament, we are impressed with the quality of these lower officers in the Roman army. The centurion whose servant Jesus healed (Matthew 8:5-13), the centurion at the cross who acknowledged Jesus as the Son of God (Matthew 27:54), and the centurion who accompanied Paul on the voyage to Rome (Acts 27:1, 3, 37-

32, 42-44) immediately come to mind. All of them seem to have been intelligent men of integrity.

We learn some important information about Cornelius' religious commitment in Acts 10:2. He, along with his household, was a devout man and God-fearing. This latter expression was frequently used to describe those who had been attracted to Judaism either by its high ethical standards or its monotheism. They often were permitted to attend the synagogue worship and sometimes became acquainted with the Greek Old Testament, even though they did not become full proselytes to the Jewish faith. These were sometimes referred to as "proselytes of the gate," suggesting that the Jews looked upon them only as standing at the gate. They were still considered Gentiles, since they had not submitted to the entire law of Moses, including circumcision. Cornelius' faith was more than just a religious fad. He demonstrated his faith by his generous contributions to the poor and his regular prayers.

One day about the ninth hour (3 P.M. our time) Cornelius was in prayer. In the midst of his prayer period, he saw a vision. An angel of God came to him and called him by name. We can speculate that God used such a dramatic way of delivering the message because this was to be the occasion that opened the church to Gentiles. Cornelius was wide awake, not asleep or in a trance, when the angel appeared. His immediate response was one of fear, a quite characteristic response when a human is confronted by the divine.

Most translations have Cornelius addressing his visitor as "Lord." The Greek word *kurios* may be translated either as "sir," a term of respect, or "Lord," referring either to God or Jesus Christ, His divine Son. "Lord" seems appropriate here because, even though Cornelius did not know the identity of his visitor, he had every reason to believe that the visitor was from God.

Cornelius' prayers and alms had gained the attention of God. This is not to suggest that his good deeds had earned the special favor of God, but they did indicate the condition of his heart. His life demonstrated that his heart was ready to receive further truth from God. His prayers may have contained a petition for further enlightenment, a petition that all of us ought to offer up regularly.

It is worth noting at this point that Cornelius' life was exemplary. He was a man of integrity, a pious man whose religious convictions led him to serve his fellow men. Almost any church would be pleased to have him as a church officer. Yet this was not enough. It is hard for us to realize that the good deeds of even the most pious person cannot merit salvation. Salvation comes only through God's grace. Cornelius was not selected to receive God's revelation because he was good enough to deserve it. The angel of God came to him because God knew his heart was ready to receive His message.

Note also that the angel did not preach the message of salvation to him. Rather, this task was left to human instrumentality. All the angel did was to bring instructions about how Cornelius was to summon Peter, who was to be the messenger to bring the gospel to him. The instructions were quite explicit, even telling where Peter was to be found.

Cornelius lost little time in carrying out the instructions. He called two servants and one of his aides, himself also a devout man, told them what had happened, and sent them on their way to find Peter.

Joppa was nearly thirty-five miles from Caesarea, and so the men must have left immediately and walked much of the night in order to have reached Joppa by noon the next day.

Peter's Vision (10:9-23)

God was already at work to time their arrival at the house of Simon the Tanner so that it would exactly coincide with Peter's trance. Peter had gone up onto the top of Simon's house to pray. The flat roofs of Palestinian houses were commonly used as places of rest and meditation. The housetop was above the street level so that persons resting there would receive the benefit of any breeze that might be stirring. The roof was usually surrounded by a parapet that gave persons privacy from the street. Many Palestinian houses are still built this way. Sometimes a vine is trained over the roof or a canopy is stretched above it to provide protection from the sun. It is likely that Peter was protected in this fashion when he retired there at the noon hour to pray. Jews often observed 9 A.M. and 3 P.M. as times of prayer, but devout Jews also observed a prayer period at noon.

As Peter began his devotion period, he became very hungry. The hosts were at that time preparing a meal; perhaps the odors wafting up from below whetted his appetite. In any event, he fell into a trance. Our English word *ecstasy* is derived from the Greek word used here for *trance*. Literally, it means "to stand outside oneself." It describes a condition in which one's normal sensations of the physical world are suspended. In that condition, one is keenly alert to a different dimension of experience. Peter was not dreaming, for he was wide awake, not asleep, when he saw what Luke called a "vision" (Acts 10:17).

Some commentators believe that Peter's vision was suggested by the situation. The sheet that descended may have been suggested by an awning that stretched above his head and the act of killing and eating may have been suggested by his hunger at the time. Certainly it is within God's power to use physical elements to reveal His will. But that should not obscure the fact that the revelation was supernatural, not something simply conjured up in Peter's own mind. It had to be supernatural to overcome Peter's prejudice against Gentiles.

In the vision, Peter saw a large sheet containing all kinds of mammals, reptiles, and birds lowered to the earth. Then came the shocking command to arise, kill, and eat. It was shocking because the sheet contained animals that were declared unclean by the law of Moses. Even though Peter addressed the speaker as "Lord," he was not willing to obey the command and violate the provisions of the law that he had observed all of his life.

The response of the voice to Peter's objection must have been an even greater shock to him: "Do not call anything impure that God has made clean" (Acts 10:15). Obviously, Peter did not have the slightest idea about all the implications of this scene. It was repeated two more times, probably accompanied each time by Peter's refusal to eat. This reminds us of Peter's three denials of our Lord and his three responses to Jesus' question on the shore of the Sea of Galilee (John 21:15-17).

The implications are obvious enough for us, living as we do after the event. It meant that the Mosaic law was passing away. The dietary provisions that were designed to create a separate nation of the Israelites were only temporary. They had served their purpose and were no longer needed. It is also clear to us that much more than dietary laws were involved. If the dietary laws, designed to create a separate people, were no longer binding or necessary, then the logical conclusion was that God no longer chose to maintain a nationally or politically separate people. If the animals designated as unclean by the law of Moses were now declared clean, then the Gentiles, considered by the Jews as unclean, were now also acceptable to God.

Given enough time, Peter might have come to this conclusion on his own. But God's timetable was in too big a hurry to allow Peter the time to work his way through his prejudices. God had already taken steps to hasten Peter to this conclusion. Even as Peter pondered these things, the men sent by Cornelius were already at the gate. They called out, probably to Simon the tanner, asking if Simon Peter was there. Apparently, Peter did not hear them call; so the Spirit interrupted his thoughts and told him to go down and greet the three men and prepare to accompany them when they left.

Peter went down as the Spirit had told him to, identified himself, and then asked them their mission. They then told of Cornelius, the appearance of the angel to him, and their subsequent mission. To make Peter more receptive to their request, they assured him that Cornelius was a God-fearing man, respected by the Jews. Their mission was to bring Peter back with them so that he could speak to Cornelius.

Once they had explained their mission, Peter took it upon himself to speak for Simon and invited them into the house. This was an unusual act, for orthodox Jews did not invite Gentiles into their homes, but a little glimmer of light had penetrated Peter's prejudices; the pieces of the puzzle were beginning to fall into place.

Peter in the House of Cornelius (10:23-48)

The men sent by Cornelius had traveled for many hours and were tired. Thus, a decision was made to delay their return with Peter until the next day. We can't help wondering what Peter and his guests talked about the rest of the day. Peter may have called in some of the Christians at Joppa to share in the conversation, for several of them accompanied him on his trip to Caesarea.

It was a long walk from Joppa to Caesarea. No doubt, the men left early in the morning. Six of the brothers from Joppa went with them (Acts 10:23; 11:12), making a party of ten. The next day, they arrived in Caesarea and made their way to the house of Cornelius, where he was waiting for them. He was not waiting alone, but had brought together his family and many of his close friends.

As soon as Peter entered, Cornelius fell before him in reverence (Acts 10:25). Several translations say that Cornelius "worshiped" him. The Greek word used means to bow down before someone or something, usually as an act of worship. While we cannot know exactly what Cornelius had in mind, it seems evident that he looked upon Peter as some kind of divine messenger.

It is also clear that his actions did not meet with Peter's approval. Although the apostle must have understood the centurion's humility, Peter was certainly embarrassed by this kind of treatment and immediately assured him that they were equals: "'Stand up,' he said, 'I am only a man myself'" (Acts 10:26). We could wish that the so-called successors of Peter exhibited the same kind of humility.

When Peter entered the house, he found several people assembled and waiting for him. Then he informed Cornelius that it was unlawful for a Jew to enter the home of a Gentile, a fact that Cornelius was certainly aware of. Actually, the Mosaic law did not specifically prohibit a Jew from entering a Gentile home, but parts of the law did serve to keep Jews and Gentiles separated. Long-standing custom had formalized this into a practice that was universally recognized and had the force of law. Yet Peter now indicated that he was deliberately and knowingly setting aside this custom, or more precisely, he acknowledged that God had led him to set it aside. Peter's vision on the housetop had got through to him.

When the messengers came from Cornelius to Peter, they told Peter their purpose in coming. But upon his arrival, Peter wanted to hear the reason directly from Cornelius. This would further reassure him that his mission was not some wild goose chase.

This chapter demonstrates the power of the gospel to break down barriers. One barrier fell when Peter invited Gentiles to enter and be entertained in the house of Simon. A second fell when Peter himself crossed the threshold of Cornelius' house. In the first century, the gospel had tremendous power to break down the walls that men had built to separate themselves into little isolated groups. Do we have any doubt that the gospel still has this power? Missionaries and evangelists around the world can cite numerous examples when barriers of race, social and economic status, and language have been swept aside by the good news. As Paul stated, He "has destroyed the barrier, the dividing wall of hostility" (Ephesians 2:14).

Peter's question as to why Cornelius had sent for him prompted Cornelius to explain to him his recent experience. He told how four days ago at that very hour (3 P.M.), he had been praying when, suddenly, a man in shining clothes appeared. Luke, when he related this incident, referred to this visitor as an angel, an angel of God. Angels are invariably described in the Scriptures as men. Cornelius recalled how he was told to send for Peter, an order he made haste to carry out. Then he indicated that he, his family, and his friends were ready and prepared for what Peter might say. How could any preacher ask for a better prepared audience than this?

Peter's Sermon (34-43)

Peter was never reluctant to take advantage of an opportunity to preach. Some of his opportunities, such as the occasion before the Sanhedrin (Acts 4), did not provide him with such a receptive audience. Peter seemed to be quite aware that what he was doing—preaching to Gentiles—was breaking new ground. He prefaced his message with the observation that God does not play favorites. The word used to describe the act of playing favorites is a compound word used in the New Testament only by Luke. It literally means "to take hold of one's face." It might, for example, be used to describe a judge who looks a man squarely in the face and renders his decision, not on the merits of the case, but on the basis of whether or not he likes the looks of the man. God, Peter emphatically states, is not this kind of a God. Thus, God is willing to accept from any nation persons who fear Him and do what is right.

The Jews believed that they enjoyed God's special favor. After all, God had called them and blessed them in special ways. They had come to believe that God had chosen them because of their unusual qualities. Actually, the reverse was true. Peter pointed out that God had called the Israelites for the purpose of making them vehicles of the "good news of peace" (Acts 10:36).

The good news came through the Lord Jesus Christ. Peter pointed out that his hearers already knew the general outlines of that good news. Although there is no record that there were any Christians in Caesarea prior to Peter's visit, travelers had undoubtedly brought news of Christ's ministry. Roman soldiers who had been present at His crucifixion would surely bring back stories about Jesus when they returned to Caesarea from Jerusalem. Further, Galilee was less than fifty miles from Caesarea, and stories about Jesus and His ministry certainly would be carried that far.

Peter dated the beginning of Jesus' ministry from His baptism at the hands of John the Baptist. Jesus had been anointed by God with the Holy Spirit and power. (The word *power* often is used to indicate miracles.) As a result, He went about doing good and healing those who were possessed by the devil. Peter was not reporting pious rumors about what had happened, but pointed out that he, along with the other apostles, were witnesses of Jesus' activities during His ministry and of His death on the cross. Unlike his sermon on Pentecost or his sermon before the Sanhedrin, Peter did not accuse his listeners of being responsible for Jesus' death. As non-Jews and as residents of Caesarea, they could hardly have been involved in the crucifixion.

But Jesus' death "on a tree" (Acts 10:39), if the story ended there, would not be good news. On the third day, God raised Him up and presented Him to witnesses—that's the good news! God did not show Him to all the people, only to a select group of witnesses (Acts 10:41; see 1 Corinthians 15:5-8 for a list of some of these witnesses). We may wonder why God did not present Him to the multitudes. One important reason is that God wanted persons who would qualify as a competent witnesses. Those who had been with Him during His ministry and knew Him intimately would be able to affirm beyond a shadow of a doubt that the man they ate and drank with was indeed the man He claimed to be. Peter specifically mentioned eating and drinking, activities that would assure that He was not some kind of apparition or ghost.

After His resurrection, Jesus commanded His apostles to preach to the people. Then Peter added an element that he had never stated in his earlier sermons. Jesus had been appointed by God to be the judge of the living and the dead (Acts 10:42). This fact was never explicitly stated in any version of the Great Commission. However, Jesus stated it in His ministry (Matthew 24:30-51; 25:31-33; John 5:24-30). Several of His parables teach of a coming judgment, giving Peter a solid basis for his statement. In addition to the witnesses who testify to His resurrection and His coming in judgment, Peter pointed out that the prophets testified about Him, declaring forgiveness through His name to those who believe in Him. This statement by Peter would seem to indicate that Cornelius had some knowledge of the Old Testament. In his sermon, Peter may very well have quoted some of these Old Testament prophets, but Luke does not include this information in his summary of the sermon.

Cornelius' Response (44-48)

At this point, Peter's sermon was interrupted by the coming of the Holy Spirit upon his hearers. In some ways, the coming of the Holy Spirit here parallels His coming at Pentecost; in other ways, His coming is different. At Pentecost, the Holy Spirit came upon the apostles, enabling them to speak in the various languages of those present. Here it came upon those who were candidates for conversion, and we are told that they spoke "in tongues," perhaps suggesting that they spoke in unknown tongues rather than known languages. Yet the purpose of the coming of the Spirit was the same in both cases—to give evidence that God approved what was taking place. Along with their speaking in tongues, they also raised their voices in praise of God.

The men who had accompanied Peter from Joppa stood amazed at what they were witnessing. No doubt, they had entered the house of Cornelius with some reluctance, sharing with Peter the Jewish prejudices against Gentiles. But this phenomenon, which they readily recognized as coming from God, must have reassured them. Their presence there was certainly providential, for they were later to play an important part in confirming Peter's report about the incident (Acts 11:12).

Seeing this display of the coming of the Spirit, Peter logically concluded that Cornelius and his household were appropriate candidates for baptism. He saw the full implications of his house-top vision. We may take as rhetorical his question, "Can anyone keep these people from being baptized with water?" He was not asking his companions for their approval. He had his answer.

So those present in the house were baptized. Included were Cornelius, his immediate family, and his close friends. Since infants or small children are not mentioned, nothing in this passage can be construed to include infants among those who were baptized. We need to note that this was a special outpouring of the Spirit to open the church to the uncircumcised. It was not the "gift of the Holy Spirit" (Acts 2:38), which believers receive at baptism. Following the baptism, Peter remained in Cornelius' house a few days. We can be sure that this time was spent in further teaching to help Cornelius grow in the faith. Luke gives us no further clue about what happened to this band of believers. We know that Philip the evangelist later lived in Caesarea, and apparently there was a church there (Acts 21:8-16). Perhaps Cornelius, his family, and his friends were charter members of that church.

CHAPTER ELEVEN

Meeting Problems in a Growing Church

Acts 11

Peter Asked for an Accounting (Acts 11:1-18)

What happened in the house of Cornelius was a landmark in the history of the church. Up until that time, the membership of the church had been drawn exclusively from the Jewish people. They brought with them their Jewish exclusiveness, and, as a result, the church almost became just another Jewish sect. By intervening miraculously, God changed things. But even though Peter had been convinced by his experience, the struggle to open the church to all people was far from being won; it was just beginning. The majority of the Jewish Christians were still not ready to follow Peter's lead.

Charges Against Peter (1-3)

Even in a day that had no telephones or radio communications, rumors traveled quickly. During the few days that Peter remained in the house of Cornelius in Caesarea, word of his actions had already got back to Jerusalem. We don't know who brought the news back to Jerusalem nor why it was so readily believed. One would think that the leaders in the Jerusalem church would not be inclined to believe a report of such a serious breech of proper conduct by a trusted leader. We can only conclude that the news about Peter's actions was thoroughly substantiated by the reports of numerous witnesses.

We might pause and raise a question about how we would have handled this matter. Are we sometimes inclined to believe the worst about our fellow Christians? Do we on occasion accept reports about others without giving them an opportunity to explain or defend their actions? There seems to be lodged in most of our hearts a bit of envy that often causes us to believe the worst about others.

In every group or organization there seem to be those whose chief concern is to maintain and defend that group's orthodoxy. Of course, sound doctrine is a matter of great importance, and true doctrines must be defended. Yet, when the defense of the faith becomes the all-consuming concern, even to the point that the faith ceases to be lovingly and winsomely proclaimed, then narrow legalism usually results. Perhaps at this point in the history of the church, the "circumcised believers" mentioned here did not constitute a separate party within the church. But their Jewish prejudices later led to the emergence of a group known as the *Judaizers,* who legalistically insisted that all must conform to the law of Moses before they could become members of the church.

The word that is translated "criticized" means "to take sides against" or "to separate oneself apart." In other words, those who contended against Peter were displaying a divisive spirit. The immediate bone of contention was not that he had preached to Gentiles. This, presumably, was acceptable so long as the ultimate objective was to convert Gentiles to Judaism. The thing that aroused the circumcised believers was that Peter had gone into the home of an uncircumcised man and eaten with him and his Gentile family and friends. Sharing a meal with a person of another faith involved a level of social intimacy that they were unwilling to countenance.

We must not deal too harshly with them, however. They had been brought up to believe that their whole religious lives, indeed, their whole lives, revolved around the keeping of the law. Peter's actions were not some minor detail on the periphery of the matter. His actions struck at the very heart of their values system and, if unchallenged, threatened to undermine the whole system. Men usually become contentious when their whole philosophical system is threatened. We can understand their position even if we do not approve of it.

We can see in our own country and in other places in the world the terrible effects of racial prejudice. We have seen the strong resistance that many have offered when challenges came to the structures that sustained racial prejudices. Yet—praise the Lord— we have seen people change. The gospel of Jesus Christ has marvelous powers to change men's hearts and minds. Let us never forget this fact when our own efforts to achieve justice in this world seem so often to fall short.

Peter's Explanation of His Actions (4-17)

It is quite likely that Peter anticipated some reaction to his breach of the law when he returned to Jerusalem. After all, he knew his own feelings against anything common or unclean. He certainly knew also the intensity with which his fellow Jews held on to their beliefs. Knowing these things, he wisely chose not to resort to sophisticated theological arguments to make his case. Instead, he related in a straightforward manner just what had happened to him.

It seems likely that Peter told his story before the whole congregation rather than just to his critics. It was, after all, a matter that involved the whole congregation. Peter repeated the account as we have it in the previous chapter, although he naturally told it in the first person. Since he was giving an account of only his own action, he did not mention the appearance of the angel to Cornelius. He also added a fourth category of animals—wild beasts—that was not mentioned in the previous chapter.

In mentioning the voice that told him to arise and eat, Peter attempted to leave no doubt that the voice was that of the Lord. In rejecting the invitation, he did so in terms that his audience would identify with. They would know the sense of revulsion that any Jew might feel at the invitation to eat non-kosher food. Yet the insistent voice from Heaven admonished him three times not to reject as unclean what God had made clean. At this point, many in Peter's audience must have wondered what this vision had to do with the criticism brought against him. Of course, when he experienced it, Peter himself had questions about its meaning. Only as the actions unfolded did Peter begin to comprehend the full meaning of his vision. By the time Peter had finished his entire account, most of his audience had also caught the implications of his vision.

After telling of this vision, Peter then mentioned the three men who had come from Cornelius. As Peter prepared to accompany them, he may still have entertained some reservations about going with them. But this was dispelled by the Spirit, who told him to go without any hesitation. At this point in his story, Peter introduced the six men from Joppa who had accompanied him. Taking them along had been a wise move (Jesus had urged the apostles to be as wise as serpents [Matthew 10:16]), and now that wisdom was paying off as their presence in Jerusalem corroborated Peter's account.

The climax of Peter's story came when he told how the Holy Spirit came upon those in the house of Cornelius just as it had upon the apostles "at the beginning" (Acts 11:15), that is, at Pentecost. This was touching a familiar group, for many if not most of his hearers would know about Pentecost. Then Peter added another idea that his hearers would know about. John the Baptist had created no small stir among the people, and although he had been dead for several years, most would know about his ministry. In recalling Jesus' words about John, Peter touched a responsive note with the people. Peter's point was that the promise of John and Jesus had been fulfilled at Pentecost, but it had also been fulfilled again in the house of Cornelius. This would have settled the argument for many people in the audience.

The dilemma Peter faced was clearly set forth. Either he had to remain loyal to his Jewish background and "oppose God" (Acts 11:17), or he had to obey God at the cost of abandoning his Jewish practices. To go against his Jewish upbringing may not have been easy for Peter, but to oppose God was unthinkable. Step by step, Peter had led his audience to this same conclusion, and they responded accordingly. Dropping their objections, they raised their voices in praise to God because He had offered life to the Gentiles on the same basis He had offered it to the Jews.

We must not suppose that this one public discussion settled this issue once and for all. It is a mistake to suppose that the prejudices of a lifetime can be swept away by one highly emotional meeting, as this meeting certainly must have been. Practices and prejudices that have taken years to acquire often take years to change. This was exactly the situation at the church at Jerusalem. So far as we know, the church did not make any concerted effort to reach Gentiles as a result of this meeting. In fact, when the church at Antioch did begin to have some success in reaching beyond the Jewish community, serious repercussions developed in the Jerusalem church, leading to the conference in Jerusalem reported in Acts 15. Our own efforts to deal with our own prejudices should prepare us for what happened in the Jerusalem church. But at least Peter made a start in the right direction, which ought to serve as an example for us today.

Gospel Victories in Antioch (11:19-30)

Now our attention turns away from Jerusalem to Antioch. The Jerusalem church remained a strong and influential church at least until the destruction of the city in A.D. 70. But the future of the church lay beyond the boundaries of Palestine, and, as a good historian, Luke quite properly directed attention to the events that prepared the way for this transition.

Church Growth in Antioch (19-21)

The persecution of the church following the stoning of Stephen had unexpected results. Saul's efforts to destroy the church by persecution actually served to spread the church. Persecuted Christians fled to Phoenicia, Cyprus, and Antioch, where they spread the gospel. At first, they worked exclusively among Jews. But then, some from Cyprus and Cyrene came to Antioch and began to share the good news with the Greeks. The term here translated "Greeks" was used earlier in the book of Acts to designate Greek-speaking Jews. Here, however, since it stands in contrast to those who did evangelistic work among Jews, its use would lead us to believe that Luke had in mind Greek-speaking Gentiles instead. Just why those from Cyprus and Cyrene were more eager than others to reach Gentiles we are not told. It is possible that Christians in Antioch had heard of the conversion of Cornelius and the subsequent acceptance of Peter's actions by the Jerusalem church. But if this was the case, it is not mentioned.

Several ancient cities bore the name Antioch. The Antioch mentioned here was located on the Orontes River in Syria, about sixteen miles from the Mediterranean. It was founded about 300 B.C. by one of the Seleucid rulers. It always had a mixed population, including a large number of Jews, many of whom had fled there during the Maccabean wars. In 64 B.C., it fell to the Roman general, Pompey, who made it a free city. Because of its location at the eastern end of the Mediterranean Sea and because it was the western terminus of roads that extended across Asia Minor, the city grew and prospered. By the period covered in the book of Acts, Antioch, with a population that may have reached 500,000, was the third most populous city in the Roman Empire, behind Rome and Alexandria. Near the city were the groves of Daphne, a center for the worship of Apollo. The sexual rites accompanying this worship gave Antioch a reputation for immorality.

Yet this large energetic, commercial, and immoral city became one of the important centers of Christianity well before the end of the first century. One of the reasons for the success of the church at Antioch was surely its aggressive evangelism that did not limit

117

its efforts to Jews. The city was famous as a center for Biblical studies during the third, fourth, and fifth centuries, and it remained a major Christian center until it fell to the Moslems in A.D. 635.

The fact that the Christians at Antioch were willing to take the message of hope to the Gentiles as well as to the Jews meant that they had a much larger mission field to work in. Thus, it should not come as a surprise that the church grew very rapidly. Those who are concerned about church growth might well take this lesson to heart. A church that is willing to break out of its socioeconomic, racial, and cultural limitations has a much better chance of growing because it has a much larger field in which to work.

Barnabas Sent to Antioch (22-24)

Travelers and merchants made their way from Antioch to Jerusalem; so it is not surprising that news of the growth of the church there soon reached the ears of members of the Jerusalem church. Their interest was naturally aroused, and seeking to gain more information about the situation, they dispatched Barnabas to Antioch just as they had earlier sent Peter and John to Samaria. The choice of Barnabas was a wise one. He was "full of the Holy Spirit" (Acts 11:24). He was a generous, open-hearted man (Acts 4:36, 37; 9:27) who would be a fair and wise observer of what was happening in Antioch.

When Barnabas saw what was happening at Antioch, he rejoiced. Unhampered by any Jewish legalism, he gave his encouragement to the people. Since the church at Antioch was taking into its fellowship many Gentiles who lacked the understanding about God that Jews would have, Barnabas exhorted them to remain faithful. Leaders of the church today need to follow the example of Barnabas, because many who come to Christ from the contemporary situation are just as pagan in their outlook as were these Greeks in Antioch.

Saul Brought to Antioch (25, 26)

The original mission of Barnabas may have been simply to investigate what was going on in Antioch and report back to the church at Jerusalem. But the church continued to grow, and Barnabas became increasingly involved in the work of the congregation. His teaching load became heavier, to the point that he needed help, and he knew where he could find that help. Saul had returned to his hometown of Tarsus after his brief visit to Jerusalem. During this time, which may have been several months or even several years, nothing was recorded about him. Barnabas knew that Saul was a capable teacher, and he also knew that Saul had been especially called to evangelize among the Gentiles. Nowhere in the church was one better qualified to assist Barnabas than Saul of Tarsus.

Knowing Paul's zeal, we are safe to assume that he had been actively engaged in evangelism in Tarsus. How, then, could Barnabas have been justified in asking him to leave if Saul was laboring in a place that needed evangelism? The only proper reason for him to leave would be that he could be more effective in another field. Since we hear nothing of the success of Saul's efforts in Tarsus, we are led to conclude that his efforts had not enjoyed great success. This surely would have been a frustrating situation for Saul. The invitation to enter a new and more promising field must have come at a most opportune time.

The move proved to be a wise one. For a year, they worked together, teaching the growing number of converts. These converts probably came from among Jews and Gentiles alike, but as a part of the church, their differences were minimized. At least, there is nothing to indicate that a continued outreach among the Gentiles created any problems. Only later, when Judaizers from Jerusalem came, was there trouble. The people of Antioch were more cosmopolitan than the people of Jerusalem. In the day-by-day business activities, Jews and Gentiles were in regular contact with one another and had therefore adopted a more tolerant attitude toward one another.

It is in this situation that the disciples were first called Christians (Acts 11:26). Scholars debate whether the name *Christian* was a divinely given name, whether the disciples gave that name to themselves, or whether outsiders gave it to them as a nickname. Regardless of the origin of the name, it is most appropriate, for it means "one who belongs to Christ." In view of this, it is surprising that this designation came so late—ten or fifteen years after Pentecost—and is used so infrequently in the New Testament. The name is used only two other times in the New Testament: once by Herod Agrippa (Acts 26:28) and once by Peter (1 Peter 4:16). In the centuries that have followed, the name *Christian* has been exalted by those who have been willing to die for it, but even more by those who have been willing to live for it. The followers of Christ are divided a hundred times over and bear sectarian names to designate their differences. Yet they all stand united in being willing to bear the name Christian above all other names. May the day soon come when they will all be Christians only, nothing but Christians, freed from their sectarian and divisive names.

Benevolence of the Antioch Church (27-30)

As the work of Barnabas and Saul bore a rich harvest, a group of prophets came to Antioch from Jerusalem. Some students distinguish between the office of the prophet and the gift of prophecy. The gift of prophecy apparently was available to all Christians. At least, Paul urged all Christians to seek it (1 Corinthians 14:1). On the other hand, the office of prophet was bestowed upon only a limited number of people. Paul lists it as one of the important offices of the church (Ephesians 4:11), but the office of prophet did not enjoy the prominence in the New Testament that it had known in the Old Testament. New Testament prophets, like Old Testament prophets, functioned under the direct inspiration of the Holy Spirit. They served primarily as proclaimers of God's truth, but they also had the power to predict the future.

One of the prophets who came from Jerusalem, Agabus, had this predictive power. His words of prophecy were not good news, but a dire warning of problems ahead. A great famine was coming upon the whole inhabited earth. Luke inserted an editor's note that this famine occurred during the reign of Emperor Claudius. Secular historians corroborate Luke here; during the reign of Claudius several famines plagued the empire.

The Christians in Antioch responded generously to Agabus' warning. The giving was done individually, "each according to his ability" (Acts 11:29). The description of their giving indicates that the collection was taken over a period of time, perhaps several weeks. The famine had not yet come; so the need was not immediate. This allowed the disciples to accumulate their funds systematically. Later on, in a similar situation, Paul suggested a systematic week-by-week giving (1 Corinthians 16:1, 2).

Once the money was collected, Barnabas and Saul were chosen to take it to Jerusalem. Saul had left Jerusalem under a death threat (Acts 9:29, 30), but that had been several years earlier. Those who had sought his life apparently no longer posed a threat. It is worth noting that the gift was sent to the elders of the

120

church (Acts 11:30), not the apostles. This is the first time that the office of elder is mentioned in the New Testament church. Most of the apostles had probably left Jerusalem either out of fear for their lives or to do evangelistic work in other areas. Elders had been selected to provide leadership for the church during the absence of the apostles. James, the brother of the Lord, is specifically mentioned as one of these leaders (Acts 12:17; 15:13-21).

Although this gift from the Antioch church was designed to help the needy, it certainly did not escape the notice of the Jewish Christians that it came from a church that was largely Gentile in membership. Nothing will dissipate prejudice more quickly than acts of mercy and kindness such as this. At the Jerusalem Conference (Acts 15) some years later, this act of love by the Gentile Christians at Antioch was certainly remembered, and it undoubtedly played a part in people's thinking as they deliberated over the issue of whether Gentiles would have to obey the law of Moses. Christians today would do well to follow the example of the Antioch church.

CHAPTER TWELVE

The Church Faces New Threats

Acts 12

New Persecution Against the Apostles (12:1-19)

The church at Jerusalem had earlier faced persecution at the hands of the Jewish leaders. This persecution had been intensified after the martyrdom of Stephen. Saul was the ringleader of this persecution, which led to the execution of some Christians, the imprisonment of others, and the exiling of others. Now persecution began from a new quarter—King Herod.

James Put to Death (1, 2)

This section of Acts poses a chronological problem. A casual reading of the closing verses of chapter 11 along with the closing verse of chapter 12 might lead one to suppose that Barnabas and Saul were in Jerusalem during Herod's persecution. Perhaps the best explanation of the order of events places the coming of Agabus to Antioch at some point before A.D. 44. He predicted that soon a severe famine would engulf the world. The church spent some time collecting the funds before they were ready to send it to Jerusalem. "About this time" (Acts 12:1), Herod began his attack upon the apostles, killing James and imprisoning Peter. Then came Herod's death in A.D. 44, which can be dated from external sources. After Herod's death, Barnabas and Saul then brought the collection to Jerusalem and, after a short visit, returned to Antioch. This may explain why the collection was given to the elders rather than to the apostles. The apostles, in the face of Herod's persecution, had fled Jerusalem and had not yet returned when Barnabas and Saul made their visit.

This is King Herod Agrippa I, a grandson of Herod the Great. His father, Aristobulus, a descendant of the Maccabean line, was murdered by Herod the Great. Young Agrippa was sent to Rome for his education. While there, he became a friend of Caligula, who in A.D. 37 was made emperor. Caligula remembered his friend and rewarded him by making him ruler over the tetrarchy of his uncle Philip and over Lysanias in southern Syria. Two years later, Caligula deposed Herod Antipas, another uncle of Agrippa, and gave Antipas' former territory of Galilee and Peraea to Agrippa.

In A.D. 41, Caligula was assassinated, and Claudius came to the throne. Agrippa had won the favor of Claudius, who rewarded Agrippa by adding Judea, Samaria, and Abilene to his realm. By this time, Agrippa ruled over almost the same territory that his grandfather, Herod the Great, had controlled.

Herod Agrippa I probably enjoyed greater popularity with his subjects than did any other of the Herods. For one thing, he was very careful to avoid offending the religious scruples of his Jewish subjects, especially the Pharisees. On one occasion, he had intervened to prevent Caligula from placing a gilded statue of himself in the Holy of Holies.

His initial arrest of several Christians may have come because of his own commitment to Judaism. He saw in Christianity a serious threat to the Mosaic code and the Jewish faith it represented. Just why James was the first of the apostles that he seized, we do not know. Perhaps he was the first one available. He is designated as James the brother of John, to distinguish him from another apostle, James the son of Alphaeus, sometimes called James the Less. Whether James had any kind of trial or hearing, Luke does not tell us. Agrippa probably did not bother with the formality of a trial. He simply gave the order and it was carried out, making James the first of the apostles to be martyred.

Peter Imprisoned (3-5)

Political motivation also entered into Herod's decision. Since the execution of James pleased the Jews, he was confident that executing Peter, the leader of the apostles, would please them even more. Peter may also have been a more attractive target because he had opened the door of the church to Gentiles. Jewish leaders tended to be more tolerant of Jewish Christians who still observed many of the regulations of the Mosaic law. Peter's arrest was made at the start of the Feast of Unleavened Bread, which began at the time of the Passover and lasted seven days. Herod may have deliberately chosen this particular time to arrest Peter in order to show his concern for the Jewish religious rites.

Herod also postponed Peter's trial so as not to intrude upon the solemnity of the religious season. During this waiting period, he took special precautions to prevent Peter's escape. He may very well have been aware of the situation several years earlier when the apostles had been miraculously released from jail (Acts 5:18-20). Four squads of four soldiers each were assigned to guard Peter through the night. It was common practice for a squad to be on duty three hours at a time, after which it would be relieved. Peter was chained between two of the soldiers, and the other two guarded the door.

As Herod prepared to carry out his plan, the church was also busy, engaged in prayer. No doubt the church prayed for Peter's release, but their prayers must have been tempered by the knowledge that God may not have willed that Peter be released. They must surely have prayed for James's release also, yet clearly it had not been God's will that he be released.

But in this case, God did will that Peter not be executed. Against God's will four soldiers—even four thousand soldiers—could not stand. The night before Peter was to face trial, an angel of the Lord, accompanied by a bright light, suddenly appeared in his cell. Peter, apparently unworried about what the next day would bring, remained soundly asleep and had to be awakened by a tap on his side. The soldiers remained asleep and were not awakened either by the light or by the angel's order to Peter to get up. We are reminded of the appearance of the angel of the Lord at the tomb of Jesus. The soldiers there, who were awake, were so overcome by fear that they shook and fainted. But in this case, the soldiers remained asleep and were not even aware of the coming of the Heavenly visitor.

Peter still thought he was dreaming and had to be told to put on his clothes and sandals. Then, still obeying instructions, Peter followed the angel out of the prison, passing the first and second guards and coming to the outside gate. As they approached this iron gate, it opened miraculously for them. Once they were outside of the prison and in the city street, the angel left Peter.

Only at this point did Peter finally realize that he wasn't dreaming. The Lord really had sent His angel to rescue him. This realization moved him to immediate action. God had miraculously delivered him from the prison, but from now on, his safety required that he himself do something on his own. God still deals with people in this same way. We may call on Him to do for us the things that are beyond our power to do. But He has every right to expect us to do what we can for ourselves. Indeed, it borders on blasphemy for us to ask God to do for us what we are able to do for ourselves.

Thus, Peter quickly sought safety in the home of Mary, the mother of John Mark. We don't know where this house was located, but some have speculated that it was in the southwestern part of the city. His arrival there was unexpected, and what follows is one of those delightful little human interest stories that occur in the Scriptures. When Peter knocked on the outer gate, a servant girl, Rhoda, came to answer the knock. We can hear her asking, "Who is it?" She no doubt was surprised that anyone would be coming at such an hour of the night. She was even more surprised to hear Peter's voice in reply, so surprised that she ran back to tell the others, leaving Peter standing in the street. Her report fell on unbelieving ears. Peter here? Impossible! They all knew he was in prison. After all, that was the reason for the meeting, to pray for Peter's release. At that moment, the irony of their response did not occur to them. Here they were, meeting to pray for Peter's release, and yet refusing to believe that their prayers had been answered.

They accused the girl of being out of her mind. When they couldn't shake her story, they concluded that actually what she saw was Peter's angel. It is probably just as well not to get into their concept of angels or try to build a theology of angels on the basis of their remark. After all, their remark was made as an offhanded comment rather than as a serious theological statement. They could have settled the matter in a few seconds just by walking to the front gate. But they preferred to argue. How like them we often are! All the while, Peter stood outside the gate knocking, no doubt a bit exasperated that a simple matter of unlocking the gate took such a long time.

Finally, someone suggested that they go to the gate and see who was there. Imagine their surprise when they opened it and there stood Peter. They became so noisy in their excited response that he had to motion for them to be quiet so that he could tell them what had happened. Once he had completed his account, he instructed them to get word to James and "the brothers" about his escape. This James is the brother of the Lord who already was a recognized leader in the Jerusalem church and who later played such an important role in the Jerusalem Conference (Acts 15).

The brothers probably were other leaders in the Jerusalem church, who may themselves have been in hiding. Peter then immediately left for another place. It was probably well known that Mary was a disciple. Her home would be one of the first places the officials would look for Peter once they learned of his escape. He probably found refuge in a less obvious place in Jerusalem. There is no evidence that he left Jerusalem at this time.

Herod's Wrath at Peter's Escape (18, 19)

It was morning, probably at the changing of the guard at 6 A.M., before Peter's escape was noticed. We can scarcely imagine Herod's anger when this news reached him. The stage had been set for Peter's trial and his execution, all to curry favor with the Jewish establishment. Now the opportunity had been lost, and the angry king wanted to know why. The most obvious answer was that the guards had been bribed. Such deals were not unknown in the ancient world—or our own, for that matter. But in this case, that was not a very logical explanation because the guards were still there and would have to bear the brunt of the accusation.

After a thorough search for Peter proved fruitless, the guards were brought before Herod for detailed questioning. They must have insisted that they knew nothing about how Peter had escaped, but such testimony must have seemed ridiculously fabricated to Herod. The poor guards could not even report the coming of the angel and the miraculous opening of the gate because they had slept through the whole affair. Dissatisfied with their answers, Herod ordered them, literally, to "be led away" (Acts 12:19). The Greek Scriptures do not state that they were executed, but this expression often means to be led away to execution, and most translations, including the New International Version, so render it. This is a logical conclusion in view of the common practice of making guards responsible even with their own lives should their prisoners escape. The Philippian jailer, who was ready to take his own life when he thought his prisoners had escaped, illustrates this dramatically (Acts 16:27).

Some have raised a moral issue over this incident. They point out that God's divine intervention placed the lives of the guards in jeopardy. To respond to this charge, we need only to examine Herod's actions. His arrest of Peter for no other reason than to gain favor with the Jews set in motion the whole unfortunate chain of events. Then, after the escape, a careful examination of the facts would have exonerated the guards. But to do this, Herod would have had to recognize that God had acted in ways that did not meet with his approval. Thus, Herod and Herod alone must bear the responsibility for the execution of these men.

Herod's Death (12:19-23)

The church might have expected a period of severe persecution following Peter's escape. But for some reason, Herod did not pursue the matter further. He may have felt that his execution of James and the imprisonment of Peter would be adequate to keep the Jews satisfied for a while. Or, as seems more likely, pressing matters of state required that he return to Caesarea.

Herod's Negotiations with Tyre and Sidon (19, 20)

Herod may have returned to Caesarea from Jerusalem in order to deal with a problem that had arisen with Tyre and Sidon. These two ancient cities on the eastern coast of the Mediterranean were important commercial centers. They enjoyed considerable autonomy in dealing with neighboring powers, and in some way, perhaps in their commercial pursuits, they had angered Herod. They sought to patch up their affairs with him because they were dependent upon his realm for food supplies. Working through Blastus, Herod's personal servant, they gained an audience with him and asked for peace.

Josephus informs us that Herod arranged a festival in honor of Emperor Claudius. It was on the second day of this festival that he wore his royal robes and sat on his throne. Josephus describes Herod in these words: "He put on a garment made wholly of silver. . . . and early in the morning came into the theater, at which time the silver of his garment, being illuminated by the first reflection of the sun's rays upon it, shone after a surprising manner, and was so resplendent as to spread horror over those that looked intently on him."

After Herod delivered a speech to the crowd, they began to cry out that he spoke with the voice of a god and not of a man. Such flattery most certainly must have come from pagan Gentiles rather than Jews, who would never have brought themselves to have addressed even Herod in such idolatrous terms. Herod's Jewish training should have led him to have rejected such adulation immediately. Yet pride has a way of blinding one to the most obvious truths.

Herod was guilty of exhibiting overweening pride, a condition the Greeks termed *hybris*. In the typical Greek tragedy, a display of hybris was followed by disaster. Complete disaster was not long in coming to Agrippa. He was stricken by an angel of the Lord and "eaten by worms" (Acts 12:23). Whether it was a literal description of his demise or a figurative expression to describe some loathsome disease we cannot be certain. Josephus tells us that Herod was smitten by a severe pain in the belly and died five days later. Just as Luke does, Josephus attributes Herod's sudden death to his blasphemous acceptance of praise properly due to God.

Summary of Church Activities (12:24, 25)

Following Herod's death, much of his realm was placed under the control of a Roman procurator. In this political turmoil, the church enjoyed a respite from persecution.

We are given at this point yet another summary of the church's activities. Without giving us any specific statistics, Luke informs us of two important facts (Acts 12:24): the word of God increased, and it spread--or more literally, it "multiplied." This suggests that the church not only increased in numbers but in its outreach into new areas.

Luke dealt with the items in the closing verses of Acts 11 and in this chapter in a topical rather than in a strictly chronological pattern. It seems best to understand that Barnabas and Saul came to Jerusalem after the death of Agrippa rather than during the time of his persecution of the church. Saul, had he been there during the persecution, certainly would have been one of the king's prime targets, making it very difficult for him to carry out his mission of benevolence. Once Barnabas and Saul had delivered the funds to the elders of the Jerusalem church, they returned to Antioch, where a new and exciting ministry awaited them. On the return trip, they took John Mark with them. Mark was a nephew of Barnabas, and it was to Mark's mother's house that Peter came when he was miraculously released from prison. As he often does in the book of Acts, Luke introduces Mark more or less incidentally before bringing him into the main narrative.

CHAPTER THIRTEEN

A Great Missionary Effort Begun

Acts 13

Barnabas and Saul Set Apart for Missionary Work (13:1-3)

Acts 13 introduces us to the second major part of the book of Acts. The first twelve chapters tell of the beginning of the church in Jerusalem, its spread into Judea and Samaria, and the establishment of the strong church at Antioch. The mission of the church in these chapters is mainly to the Jews.

At this point, all this changes. With Antioch as the center, the main thrust of the church turned to the Gentile world of the Roman Empire, and eventually even beyond the boundaries of the Empire. Instead of individual Christians evangelizing as they traveled from Jerusalem, an organized effort was made to spread the gospel. This is not to suggest that the methods used in the first twelve chapters were wrong or inadequate. Indeed, under the pressure of persecution, a more structured effort might very well have been impossible. But the Gentile world of the Roman Empire offered a different challenge that required different methods.

The church at Antioch was blessed by a number of capable leaders, a few of whom are mentioned in this chapter. It is interesting to note that the existence of elders is never mentioned in the church at Antioch. Perhaps at this time, no leaders had been designated as elders. Or it may have been that at this time prophets and teachers were so prominent that they overshadowed the elders. Scholars differ about whether the prophets and teachers were separate offices or were simply different functions of the same office. Paul, writing at a later time, seems to indicate that the two were distinct offices (Ephesians 4:11). An important function of the prophets was to proclaim the Word of God, but in the New Testament at least some of the prophets had the power to predict the future (like Agabus, Acts 11:27, 28). The main function of teachers was to help the people apply the Word of God to their lives. It is debated by some whether all five men mentioned were both prophets and teachers or the first three were prophets and the latter two, teachers.

The five men named are an interesting and diverse lot, attesting to the heterogeneous nature of the church at Antioch. Barnabas, of course, we have already met in earlier chapters of Acts. He was a Jew from Cyprus. Simeon is one of several by that name who are mentioned in the Scriptures, but he is not to be positively identified with any of them. He was given the nickname Niger, which is a Latin term meaning black. This has led some to suppose that he was from Africa. A further supposition identifies him as Simon from Cyrene, who was forced to carry Jesus' cross. But Luke does not indicate that he was from Cyrene, and so this supposition may be rejected. Lucius was from Cyrene, an area in North Africa west of Egypt. Some identify him with Luke, the author of Acts, but this is highly improbable. Manaen is an interesting person. We are told that he was brought up with Herod the tetrarch, also known as Herod Antipas, who ruled over Galilee and Perea during the ministry of Jesus. This would indicate that Manaen was either of the royal family or of a noble Jewish family. Since he was probably the same age as Herod and Herod was born in about 20 B.C., Manaen would have been at least sixty-five years old at this time.

Of these five leaders, only Barnabas and Saul are mentioned again in the book of Acts. But even though they are not mentioned by name, it is reasonable to believe that they played an important part in the continued growth of the church at Antioch and in the dispute that developed with the Judaizers. One reason for the rapid growth of this church certainly must have been its cosmopolitan leadership. Barnabas was a Jew from Cyprus with an open mind and heart. Simeon may have been an African. Lucius was a Cyrenean, and Manaen was an elderly, well-educated member of the Jewish aristocracy. Add to this group Saul, a brilliant Pharisee and former persecutor of Christians, and we can see the diverse leadership enjoyed by the church. Does this suggest that the leadership of our churches today might be more creative if the leaders came from more varied backgrounds?

The church at Antioch undoubtedly met regularly for worship, and on one of these occasions, the congregation received a special revelation from the Holy Spirit. The word here translated "worshiping" means to perform a public service and was sometimes used to describe the activities of a priest as he offered sacrifices at the altar. Our English word *liturgy* comes from this Greek word. It is likely that the church had developed a definite pattern for its public worship that included the Lord's Supper, prayers, singing, preaching, and Scripture reading. These would be considered as a service rendered to the honor and glory of God.

During this public service, the Holy Spirit in some fashion indicated God's wish that Barnabas and Saul be set apart for a special mission. Whether this message came as an audible voice or in some other manner we are not told, but there seems to have been no doubt in the mind of the church that the Spirit had made His will known. The congregation acted at once to carry out the Spirit's bidding. The people fasted and prayed, no doubt asking for further guidance about this mission and for the health and safety of the two missionaries. Then, before sending them on their way, they laid their hands upon them in a public service, thus indicating to all their blessing and approval upon this mission.

Finally, the time arrived for the departure of the two missionaries. It is not likely that either of the two men or the church had any idea of the eternal significance of this event. Yet as we look back on it, we can say without hesitation that this was one of the most decisive moments in the history of the world. It marked the point at which the expansion of the church became a united, organized effort, rather than being a matter of individual choice. It also marked the point at which the church deliberately moved out of its narrow Jewish circles and reached out into the wider Gentile world.

Two or three things ought to be noted about this new and different missionary enterprise. First of all, it was instigated by the action of the Holy Spirit, not by the congregation. However, the church gladly gave up its two most talented leaders for this new mission. (Modern churches might well emulate this example.) In the second place, the laying on of hands was not an ordination service, nor did it impart to the two men any special authority or power. Its main purpose was to indicate to the whole membership and anyone else present that this missionary effort had the approval of the church. Finally, there is nothing specifically mentioned to indicate that the church provided any financial support for the two men when they left. It would be safe to assume that at least some support was provided, but we do know that on some of his later missionary journeys, Paul found it necessary to support himself with the labor of his hands. At this point, many modern churches seem to have patterned their missions programs after the church at Antioch. They are willing to pray for missionaries and even fast for them, but they don't provide them much financial undergirding.

Barnabas and Saul in Cyprus (13:4-12)

We are not given any hint about how the men chose the field in which they would serve. Perhaps the Holy Spirit gave them specific directions about where to go. But the Holy Spirit more often works indirectly to carry out God's will. That may have been true in this case as the men used their God-given intellects to make the decision. Regardless of how it was made, the decision to go first to Cyprus was a logical one. First of all, Cyprus was close by and readily accessible. There is no reason to travel to distant fields to serve when equally needy fields are close at hand. Another compelling reason for them to go to Cyprus was that this was the home of Barnabas. This meant that they would not have any formidable cultural or linguistic barriers to surmount as they sought to share the gospel with the people there. Modern students of missionary strategy generally recognize that people are more receptive when the cultural barriers are slight. This is not to suggest that difficult fields ought to be neglected, but it does seem to indicate that when time, personnel, and resources are limited, these ought to be used in the areas most likely to receive the gospel.

Antioch was more than a dozen miles inland, and to reach the seaport of Seleucia, the two men may either have walked or taken a smaller vessel down the Orontes River. At Seleucia, they caught a ship sailing for the port of Salamis on the island of Cyprus, which lay about a hundred and twenty miles south and west of Seleucia.

Cyprus is a large island, a hundred and fifty miles long and ranging from five to fifty miles wide. In ancient times it had been controlled by various peoples and was prized as a source of copper. In 58 B.C. it fell to the Romans, and in 27 B.C., when Caesar Augustus came to power, it became an imperial province.

Having arrived in Salamis, Barnabas and Saul preached in the synagogues of that city. They went first to the synagogues because they were more likely to get a sympathetic hearing there. This was to be their practice throughout the first missionary journey. The fact that there was more than one synagogue in Salamis indicates a sizable Jewish population in the city. It is at this point that we first learn that John Mark, Barnabas' cousin, was accompanying them as a helper. Luke does not give us any information about the results of their efforts, but we know that there were churches in the area later, indicating that the seeds they had planted took root.

From Salamis, the missionary team journeyed the length of the island to the city of Paphos, the seat of the Roman government. From ancient times, Paphos had been a center for the worship of the goddess of love, Aphrodite or Venus. It doesn't take much imagination to realize what the moral level of the community must have been. As Barnabas and Saul began to preach there, they attracted the attention of the proconsul, Sergius Paulus. The title of proconsul was given to those rulers sent out by the Roman Senate. We now know that Cyprus was a senatorial province at this particular time; so here we have evidence of Luke's accuracy as a historian.

The missionaries had an invitation to the proconsul's court, an invitation they must have accepted with enthusiasm. But there were problems. Attached to the court of Sergius Paulus was Bar-Jesus, described as a "Jewish sorcerer and false prophet" (Acts 13:6). He saw in the missionaries a threat to his influence with the proconsul, and he did his best to turn him away from the gospel. Sergius Paulus is described as "an intelligent man" (Acts 13:7); so it may surprise us that he was so influenced by a sorcerer. But the ancient Romans were much given to sorcery and divination. Apparently, the proconsul was simply reflecting his culture.

Throughout the narrative, until this point, the man that we know as Paul has been called Saul. Here, without any explanation, Luke began to call him Paul, and used this designation through the rest of the book. It is also the name that Paul himself used in his epistles. Why the change at this particular time? We simply don't know.

Some have speculated that as a Roman citizen Paul had three names. Paul, or Paulus, is a Roman name, and some feel that this name change signaled his increasing involvement with the Roman world and thus the need to use a Roman name. Others have suggested that the name, which means "small," was given to him as a nickname because he was small of stature. Still others have suggested that he took the name out of deference to Sergius Paulus. Whatever the reason, from this time on through the book

135

of Acts and for the rest of history, it was no longer Saul of Tarsus but the apostle Paul.

Paul wasted no time in meeting the problem. Looking the man straight in the eye, Paul called him a child of the devil, indicating that Elymas was under the influence of Satan. He was guilty of deceit and trickery. He knew very well that the claims he made for his practice of sorcery were fraudulent, but he deliberately used these skills to mislead people for his own selfish purposes. Paul then hurled a rhetorical question to him: "Will you never stop perverting the right ways of the Lord?" (Acts 13:10). The implication was obvious: Elymas had no intention of ceasing his wicked practices. He had sold himself into bondage to the devil, and Paul's words of condemnation would not change him.

Since the man could not be reached by words, he must be reached by actions. Paul, filled with the Holy Spirit, pronounced judgment upon him. Elymas would be blind for a season. As severe as this judgment was, it was not irreversible, and it did give him time to repent. As soon as Paul spoke the words, darkness came upon the man, and he needed help to find his way about. Luke makes no further mention of Elymas; so we don't know how long he suffered this affliction or what became of him.

The miracle was not lost on Sergius Paulus. Although he had been beguiled by Elymas, now the sorcerer's spell over him had been broken, and he was free to accept the message that Paul brought. Luke informs us that the proconsul "believed" (Acts 13:21). Scholars have long debated whether he believed only in the intellectual sense or whether he became a convert to Christianity and was baptized. The same word *(believed)* is used several times in the book of Acts to describe the actions of those who did become Christians. It has been argued that a Roman official in such a high office could not become a Christian because his official duties often involved homage to pagan deities that would be impossible for a Christian. Yet, in the first three hundred years of the church's existence, many high officials did become Christians. Undoubtedly, some compromised their faith; others resigned or were removed from office; a few died for their faith. Here, as in many other places in the book of Acts, we may wish that Luke had given us more information. We must conclude, however, that the Holy Spirit chose not to give us this information. At this point, all we can do is wait patiently, knowing that someday everything will be revealed to us.

Paul and Barnabas in Asia Minor (13:13-52)

The previous section indicated a change in name from Saul to Paul. In this section another significant change occurred. Until this point, Barnabas had apparently been the leader. He took the lead in calling Saul to minister with him in Antioch, and he seems to have been the leader when the missionary team left Antioch. At least, his name was always stated first. But here Paul's name was listed first, and in the activities that would follow, Paul was increasingly the leader. This change in leadership seems to have stirred no resentment on the part of Barnabas, further evidence of his generous and humble nature.

Traveling to Antioch (13, 14)

We don't know how long Paul and Barnabas remained in Cyprus after their confrontation with Elymas. It would appear that they spent some time teaching Sergius Paulus, who was "amazed at the teaching about the Lord" (Acts 13:12). It is also likely that they spent time teaching other converts and gathering them into a fellowship. Some allow a few weeks for this; others, a few months.

From Paphos, Paul and his companions, Luke and Mark, sailed for Perga in Pamphylia. Pamphylia was a district on the southern shore of Asia Minor. Perga was a few miles inland on the Cestrus River, which in ancient times was navigable by small ships. At Perga, John Mark left the party and returned to Jerusalem. No reason is given for his departure; so we are left to speculate about it. Some suggest that he was afraid of traveling to the interior because of the reputation it had for harboring bandits. Others think he resented Paul's replacing his uncle as the leader of the group. Another view is that he felt that the commission applied only to Cyprus, and did not include Asia Minor. Or perhaps he suffered a severe case of homesickness. Whatever the reason, Paul felt it unworthy and later refused to have him as a traveling companion (Acts 15:37-39).

The missionary team did not remain in Perga (perhaps there was no synagogue there) but traveled about a hundred miles north to the city of Antioch. This city, located at an elevation of more than 3,500 feet above sea level, was founded about 300 B.C. by one of Alexander's officers. Jews had been encouraged to settle there, and later Augustus had made it a Roman colony. The city was actually located in Phrygia, but it lay near Pisidia and was therefore referred to as Pisidian Antioch, to distinguish it from other cities that bore the same name, including Antioch of Syria.

Paul's Preaching in the Synagogue in Antioch (15-43)

When the Sabbath arrived, Paul and Barnabas made their way to the local synagogue. In synagogues of that day, it was the usual practice to read first a selection from the Law (the first five books of the Old Testament) and then one from the Prophets, the second major section of the Hebrew Old Testament canon. This was then followed by a lesson or sermon by one of the leaders of the synagogue or by a visiting teacher. It seems that the leaders of the synagogue had met Paul and Barnabas earlier in the week and, knowing something about them, extended them the courtesy of addressing the congregation. Paul did not hesitate to take advantage of this opportunity.

Luke provides us a summary of the message. Paul, just as Stephen had done in his sermon before the Sanhedrin, began with a brief review of Hebrew history. This served two purposes. It got the attention and won the approval of the people, who never tired of hearing about how God had dealt with them in the past. His second purpose was to lead the people to see how Jesus was the Messiah, whose coming was prophesied in the Old Testament. Stephen's and Paul's messages differ in one respect, however. Stephen used history to show that time and again the people had resisted God and that the Jewish leaders to whom he spoke were doing the same thing. Paul, on the other hand, was more conciliatory, seeking to lead the people to accept Christ.

As Paul arose to address the people, he made some kind of a gesture with his hand to get their attention. His opening words indicate the nature of his audience (Acts 13:16): Jews ("men of Israel") and proselytes ("Gentiles who worship God"). He first told how God had chosen the people of Israel, how they had prospered in Egypt, and how with mighty power (literally, the Greek says "with a high arm"), He had led them out of Egypt (Acts 13:17). In the desert, God "endured their conduct" (Acts 13:18), an interesting way of describing their grumbling and disobedience. Interestingly a variant reading, carried as a footnote in the Revised Standard Version, says He "cared for them" in the wilderness. Both readings accurately describe what happened in the wilderness. God certainly did care for them, or they would not have survived. But He also had to put up with a great deal of disobedience on their part. And, come to think of it, both readings describe God's actions toward us today.

The sojourn in Egypt, the wanderings in the desert, and the beginning of the conquest of Canaan took about 450 years (Acts 13:20). The King James Version makes this period cover the period of Judges in addition to the Egyptian sojourn, the desert wanderings, and the beginning of the conquest. Such a reading is impossible to square with Biblical chronology, and so it is better to follow the New International Version here. After the conquest came the judges, then Samuel and King Saul, and finally David. This is an important point in his message, for not only was David a man after God's own heart, but it was through his descendants that the Savior came.

Before the arrival of the promised Savior, John the Baptist came preaching repentance and baptism. Brief though his career was, John's reputation may have reached even to this Jewish community; so Paul did not have to give a lengthy explanation about John and his ministry. John's mission was to announce the coming Messiah, and with the beginning of Jesus' ministry, John was prepared to fade into the background.

Jesus came bringing a message of salvation. Tragically, neither the people of Jerusalem—at least the majority of them—nor the leaders recognized who Jesus was, and as a result conspired to have Him executed by Pilate. Paul pointed out that in so doing, the people were actually fulfilling the Old Testament prophecies. But the cross was not the end. Indeed, the cross was a necessary prelude to the victory of the empty tomb. Paul was quick to show that the account of the resurrection was not some idle wives' tale but was attested to by many credible witnesses (Acts 13:31). Many of those witnesses who had been with Jesus during His ministry were still alive and still bearing witness to His resurrection.

Now for the good news. The promise that God had made to the fathers and renewed many times across the centuries was now available to them. Paul quoted a number of Old Testament texts to prove his point. He used Psalm 2:7 to show that Jesus was the Son of God and Psalm 16:10 to show that Jesus would not see corruption in the grave. This latter verse was used in a similar way by Peter on Pentecost (Acts 2:27). Just as Peter had done, Paul pointed out that David, who wrote this psalm, could not have been speaking of himself, for he died, and his tomb was still there in Jerusalem. Because Jesus had not remained in the grave but

139

had arisen, He was empowered to offer forgiveness of sin to them.

Then came the theological blockbuster. Man is justified by faith in Jesus Christ, not by the law of Moses. For the first time in the book of Acts we meet the Greek word *dikaion,* which means "to justify" (Acts 13:39). In the New Testament, this word is used exclusively to describe the process whereby God declares the sinner free from the guilt of his sins, not by virtuous deeds but by faith in Jesus Christ. Although this word is not used frequently in Acts, it becomes the cornerstone of Paul's great theological treatise—the book of Romans. It is succinctly summed up in Romans 3:28: "For we maintain that a man is justified by faith apart from observing the law."

It is not likely that many in the audience that day realized the full implications of what Paul was saying. Yet his words were different enough that their curiosity was aroused to the point that Paul and Barnabas were asked to return the following Sabbath. But discussion did not end with the benediction. We can well imagine the discussions that filled the intervening week. Both Jews and proselytes seemed eager to hear more. Some, no doubt, readily accepted this startling new message and rejoiced in it. Others, we can be sure, wanted more evidence, more Old Testament prooftexts before they were willing to believe. And we can be sure that some, in spite of all the persuasive arguments that Paul and Barnabas could advance, still were unwilling to believe.

The fact that some were unwilling to believe should not surprise us. Wherever the gospel has gone, it has always met those who come to faith only slowly and after much struggle. Others never are willing to achieve that faith, and some openly and aggressively oppose it.

Opposition Aroused (44-48)

On the following Sabbath, a record attendance awaited Paul and Barnabas when they returned to the synagogue. The news of Paul's sermon had circulated widely, and this, along with the continued activities of the two missionaries during the previous few days, had stirred up an unusual amount of interest. Luke was so impressed that he resorted to a bit of hyperbole to describe the crowd: "almost the whole city gathered" (Acts 13:44). Most of the added crowd that day were Gentiles, who were especially attracted because they understood Paul's message to mean that they could enjoy the blessings of God's salvation without first becoming obedient to the law of Moses.

But not everyone was pleased with Paul's message, and not everyone was happy about the increased attendance at the synagogue service. Luke indicates that it was the latter that most upset them. They were "filled with jealousy" (Acts 13:45). This seems to have been the main motivation for their opposition to Paul's teaching. This reminds us of the trial of Jesus. The Jewish leaders had no real basis for their charges, and Pilate easily saw through their flimsy charges, realizing that it "was out of envy that they had handed Jesus over to him" (Matthew 27:18). How many of the issues that divide believers today actually have their roots in jealousy rather than in real doctrinal differences? Would we be more likely to heal these divisions if we concentrated on this aspect of the problem rather than continuing to debate doctrinal issues?

Those who opposed Paul and Barnabas "talked abusively" (Acts 13:45) against what they were saying. The word used here actually means "to blaspheme." In its strictest sense, blasphemy is speaking in a derogatory manner about God. By extension, it also means speaking against a representative or spokesman of God. It would seem here that the sin of the nonbelieving Jews lay in attacking the message Paul brought, but, of course, the messenger probably did not escape abuse either.

This opposition did not prevent Paul and Barnabas from carrying out their ministry. Instead of continuing to argue with those whose minds were already made up, they turned to the Gentiles. In every community they entered, the missionaries tried first to reach the Jews. When they were rejected, they were free to reach out to the Gentiles. There was a practical reason for preaching to the Jews first. They believed in the one true God, and the Old Testament pointed to the coming Messiah. But beyond this practical reason, there seems to have been a theological reason. In His last words to His disciples, Jesus instructed them that they would be His witnesses first in Jerusalem and then in Judea before they went to Samaria and then to the ends of the earth (Acts 1:8).

In rejecting God's spokesmen and the message of hope they brought, the Jews had called forth a severe judgment upon themselves. Paul put it bluntly: they did not consider themselves worthy of eternal life. Of course, they didn't see the situation that way at all. They were quite convinced that they already had eternal life and that Paul's message only confused the issue. In announcing to the Jews that he was turning to the Gentiles, Paul made it clear that he was not taking this action because of his own feelings in the matter. Rather, the Old Testament (Isaiah 49:6) had made it clear that the Jews were to become a light to the Gentiles. The irony was that having served as God's vessel to bring the light, so many of the Jews themselves rejected it.

When the gospel is preached, it always brings consequences, not only for the believer but also for those who reject it. Persons who reject the good news often harden their hearts and become, for all practical purposes, impervious to it. The messenger always faces the practical problem of how long to work with such persons, especially when others more receptive are eager to hear. Most of us probably know of persons who have finally come to accept the gospel after rejecting it for years. They were reached because someone patiently and lovingly continued to witness to them. There is no easy solution to the dilemma about how long we should work with a difficult person when eager, receptive persons await the message. This was the dilemma that Paul had to face. But he had one advantage that we lack; he had more immediate and direct leading of the Holy Spirit than we can claim. Luke has given us a rather detailed account of the situation in Antioch because it is a pattern that developed in several other places visited by Paul and Barnabas.

In contrast to the Jews, the Gentiles were "glad and honored the word of the Lord" (Acts 13:48). Many of these had long since abandoned their old beliefs in the pagan deities of their ancestors and had turned to the synagogue in search of the true God. Yet the Jews' insistence that they become obedient to the law of Moses had become a serious barrier to their complete acceptance by the Jews. Now the message that Paul brought swept these barriers aside, giving them complete freedom to come to the one true God. Their enthusiastic response indicated the depth of their commitment to their new faith.

Paul and Barnabas Forced to Leave Antioch (49-52)

As the result of their enthusiasm, the word of the Lord spread throughout "the whole region" (Acts 13:49). We don't know how extensive this area was, but it would certainly have included Antioch and the area immediately around the city that depended upon it for trade and employment. Unable to answer Paul's logic in free and open discussion, the Jews resorted to political subterfuge to rid the city of him. In many cities in that part of the world, Gentiles—but especially Gentile women—had been attracted to Judaism. The Jews were able to persuade them to influence their husbands and the "leading men of the city" (Acts 13:50) to bring pressure to bear on the missionaries. Luke does not explain to us the nature of the persecution. It may have been physical abuse. In 2 Timothy 3:11, Paul mentions persecutions in Antioch and in 2 Corinthians 11:25 he mentions having been beaten with rods. Since beating with rods was a form of punishment frequently used by Romans, and since Antioch was a Roman colony, he might very well have suffered such a physical beating. On the other hand, the persecution may have been political. By manipulating the law, the leading men succeeded in getting Paul and Barnabas expelled from the city. In either case, the punishment came because they were accused of disturbing the peace.

This action against the missionaries made it impossible to remain in Antioch, so they left at once for Iconium. But before leaving, they paused long enough to shake the dust from their feet as a symbolic gesture that they would no longer attempt to work in that city. The dust left behind testified that the city had lost its great opportunity to receive the Word of God. When Jesus sent out the twelve to preach in Galilee, He instructed them to shake the dust off their feet in any town that would not receive them. This action was a sign of the judgment that God would eventually bring upon that town (Matthew 10:14, 15). As painful as this departure was for Paul and Barnabas, it did not have the devastating effect on the church that the Jews hoped for. Instead of sinking into despair, the Christians were filled both with joy and with the Holy Spirit. As the two missionaries made their way to Iconium, they left behind a glowing, growing group of Christians. Some months later, on their way back to Antioch of Syria, they passed through Antioch and ordained elders from among the membership, signifying the growing maturity of the church (Acts 14:21-23).

FIRST MISSIONARY JOURNEY

GALATIA

ASIA

CAPPADOCIA

Antioch

Iconium
Derbe

Lystra

Attalia

Perga

CILICIA

Antioch

Seleucia

LYCIA

PAMPHYLIA

SYRIA

Paphos

Salamis

CYPRUS

MEDITERRANEAN SEA

- - - - - Paul, Barnabas, and John Mark
————— Paul and Barnabas

CHAPTER FOURTEEN

A Successful Missionary Journey Completed

Acts 14

Paul and Barnabas in Iconium (14:1-7)

Forced to leave Antioch, Paul and Barnabas had several options from which to choose. They could have returned to Perga and from there back home, where they could have reported a quite successful journey. Or they could have gone westward to Ephesus, an important city that Paul did visit on a later trip. They chose, however, to travel south and east about eighty miles to Iconium (modern Kenya). This choice was probably made on the basis of Paul's usual practice to go to those population centers that were located on important highways and where he could find a Jewish synagogue. Iconium had at various times in the past been considered a part of Phrygia or of Lycaonia. In 25 B.C. it was made a part of the Roman province of Galatia.

Upon their arrival in Iconium, the missionaries followed their usual practice and went to the synagogue on the first Sabbath after their arrival in the city. Luke does not recite any of the details of this visit, giving only a summary. Probably when they were recognized as learned in the Hebrew Scriptures, they were invited to speak. The sermon must have followed the pattern of Paul's message at Antioch. The results were gratifying, as a great number of both Jews and Greeks believed.

But not everyone believed. As in Antioch, some of the Jews rejected the message, and, not being content just to oppose Paul and Barnabas, they worked to turn the Gentiles against them. It took a little while, however, to involve the Gentiles in this dispute. During this time, the missionaries chose to remain as long as they could to encourage the new Christians. Their preaching was confirmed by miracles, which may have worked to silence some of the opposition, especially since these were in all likelihood miracles of healing. People are less inclined to believe evil about persons who are doing good deeds. This lack of opposition allowed them to spend "considerable time" there (Acts 14:3). They may have stayed several weeks or even months; Luke does not say.

But the Jewish opposition was busily at work trying to undermine the work of the missionaries. Finally, they succeeded in dividing the populace--some supporting the Jews and some the apostles. The gospel, when it is faithfully preached, often has this divisive effect, just as Jesus said it would (Luke 12:49-53).

It is worth noting that Luke refers to Paul and Barnabas as "apostles" (Acts 14:4). Paul, of course, was quite commonly referred to as a special apostle to the Gentiles. His call at the time of his conversion specifically was to proclaim the good news to the Gentiles. Barnabas, on the other hand, had no special call and did not meet the qualifications of the original Twelve. In what sense, then, was he an apostle? Apparently, the term is used here in the more general sense of "one who is sent." Strictly speaking, Barnabas was not an apostle of Christ but an apostle of the church.

The Jews finally succeeded in their efforts to arouse the city against Paul and Barnabas, and a plot was hatched to get rid of them. From the description of what they planned, it appears this was a mob action rather than any legal action by the city officials as had been the case in Antioch. Getting wind of this plot, the pair wisely chose to leave town rather than face a bloodthirsty mob. Their destination was Lystra and Derbe, cities lying south and east of Iconium.

Paul and Barnabas in Lystra and Derbe (14:8-20)

Lystra and Derbe lay in Lycaonia, which in turn had been incorporated in the Roman province of Galatia. Although Augustus had made Lystra a Roman colony, neither city was as large or as important as Antioch or Iconium.

A Cripple Healed in Lystra (8-10)

Lystra was about twenty miles from Iconium, about a day's journey. It was different from Antioch and Iconium in that it contained no Jewish synagogue. In this city, the missionaries would have no ready-made platform from which to launch their campaign. This meant a change in tactics for Paul and Barnabas, but a change that they were willing and able to make. This illustrates quite well the principle that evangelists must adapt their tactics to different situations.

146

Since there was no synagogue where they might gather an audience to whom they could speak, Paul and Barnabas must have used the marketplace or some other public place to begin their ministry in Lystra. It was not uncommon for itinerant teachers and religious leaders to carry on their teaching in the marketplace (the *agora);* so the people of Lystra would not have been upset at seeing Paul and Barnabas speaking there. In fact, they probably would have attracted little attention until the crippled man was healed. This poor man, like the man Peter had healed (Acts 3:1ff), had been crippled from birth. As Paul spoke, he undoubtedly mentioned the life of Christ, including some of the miracles He had performed. This aroused hope in the man's heart that he too might be made whole. Paul became aware of the man's faith, either by his expression or through some special acts of the Holy Spirit. As a result, Paul spoke in a loud voice ordering the man to stand on his feet. We can only surmise the feeling that swept over the man as he felt new strength surging through his crippled limbs, strength that he had never known before. Then, without waiting for a second command from Paul, he leaped to his feet and began to walk.

There are some interesting similarities between the two healings of lame men, one by Peter and one by Paul. For one thing, both had been lame from birth, and both were healed by apostles. These similarities have led some critics to argue that Luke made up this account and made it similar to Peter's healing in order to enhance the reputation of Paul. But if we examine the accounts more closely, we will note several differences. For example, one of the lame men was a Jew, the other a Gentile. One was a beggar, the other is not called a beggar. The Gentile had faith that Paul could heal him, while the beggar in the temple asked for alms, not healing. The immediate results were also different. In Jerusalem, many came to believe as a result of the healing. In Lystra, the healing led the people to want to worship Paul and Barnabas as gods. The conclusion should be obvious. These are two separate incidents, similar in some respects but quite different in others. Luke was a careful historian, not a writer of fiction.

The people standing about who witnessed the miracle excitedly began to shout that the gods had come down in human form (Acts 14:11). Paul had been preaching in Greek, which they could understand, but in their excitement, they reverted to their native language. The people of Lystra had an old legend that at one time

Zeus and Hermes had visited the city in disguise. An elderly couple had entertained them, not realizing that they were two gods. As a result of their being snubbed, Zeus and Hermes severely punished the rest of the people, leaving the old couple as guardians of the temple. The people of Lystra wanted to be certain that they did not make this mistake again. They hailed Barnabas as Zeus and Paul as Hermes. (The King James Version calls them Jupiter and Mercury, supposing that English readers would be more familiar with Roman gods than with Greek gods.) In the Greek pantheon, Hermes was the messenger god and often served as a spokesman for the other gods. Since Paul was the speaker on this occasion, it seemed reasonable to the Lystrans to identify him with Hermes. Because Hermes often accompanied Zeus, Barnabas was thought to be Zeus. Hermes was usually depicted as small in stature, while Zeus was an imposing figure. This has led some to speculate that Barnabas was a large man, much taller than Paul. Perhaps so.

Since the people thought Paul and Barnabas to be gods, they wanted to make certain that they received proper homage. Just outside the city gate was a temple of Zeus, and the priest—probably the chief priest—wanted to take full advantage of the situation. He immediately brought bulls festooned with garlands for the purpose of offering them as a sacrifice. Because of language differences, Paul and Barnabas did not at first realize what was happening. When they did, they tried to put a stop to the ceremony. Finally, they had to take dramatic action to convince the people that they were not gods. They tore their clothing to show their distaste for the idolatrous worship that was being heaped upon them, and rushed into the crowd, shouting that they were men, not gods.

Apparently this bold action caught the attention of the crowd and stopped them, for the missionaries were permitted to give a rational presentation of their message. Up to this point in their journey, Luke has reported only the messages they gave to Jewish audiences. The Jews already believed in the one true God, and they believed in the Old Testament Scriptures. From these fundamental beliefs, Paul and Barnabas could begin to explain that Jesus was the anticipated Messiah, the fulfillment of Old Testament prophecies. But speaking to Gentiles who believed in many gods, the worship of which was often quite immoral, they had to take a much different approach. We see a similar situation in Acts

17, when Paul addressed the philosophers of the Areopagus in Athens. Like Paul, we would be wise when we are witnessing to adapt our message to the needs of our listeners.

Paul and Barnabas appealed to the crowd in Lystra by informing them that they were bringing good news. It is interesting to contrast Paul's approach to that of the Old Testament prophet Jonah, who preached to a pagan audience in Nineveh much like this one. But Jonah's message was not good news; instead, it was the bad news of God's impending judgment on the city. After announcing that he was bringing good news, Paul went on to tell that the true God created heaven, the earth, and everything in them. This contradicted some of the mythological tales of creation prevalent among pagans. Yet pagan philosophers had already challenged many of these myths; so Paul's statement was not all that shocking.

In the past, God had permitted the nations to go their own ways, not out of indifference but because of His patience. Yet even as He permitted them to fall into idolatry, He kept giving them evidence of His loving concern for them. He had sent the rain and the seasons; He had provided food and other reasons for joy. But even after all of this, Paul and Barnabas had difficulty in keeping the people from worshiping them. Lives that have been spent entirely in the darkness do not readily accept the light when it first shines upon them. Yet some were convinced by this message and other teaching that must have followed, and they became "disciples" (Acts 14:20).

Paul Stoned (19, 20)

What happened shortly after this incident shows how fickle people are. Within a short time—perhaps only a few days—word got back to Antioch and Iconium about the work of Paul and Barnabas in Lystra. As a result, they dispatched a squad whose purpose was to create problems for the missionaries. Luke does not mention a synagogue in Lystra, but if there was one there, it would have been the base of operations for this squad. They were successful in turning the people against the missionaries, so successful that the crowd was persuaded to stone Paul. Since Paul had been the chief speaker, he was the target of their wrath. Paul was knocked unconscious by the attack and dragged outside the city, where he was left for dead like an animal. The crowd that only a short time before had wanted to worship Paul and

Barnabas had turned into a lynch mob demanding Paul's blood. The action of this crowd should caution us about relying on miracles or other dramatic events to win persons to the Lord. Such easily-won victories can turn just as easily to defeats.

As Paul lay unconscious outside the city, a little band of disciples, torn by various emotions, gathered about him. The more practical ones were probably beginning to consider plans for burying the body. The more optimistic ones may have been hoping against hope that Paul was only unconscious, not dead. The most optimistic ones may have hoped for a resurrection in case he was dead. It is possible that young Timothy was among these disciples. Paul later on speaks of him as "my son whom I love" (1 Corinthians 4:17), perhaps indicating that Paul had converted him. When Paul returned to Lystra on his second missionary journey, Timothy was mature enough as a Christian to become one of his traveling companions (Acts 16:1-3). What joy must have been felt when Paul painfully began to move and finally opened his eyes. Luke passes over this scene with remarkable brevity, and he does not suggest that a miracle occurred. Had Luke been writing fiction, he certainly would have highlighted this as a miracle in order to enhance the reputation of Paul. Think what a modern public relations man could do with a story like that. "Apostle Raised from the Dead to Speak!" would read the headlines. Alas, we have to forego such attention-getters. Paul may have been providentially spared but not miraculously raised from the dead. And since no miracle was performed bringing instant healing, Paul must have gone through agony as he was helped to his feet and led haltingly back into the city. Paul later referred to this incident in listing some of the suffering he had experienced (2 Corinthians 11:25). He may also have had this in mind when he wrote, "I bear on my body the marks of Jesus" (Galatians 6:17). In Lystra, the mob did not use Styrofoam facsimiles of stones, but real stones, which were certain to have left cuts and bruises.

The Missionaries in Derbe (20, 21)

It may have been late in the day by the time Paul, accompanied by his friends, was able to limp back into the city. He would be safe there during the night, but he knew that he could not stay long in Lystra. The next day, he and Barnabas set out for Derbe. At one time Derbe was identified with a tell or mound about twenty miles from Lystra. As a result the older translations read that Paul and Barnabas went to Derbe the next day. But now, the New Testament site of Derbe has been identified with a tell about sixty miles from Lystra. Thus, the New International Version correctly renders the last part of Acts 14:20, "The next day he and Barnabas left for Derbe." Fresh agony from the wounds and bruises would have accompanied Paul every step he took; so it must have taken three or more days to walk the distance to Derbe.

Their efforts met with success in Derbe, and a large number became disciples. If they met any serious opposition there, Luke does not mention this fact. Unhampered by the persecution they had faced earlier, they were able to preach openly, and the results were gratifying. Gaius, one of Paul's traveling companions when he traveled from Greece to Jerusalem (Acts 20:4), was from Derbe. It is entirely possible that Gaius was converted in this visit of Paul to Derbe.

Paul and Barnabas Return to Antioch (14:21-28)

Luke gives us no clue about how long Paul and Barnabas ministered in Derbe. Perhaps several weeks or even months elapsed. At least enough time had passed that they deemed it feasible to return to the cities where they had suffered so much abuse. It is likely that the magistrates in some of the cities had changed in the months that had elapsed, and new officials without any knowledge of Paul and Barnabas would be less likely to renew the persecution against them. Further, these were brief visits, and by this time, the churches were meeting in houses or less obvious locations. By keeping a lower profile, the missionaries were less likely to attract the attention of their persecutors. Yet with all these precautions, a return to the places where they had been persecuted took a great amount of courage.

Strengthening the Churches (21-23)

Paul was an able evangelist, but he did not consider his work done when he had made converts. These converts needed to be organized into congregations and strengthened in the faith. This was exactly what Paul proposed to do as he and Barnabas made their way back through Lystra, Iconium, and Antioch. The missionaries reminded the young Christians that the way to Heaven led through difficulties and hardships (Acts 14:22), or as someone has put it, "No cross, no crown!" Their sufferings were but a

151

small foretaste of what the church would endure across the centuries.

Not only was Paul an evangelist, he was also an able administrator, qualities that are not always found together in the same person. The churches were organized and elders were appointed in each of the congregations. The verb translated "appointed" (Acts 14:23) means "to choose by raising hands," suggesting that the congregations had a part in the selection of their elders. A footnote in the New International Version reads "had elders elected." It is certainly appropriate that the members of the congregation share in the selection of their officers. They are more likely than anyone else to know who from among them are qualified. They also know better than outsiders what persons they can work with more effectively.

It is usually not wise to select leaders from among those who have been Christians only a short time, in this case just a few months. In fact, Paul himself specifically warned against this (1 Timothy 3:6). But the actions of Paul and Barnabas were entirely justified in these churches. Most of the leadership came, not from among pagans, but from among Jews. They already believed in and worshiped the true God, and they were familiar with the Old Testament, which pointed them to the Messiah. In just a short time, men with these qualifications would be mature, able leaders. Once the elders were selected in each church, the members joined in prayer and fasting as they committed their leaders to the Lord.

Returning and Reporting to the Church in Antioch of Syria (24-28)

After Paul and Barnabas had visited the churches in Lycaonia and Pisidia, they retraced their steps through Pamphylia to Perga, where John Mark had left the party to return to Jerusalem. Paul and Barnabas had not preached in Perga on their initial visit. Now they took time to share the good news with the people there. Luke does not mention any opposition in connection with this preaching, nor does he record any results. But it is quite likely that a band of believers was left behind there.

Traveling on to Attalia, they took a ship there and sailed to Syrian Antioch. What an exciting homecoming this must have been. They had been absent for many months, and so far as we know, they had had no communication with the home church during this period. At last the church would have an opportunity to learn about all that had befallen the missionaries on their journey. In our day, as well as in Paul's day, the personal contact between the missionary and the sending church is important. By this means, the members of the congregation learn about the problems and needs of the mission field. As a result, they are able to provide for many of these needs and to undergird the effort with intelligent prayer support.

One important part of the missionaries' report was how God had opened the door of the church to Gentiles. Of course, Gentiles had become members of the church before this, but most of these had been proselytes, Gentiles who came to the church through Judaism. But it is evident from this report that a great number, perhaps the majority, of these new members were Gentiles who had previously had no connection with Judaism. This change would soon stir serious controversy, but it would also allow the church to reach beyond the narrow confines of Judaism into the whole world.

CHAPTER FIFTEEN

The Jerusalem Conference

Acts 15

The Occasion of the Conference (15:1-4)

Everyone agrees that the Jerusalem Conference is a crucial event in the life of the young church. The amount of emphasis that Luke gives to the conference further substantiates this conclusion. Had the Jewish Christians refused to accept any Gentiles but those who were willing to conform to the law of Moses (including circumcision), Christianity almost certainly would have remained a Jewish sect. As a Jewish sect, it could never have carried out our Lord's marching order to go into the whole world. In all likelihood, it would have long since taken its place among the other Jewish sects that have arisen briefly and then disappeared. And because it would have failed to evangelize the world as Christ commanded, its disappearance would have been justly deserved.

The issue discussed and dealt with at the Jerusalem Conference was more than just a question about obedience to the law of Moses. It touched the very heart of what Christianity is about. The basis for salvation, as the Jews interpreted the law of Moses, was good works. One would be saved by what he did, not by what he believed or what he was. On the other hand, the teachings of Jesus and of the inspired apostles make it clear that salvation is by grace through faith in Jesus Christ as the divine Son of God. Works result from salvation; they don't produce it.

The Jerusalem Conference for all practical purposes settled the matter of obedience to the Mosaic code as a basis of salvation. However, it did not settle permanently the issue of works versus grace. Again and again, in one form or another, this issue has appeared in the church to create controversy and division. Even today, this issue continues to appear in modern garb to plague our churches.

155

Controversy at Antioch (1, 2)

Things were going well at the church in Antioch. The church was continuing to grow, and Paul and Barnabas had returned to bring a report of a highly successful missionary journey. But Christians need especially to be alert when things are going well, for such a situation invites attack from Satan. The devil doesn't worry much about dead churches; they do his kingdom little harm. But the alive, active churches—they are another story. They pose a serious threat to his empire. Logically, then, he concentrates his efforts against them.

These teachings of the Judaizers directly attacked Paul and Barnabas and the great work they had done. The Judaizers seemed to be repudiating the converts these two missionaries had won and the suffering they had undergone. It should not surprise us that Paul and Barnabas strongly opposed these false teachings, but their arguments did not faze the Judaizers, who firmly held to their position. This might surprise us, for several years earlier, Cornelius, an uncircumcised Gentile, had been admitted into the church through the work of Peter.

Two things we need to keep in mind. The Judaizers were apparently willing to accept a few Gentiles so long as they remained a small, obscure minority. But they saw that the work of the Antioch church was bringing such large numbers into the fellowship that Gentiles would soon be a majority, and the Jews would be a minority. What should have been a source of rejoicing was to them a serious threat.

Second, we need to keep in mind that prejudices die slowly. And the more firmly a prejudice is held, the longer it is likely to take to excise it. Our own times have provided numerous illustrations of this fact. While some of the Pharisees may have been hypocrites, the majority of them were committed to a life-style that saw no virtue in any other life-style. Their very sincerity made it more difficult to give up their prejudices. The admission of Gentiles into the church was not just a minor concession for them; rather, it struck at the heart of their life philosophy.

Delegation Sent to Jerusalem (3-5)

Since the issue raised was so divisive, and since it could not be settled in Antioch, the church decided to send Paul and Barnabas to Jerusalem as the head of a delegation to pursue this issue further. As the group traveled to Jerusalem through Phoenicia and Samaria, they received words of encouragement on every hand. When they told about the numerous conversions of Gentiles, these people rejoiced. Of course, since these congregations had non-Jewish members, we would expect them to feel this way about it. Unfortunately, not everyone in Jerusalem shared this feeling.

When the party from Antioch arrived in Jerusalem, they were welcomed by the church. Instead of aggressively attacking the Judaizers, Paul and Barnabas wisely reported the victories that had been won among the Gentiles. But this did not convince the members of the party of the Pharisees. They demanded that the Gentile Christians be circumcised and become obedient to the law of Moses. Paul was in a position to understand their feelings. After all, he had been a Pharisee, an exceedingly strict Pharisee. But at his conversion, Paul had been led to see that Christianity was much more than just adding faith in Jesus Christ to the doctrines they held as Pharisees. His new faith brought him to recognize that God and man were put in a new relationship. Man was not justified by works of the law but by grace through faith. Though some of the Pharisees had come to believe in Christ, they had not understood how this faith set aside any basis for salvation by works. This was now the bone of contention.

Apostles and Elders Meet (15:6-21)

We have no idea how large the Pharisee party was. It may not have been very large, but it was outspoken. In some situations, the leaders of a church may be justified in ignoring a disruptive minority. Time and energy spent in dealing with such a group is time taken from more productive activities. But because this group was so outspoken, the leaders felt that the issue had to be dealt with openly and swiftly. For that reason, they met to discuss it.

Peter's Report (6-11)

Apparently, this meeting was open to the whole church, for Luke spoke of "the whole assembly" (Acts 15:12), which in the Greek literally means "all the multitude." After much discussion, which may have been heated at times, Peter took the floor (Acts 15:7). He was certainly the most highly respected leader in the church, and his opinion in this matter would carry considerable weight. Peter did not base his arguments on theology but on

157

experience. He indicated that God had already made it clear that uncircumcised Gentiles should be accepted into the church when He sent him to preach to Cornelius. God made this fact known by sending the Holy Spirit upon the household of Cornelius just as He had upon the Jews at Pentecost.

This should have decided the argument, but Peter was not willing to let the case rest there. He pointed out that the Judaizers were testing God by trying to fasten the yoke of the law upon Gentiles. He strengthened his point by reminding them that neither they nor their fathers had been able to bear this yoke. He concluded his presentation by showing that both Jew and Gentile were saved the same way—by the grace of the Lord Jesus.

A Report by Paul and Barnabas (12)

Following Peter's presentation, the multitude remained silent. Either the Judaizers were convinced by Peter's arguments or they were trying to find a way to answer them. Barnabas and Paul (interestingly, Luke reversed the order of the names of the two men here in Jerusalem, perhaps in recognition of Barnabas's good reputation there) took the platform next. They underscored Peter's position by relating the things God had done among the Gentiles, "miraculous signs and wonders" (Acts 15:12).

James's Speech (13-21)

Although Peter, Paul, and Barnabas had spoken, agreeing in their arguments, the decisive voice was yet to be heard. The words of James, the brother of the Lord, would carry the greatest weight. He was the recognized leader of the Jerusalem church, but more than that, we would expect him to be the most conservative, the most Jewish of all the speakers. James began his speech by referring to Peter's experience in the house of Cornelius. (James used Peter's Hebrew name, Simon, an interesting concession to the situation.) The New International Version does not convey the full impact of James's statement. He actually said "God visited the Gentiles" (Acts 15:14), an expression that indicated God's special revelation. The purpose of this special revelation was to take a "people for himself." The Jewish audience would be quite familiar with the idea of God's people. Again and again through the Old Testament, they had been referred to as God's people. Now James confronted them with the fact that God had also chosen a people from among the Gentiles.

158

But James did not conclude his argument at this point. He went on to show that the choosing of a people from among the Gentiles was not something that God devised on the spur of the moment. Rather, it was a part of His eternal plan that He had already revealed. He quoted Amos 9:11, 12 to make his point, but he might very well have quoted other Old Testament passages. In this passage Amos described how God would "rebuild David's fallen tent" (Acts 15:16). Amos did not intend to say that God would restore the ruling house or royal lineage of David. He meant, rather, that God would restore the place of worship, which was in David's day the tabernacle. In the new dispensation, this is the church. Through this rebuilt tabernacle, the church, including the Gentiles, would be able to seek the Lord.

These arguments led James to conclude that they should not impose the law of Moses upon the Gentiles. Jewish meetings were not conducted according to Robert's Rules of Order. They did not take a vote on issues as we would, but worked for a concensus of the people. When James set forth his opinion, he was expressing what he felt to be the concensus of those present. Subsequent events proved that he was right.

Although James made it clear that the Mosaic law should not be imposed upon Gentile Christians, at the same time he asked that Gentile Christians make some concessions to the sensitive consciences of Jewish Christians. Gentiles were asked to abstain from food polluted by being dedicated to idols. In pagan temples, the priests received many of the animals sacrificed. Since this often provided more meat than they could consume, the remainder was sold in the marketplace. Jews found eating such meat repulsive and tended to reject anyone who ate it. Since meat was available from other sources, the abstention would not be a serious burden. The second prohibition dealt with sexual immorality. This would include not only fornication and adultery, but marriage relations that were considered incestuous by the Jews. Fornication and adultery were not illegal in the pagan society from which the Gentiles came, nor was there any particular stigma attached to engaging in these activities. Further, sexual acts were often incorporated into pagan worship rites. James's prohibition against sexual immorality served two purposes. One purpose was to prevent the Gentiles from engaging in activities that were especially offensive to the Jews with their high standards for sexual morality. The other reason was to help sensitize the Gentiles' conscience against those things and to protect them from the temptations that surrounded them.

The third prohibition dealt with the eating of the flesh of animals that had been strangled. The Old Testament prohibited this practice (Leviticus 17:13). Jews later developed specific rules about killing animals that were to be used for food. Such food properly prepared became known as "kosher" food. The last prohibition was against consuming blood, a practice also strongly condemned in the Mosaic law (Leviticus 17:10-12). In the pagan world the drinking of blood was sometimes associated with the worship of various gods; so this practice by Gentile Christians would be doubly offensive to Jewish Christians.

James concluded his speech by pointing out that the law of Moses was universally received among Jews. Moses had been preached and read in every Jewish synagogue every Sabbath (Acts 15:21). Thus, his teachings were so drilled into Jewish people that even after they became Christians they could not readily forget or abandon the practices set forth by the law. "Since Jews have been so well indoctrinated in these teachings," James seems to be saying, "then Gentile Christians need to show their love and concern by not offending their fellow-Christians in these matters."

The Letter to the Gentile Churches (15:22-35)

James asked that his suggestions for the Gentile Christians be sent to them in the form of a letter. Undoubtedly, the brethren who had come from Antioch to Jerusalem for this meeting would convey James's sentiments to the church at Antioch when they returned, but an official letter would carry even more weight.

A Party from Jerusalem Sent with the Letter (22)

James's suggestion met with the approval of the Jerusalem church. The Judaizers either had been won over to James's position, or they had come to realize that they were a minority that could no longer have much influence on the church's decisions. In this situation, they discreetly kept silent. Yet the Judaizing party did not die out. Paul had to deal with this problem in the Galatian churches, and we see hints of it in his letter to the Romans. There developed later, in the first century and beyond, a sect called the Ebionites. Their teachings were similar to many of the teachings of the Judaizers. The persistence of these divisive, even heretical, teachings should warn us that theological views, even patently

160

false ones, do not die an easy death. Nor, for that matter, can they be quickly and painlessly excised from the church by the pronouncements of church councils.

The apostles, the elders, and the whole church concurred in the decision to send some of their own men back to Antioch with Paul and Barnabas. They chose two of their own leaders for this mission: Judas, called Barsabas, and Silas. About Judas we know little except that he was a prophet (Acts 15:31). Silas, however, is mentioned several times later in the book of Acts as a traveling companion of Paul (Acts 15:40). He is also mentioned in some of Paul's epistles, where he is called Silvanus (1 Thessalonians 1:1; 2 Thessalonians 1:1).

Contents of the Letter (23-29)

The letter was sent in the name of the apostles and elders of the Jerusalem church. The salutation in no way suggests that the church of Jerusalem was attempting to assert any kind of ecclesiastical control over the church in Antioch and other areas. Yet, because it was the mother church, and because the inspired apostles had been involved in this matter, this letter from the Jerusalem church did carry considerable weight. The letter was addressed to the "Gentile believers in Antioch, Syria and Cilicia" (Acts 15:23). The largest and most influential church was that in Antioch. This church undoubtedly had started other congregations in Syria. At this time, the eastern part of Cilicia was administered by Syria, and so the influence had also penetrated there.

The letter disavowed the men who had come from Jerusalem to Antioch, starting the dispute in the first place. Their activities had not been authorized by the church in Jerusalem. Not infrequently in the history of the church, self-appointed prophets, evangelists, and teachers have been the cause of disturbances.

The letter carried a warm commendation of Barnabas and Paul, who had risked their lives for the Lord. These gracious words about their two respected leaders would be well received in Antioch. In contrast to the unauthorized teachers who had previously come causing dissension, the church sent two of their leaders, Judas and Silas, to accompany Barnabas and Paul. These two men were coming as agents of peace and harmony, not as agents of discord and strife.

This letter carried more authority than just that of the Jerusalem church. Actually, the decision conveyed in the letter was the work of the Holy Spirit. The Jerusalem church had been merely the agent used by the Spirit. We are not told specifically how the Holy Spirit made His will known in this matter. He had, of course, directed them through the passage from Amos that James quoted. He had also spoken through the inspired apostles, who had been promised His guidance into all truth (John 16:13). We can also see the providential working of the Spirit to bring this matter to a head.

This raises some interesting questions. Through the centuries, many councils have met to discuss matters that were disturbing the church. These councils have usually claimed that they spoke with the authority of the Spirit. Yet their pronouncements have often contradicted one another and contradicted the Scriptures. Two thousand years of experience should lead us to be quite cautious about claiming the blessings of the Holy Spirit for our conciliar pronouncements.

The Holy Spirit had decreed that the Gentile Christians would not have to conform to the law of Moses. The four prohibitions that were laid upon them were the same—expressed in a different order—as those proposed by James in his speech before the congregation.

It would be difficult to overestimate the importance of this letter, brief though it was. It determined the whole future of Christianity, whether it was to remain a Jewish sect or become a world-encompassing fellowship.

The Letter Received at Antioch (30-35)

When the Antioch church sent Paul and Barnabas to Jerusalem to carry their plea for Gentile Christianity, they had no way of knowing for certain how the decision would turn out. Suppose that the Judaizers who had come from Jerusalem really had had the approval of the apostles and elders there. What then? And so they must have awaited the return of their emissaries with more than a little apprehension.

No doubt they were greatly relieved when Paul and Barnabas returned with Judas and Silas. When the congregation was assembled and the letter read, rejoicing followed. Not only had the letter lifted the burden of Judaism from their shoulders, but the tone of the letter itself was encouraging. There was nothing cold, formal, or begrudging about the letter. We might very well take a lesson from this in handling our own correspondence.

The presence of Judas and Silas contributed to the good feelings as they encouraged and strengthened the brothers. After their mission was accomplished, they were sent back to Jerusalem with the blessing of the Antioch church. Acts 15:34, in the King James Version, tells us that Silas did not return to Jerusalem but remained in Antioch. Several ancient manuscripts omit this verse, and so it is omitted in the New International Version (except for a footnote). If Silas did not remain in Antioch at this time, he soon returned, for he was available soon afterward to accompany Paul on his second missionary journey (Acts 15:40).

Paul and Barnabas Plan Another Missionary Trip (15:36-41)

With this major controversy behind them, Paul and Barnabas could now give their undivided attention to evangelism. They remained in Antioch for a time preaching and teaching, but before long, Paul became restless and began once more to look to more distant horizons.

Paul's Plan (36)

After a few weeks or months (Luke is distressingly vague about time), Paul proposed that Barnabas and he return to the churches they had started on the first missionary journey. They may have remained in Antioch over the winter, and with the coming of spring, travel would be easier and safer. Paul had a continuing interest in these churches. Not only did he want to see how they were doing, but he wanted to spend some time teaching among them. He knew very well that continued growth toward maturity required additional teaching. Young churches are tempting targets for false teachers, and Paul wanted to protect them against such men. As the Galatian letter shows, many of the people in the Galatian churches were led astray by the Judaizers. In spite of the decision of the Council of Jerusalem, these men continued to plague the churches.

Paul and Barnabas Disagree (37-41)

Barnabas was in complete agreement with Paul's idea. But it soon turned out that there was a problem. Barnabas wanted to take John Mark with them again, and Paul wanted nothing to do with him. Luke does not gloss over this sharp disagreement between these two old friends. At the same time, he does not give us many of the details of the disagreement.

163

From what we know of the two men, the dispute developed more because of their diverse personalities than over any substantive issue. The picture that the New Testament gives us of Paul is that of an aggressive, driving person. He was certainly not without emotions, but he never allowed these emotions to deter him from his goals. Today, we would call him a goal-oriented person. Barnabas, on the other hand, seems to have been a more relaxed person, generous with his possessions and loving toward his fellowmen. We would call him person-oriented.

Paul had in mind certain objectives for his second missionary journey. Mark had failed on the first journey, and Paul did not want to take along a companion who might fail again and hinder the efforts to achieve the goal. Barnabas looked at Mark differently, perhaps partly because Mark was a blood relative. But knowing Barnabas, it seems likely that he would have taken the same generous attitude even if Mark had not been related to him. He saw Mark as a young man who had failed under pressure, but who needed another chance.

Men with such diverse outlooks on life can work together successfully in many situations. In fact, they often complement one another. But in this case, neither man was willing to compromise his position. With the lines so sharply drawn, the men could not work together, and the only thing to do was for each to go his separate way. Barnabas took Mark and returned to Cyprus, and Paul took Silas and went through Syria, Cilicia, and on to Galatia. The beautiful thing about all of this is that God took human weaknesses and used them for His glory. Instead of just one missionary team in the field, there were two.

This dispute had a happy conclusion in another way. Many years later, when Paul was in prison awaiting his execution, he wrote to Timothy, "Get Mark and bring him with you, because he is helpful to me in my ministry" (2 Timothy 4:11). Barnabas was right in giving Mark a second chance, and Mark had used that opportunity to develop into a faithful minister and a writer of the Gospel that bears his name. And Paul was man enough to admit that all this was true. How we wish that all of our church disputes would end on such a happy note.

CHAPTER SIXTEEN

Paul's Second Missionary Journey

Acts 16

The Journey Begins (16:1-5)

Even though the disagreement between Paul and Barnabas had been serious, leading to the separation of the two veteran missionaries, Paul was not deterred in his plan to launch out on another journey. But with Barnabas going another direction, he needed a new partner. It did not take him long to settle on Silas as that partner. And an excellent selection it was, for Silas faithfully accompanied Paul and suffered many things with him during the second missionary journey.

Paul and Silas left Antioch and passed through Syria. They then entered Cilicia, crossing the Taurus Mountains through a pass called the Cilician Gates. This route would have taken Paul close to or even through his hometown of Tarsus, but Luke does not mention that the party stopped there. Moving into Galatia, they came first to Derbe and then to Lystra because they were traveling westward rather than eastward as they had on the first journey. At Lystra, they met the young man Timothy. His mother, Eunice (2 Timothy 1:5), was a Jewess, but his father was a Greek. Such Jewish-Greek marriages were quite rare in Judea, but were much more frequent among Jews of the Dispersion living among Greeks.

Timothy, who may have been about twenty at the time, had a good reputation, not only in Lystra but also in Iconium. For this reason, Paul wanted to take him along as they continued their journey. But a problem arose: Timothy was uncircumcised. According to Jewish thinking, Timothy would have been considered a Jew because his mother was Jewish. Yet because he had not been circumcised, he would not have been acceptable to the Jews. Why this matter had not been taken care of at Timothy's birth we are not told. Perhaps Eunice was lax in her Jewish faith, although her faithfulness in teaching her son the Scriptures would seem to refute this. Or perhaps Timothy's father had forbidden it. Timothy's problem was that the Greeks looked upon him as Jewish and yet he was not acceptable to the Jews. As a "man without a country," so to speak, his effectiveness as a missionary would have been hampered. To solve this problem, Paul arranged to have him circumcised.

Some have branded Paul as being inconsistent for taking this action. He had argued so strongly against the necessity of circumcision, and yet here he agreed to it, the critics charge. Paul's critics have missed the point of the matter completely. Paul was adamantly opposed to requiring Gentiles to be circumcised as a necessity for salvation. That was not the issue in Timothy's case. Timothy was circumcised to prevent his being offensive to the Jewish communities into which they would be going. This is an example of Paul's willingness to "become all things to all men" (1 Corinthians 9:19-23). On another occasion, however, when some of the Judaizers demanded that Titus be circumcised, Paul refused on principle, insisting that because he was a Greek, Titus did not have to conform to the law of Moses (Galatians 2:2-5). When it is a matter of free choice, we can make concessions to the feelings and beliefs of others. But when they demand that we conform, we must, in order to defend our Christian freedom, not give in. That's exactly the way Paul responded: "We did not give in to them for a moment, so that the truth of the gospel might remain with you" (Galatians 2:5).

As they traveled from town to town, they shared with the Christians the decisions made at the Jerusalem Conference. Although the letter was addressed to Gentile believers in Antioch, Syria, and Cilicia, the principles it set forth would be just as applicable in Galatia. Because of the teaching and preaching of Paul and Silas, and probably also because of the effects of the letter, the church was strengthened in the faith and grew in numbers. The continued growth of these churches gives some indication of just how well Paul and Barnabas had laid the foundations on their earlier visit.

Called to Europe (16:6-10)

When he first proposed the second missionary journey, Paul's plan was just to visit the churches in Asia Minor that had been started on the first journey. If he had any plans beyond that, we have no record that he expressed them to anyone. But once that

166

mission was accomplished, what then? Return to Antioch? That might have been a logical option for most people, but Paul was different. His soul was troubled by the fact that beyond the borders of Galatia were countless thousands—yea millions—who had never heard the gospel. To return to Antioch at this time was unthinkable.

The city of Ephesus may have beckoned. Located in the western part of the Roman province of Asia, Ephesus was a large and important city that lay on the main highway west of Pisidian Antioch. From the human point of view, it seemed to be a perfectly logical choice. But the Holy Spirit ruled otherwise, forbidding Paul to preach in the province of Asia (Acts 16:6).

Paul and his party then turned northward, coming to Mysia, the northwestern part of Asia. At this point, Paul proposed to turn eastward into Bithynia, a Roman province that stretched along the southern shore of the Black Sea. This time, Luke reported, they were prevented from going there by "the Spirit of Jesus" (Acts 16:7). There is no reason to suppose that the Holy Spirit and the Spirit of Jesus were two different persons. Luke probably used this designation to show that Jesus, through the Holy Spirit, was especially involved in guiding Paul. We are not told how this guidance came, whether by audible voice as on the road to Damascus or by some inward urging. In any event, as far as Paul was concerned, it was decisive, and he made no attempt to resist it.

With his other options closed, the party passed through Mysia and came to Troas. This city, located near the ancient city of Troy, had been made a Roman colony by Augustus. Troas was a port town and would be used by most travelers going from Asia Minor to Macedonia.

That night Paul had a vision—a vision that could change the course of history. In this vision, a man of Macedonia asked Paul to come over into Macedonia and help him and his people. The help that the man wanted clearly was spiritual help, exactly the kind of help that Paul was prepared to give. The Macedonian call was the call for which Paul was waiting. Asia, Bithynia, and other areas had been closed to any evangelistic work. Knowing Paul, we can be certain that he was eager to become involved in a new work and was undoubtedly becoming impatient at the delay.

One of our old favorite missionary hymns sings, "We have heard the Macedonian call today, Send the Light! Send the

Light!" The hymn writer seems to be saying that "the Macedonian call" is a call to worldwide missions. But that is not precisely the case. This was a very specific call to a specific area that was ready to receive the gospel. The Macedonians needed the gospel, but so did the people of Asia and Galatia and Bithynia. Why was Paul forbidden to preach in those areas and yet called to Macedonia? Since the need was no greater in Macedonia than in these other areas, we have to look to another cause. Paul was called to Macedonia because God knew that the Macedonians were ready to receive the message of salvation.

It makes good sense in our missionary strategy today to go first to those peoples who are most receptive. Only about one-fourth of the world's population is even nominally Christian. Thus three-fourths of the people need to hear the gospel. With limited resources and personnel, we cannot reach all of them immediately; we need to go first to those who are most receptive. So we ought to understand the Macedonian call, not as a call to worldwide evangelism, but a call to receptive fields.

Paul had one advantage that we do not have. He had a night vision to direct him into a field that was ripe. On the other hand, we have some tools that Paul did not have. Anthropology, linguistics, sociology, psychology, and demography are some of these tools that we can use to reach the reachable in our times. Let us then use these tools that God has put at our disposal rather than waiting for another night vision.

Paul did not need a second invitation. "At once" (Acts 16:10), which probably means the next day, he was down at the docks seeking to find passage to Macedonia for himself and his party. Since Troas was a busy port, it probably was not difficult to find a ship sailing across to Macedonia. Here in Troas the party of three—Paul, Silas, and Timothy—became a party of four, for it was here that Luke joined them. Acts 16:10 begins the first of the so-called "we passages" in Acts, in which the narrator reported the events as an eyewitness, not in the third person. We really know very little about Luke. We know that he was a physician (Colossians 4:14) and that he accompanied Paul on some of his travels. We don't know when he became a Christian or what he was doing in Troas. Paul could hardly have arranged ahead of time for Luke to meet him there, since Paul himself did not know that he was going to be there. It is safest to conclude that God in His providence arranged it.

Ministry in Philippi (16:11-40)

The Conversion of Lydia (11-15)

The ship had favorable winds, and the crossing took only two days. The first day, the party reached Samothrace, an island about halfway between Troas and Neapolis. The next day, they went on to Neapolis, the modern Kavalla. Neapolis was the port for Philippi, which was located about ten miles inland on the Egnatian Way that ran across northern Greece, connecting the Aegean and the Adriatic.

From Neapolis, they traveled inland to Philippi, a Roman colony and the leading city of that area. The beginnings of this city are lost in antiquity. In 356 B.C., it came under the control of Philip of Macedon, who renamed it. Near Philippi in 42 B.C., Mark Antony and Octavian defeated Brutus and Cassius. After the battle, many of the veterans of that battle were settled there. After the Battle of Actium in 31 B.C., in which Octavian defeated Antony, Philippi was made an official Roman colony. Its citizens were governed by the "Italian law," a special privilege conferred on only a few areas outside Italy itself. This particular legal arrangement later on worked to Paul's advantage as a Roman citizen.

When Paul visited a city for the first time, he ordinarily went to the synagogue on the next Sabbath. But since he did not do this in Philippi, we conclude that there was no synagogue in the city. The usual Jewish practice was to start a synagogue whenever there were ten or more Jewish men in the community. The absence of a synagogue in Philippi leads us to believe that very few Jews lived there. Instead of a synagogue, Paul and his party found a group of women meeting for worship outside the city beside the Gangites River. The place where they met was called a "place of prayer" (Acts 16:13), an informal place of worship. It was not uncommon for these places of worship to be located near water, needed for the washings used in connection with their services.

Paul and his companions met with the women, and Paul was invited to speak to them. One of the most attentive listeners was Lydia, a Jewish proselyte from Thyatira. She was called "a dealer in purple cloth" (Acts 16:14). Whether she was a widow or a single woman, the Scriptures do not inform us. But it is obvious that she was a woman of some means, for the purple cloth she sold was quite expensive. The dye for this costly fabric was

169

extracted from a small mollusk found in the eastern Mediterranean. Lydia came from the city of Thyatira, which is mentioned in Revelation 2:18-29 as one of the seven churches of Asia Minor. References in ancient Grecian literature mention the dyeing trade that was practiced in that area.

As Paul and his friends began to present the good news, Lydia was moved by their message. Whether she was baptized then and there is left to conjecture. We are told only that "she and the members of her household were baptized" (Acts 16:15). Perhaps some of the women attending the service by the riverside were members of her household. This is one of the household baptisms mentioned in the book of Acts. Some have used these household baptisms to argue for infant baptism, maintaining that each of these households would surely have contained infants or small children. Of course, many households did not contain infants, and no mention of infants or small children is made. An argument from silence, as this argument is, is a very thin thread from which to suspend such an important act as baptism. As soon as she and her household had been baptized, she graciously invited the missionaries to stay with her in her home. Her Christian faith was translated quickly into Christian action.

The home of Lydia became the base of operations for Paul and his three companions while they remained in Philippi. Since there was no synagogue in the city and very few Jews, they were forced to turn to the Gentile population in their evangelistic efforts.

A Slave Girl Made Well (16-18)

The practice of the missionaries seems to have been to make regular visits to the place of prayer either for worship and meditation or to preach to those who came to hear the gospel. On one of these occasions, the party was met by a slave girl who had, as Luke's words literally translate, a "spirit of a python" (Acts 16:16). This unusual expression has reference to myths about the god Apollo. One of these myths has Apollo slaying a snake that guarded the temple at Delphi. This later became the center of the famous oracles, who supposedly had the power to predict the future. This snake, or python, was sometimes used as the symbol of Apollo, and persons who had predictive powers were said to have a python.

In this case, the girl was possessed by an evil spirit, similar to cases reported in the ministry of Jesus. She cried out, "These men are servants of the Most High God" (Acts 16:17). We are reminded of the words of the Gadarene demoniac who proclaimed that Jesus was the Son of the Most High God (Luke 8:28). This poor girl continued this outcry day after day each time she saw the men. Paul was finally moved to act. Not only did he feel compassion for the girl, but he also did not want that kind of advertising.

The issue of demon possession raises a number of difficult questions for which we have no clear answers. Why, for example, did a demon enter into one person and not another? Did the person so possessed bear some moral responsibility for his condition? Why did demons recognize Christ or His servants publicly?

Even though the Scriptures do not provide us clear answers to these and other questions, we are told enough to understand that demon possession was a special effort on the part of Satan to attack Christ and hamper the spread of the gospel. This poor demon-possessed slave girl in Philippi was being exploited by her owners. It was believed that because of her affliction, she could predict the future. People were willing to pay good money for this information. Whether the demon that possessed her and supposedly gave her this power really had predictive foresight is open to serious question. At least, the demon was not able to foresee that the continued harassment of Paul would lead to his being cast out, a fate that demons dreaded (Luke 8:31, 32).

The message that the girl shouted was true. Paul and his companions were servants of the Most High God, a term Jews used to designate Jehovah God. It was also true that the message they brought in God's name did point the way of salvation. But Paul knew that this message from the lips of a demon-possessed slave girl would not in the long run work to the advantage of the gospel. In the minds of many people, the gospel would be associated with fortune-telling and even with the pagan god Apollo. This incident should cause us to be concerned about the methods we use to propagate the gospel. So Paul ordered the demon to leave the girl. Immediately, and without even a struggle, the demon departed, leaving the girl whole.

Paul and Silas Imprisoned (19-24)

Strong reaction to this cleansing was not long in coming. The owners of the girl, instead of rejoicing because she was healed, saw their profits going down the drain and blamed Paul and Silas for their loss. The world is usually willing to tolerate Christianity so long as it remains within the walls of the church. But let the church take a stand that in any way endangers the world's ill-gotten gain, and the world is ready to fight with any weapons it has in its arsenal. Whether or not the owners of the girl were present when she was healed we are not told, but in any event, they soon learned what had happened. Seizing Paul and Silas (Timothy and Luke, for some reason, were not charged in this matter), the owners brought them before the magistrates.

They did not charge the two with interfering with their profits. Such a charge would not have carried much weight in the courts. Instead, they brought two other charges against them. Paul and Silas were guilty of disturbing the peace, a relatively minor charge. The missionaries were also guilty of teaching customs that were unlawful for Romans either to receive or to practice. The slave owners also pointed out that Paul and Silas were Jews, hoping to play upon any anti-Jewish prejudice that might be present in the crowd.

What followed was more the actions of a lynch mob than the proceedings of a court of law. The slave owners had so inflamed the mob that their shouting pressured the magistrates into taking action against the two men even before their case had been heard. The magistrates ordered the men stripped and beaten without even giving them a chance to reveal that they were Roman citizens. The tumult in the court and the haste of the magistrates to appease the mob must have combined to make such an illegal oversight possible.

Paul and Silas received a severe beating at the hands of the lictors, the officers responsible for administering punishment. Then they were turned over to the jailer, who was charged to keep them securely. Why, since Paul and Silas were hardly classified as desperate or violent criminals, did they take such precautions in jailing them? Perhaps the magistrates had heard about the exorcism of the demon and feared that the men might possess more than natural power. The jailer carried out his order faithfully, placing them in the inner cell and fastening their feet in stocks. The word translated "stocks" (Acts 16:24) literally means "tree" or "wood." This seems to have been a large piece of wood or a log. Their legs were spread apart at a painful angle, and their feet were tied or chained to the piece of wood. This made it very painful for them either to sit up or to lie on their backs, which had just received the brutal stripes.

An Earthquake Opens the Prison (25-28)

The Philippian jail had never held two prisoners like these. Instead of moaning and complaining because of their misfortunes, they filled the dungeon with their songs. Between their prayers, they sang hymns that caught the attention of the other prisoners. They probably sang some of the psalms, many of which would be most appropriate for this occasion. Then, at about midnight, the very foundations of the prison were shaken by a violent earthquake. So severe was the quake that the doors of the prison were jarred open and the chains shackeled to the prisoners' feet came loose from the wall.

Earlier, God had freed the apostles from jail through an angel (Acts 5:18-20). In a similar fashion, Peter was also freed from jail (Acts 12:6-10). In these cases, God used supernatural intervention to accomplish His purpose. But in freeing Paul and Silas, God chose to use a natural agency to accomplish the same purpose. Of course, even the earthquake, happening when it did, was a miracle of timing. This should remind us that God is not limited in the agencies or the powers that He has at His disposal.

Although Luke does not mention them, it is likely that there were guards in the prison when the earthquake struck. They undoubtedly fled from the jail at the first tremors, seeking safety in the street. The jailer must have lived in a house or an apartment adjoining the jail, and hearing the commotion and feeling the tremors, he quickly ran to the jail. What he saw struck dismay in his heart. When he saw that the prison doors were open, he had every reason to believe that the prisoners had escaped. The Roman law did not deal lightly with a jailer who allowed his prisoners to escape, even though the fault was not his own. If he allowed a prisoner accused of a capital crime to escape, his own life was forfeit. Suicide was common among the Romans, and death at one's own hands was considered more honorable than a public trial and execution.

We may wonder why he so quickly prepared to take his own life. In all likelihood, he was or had been a Roman soldier. Roman soldiers were trained to size up a situation quickly and to act decisively. Thus, with the resolve that went with his profession, he drew his sword (probably the short sword that the Romans used in close combat) and prepared to commit suicide. But in the split second before the sword did its bloody work, Paul's voice rang through the darkness: "Don't harm yourself! We are all here!"

(Acts 16:28). Luke, for the sake of brevity in giving us this account, leaves us wondering about some of the details. How could Paul see the jailer when the jailer could not see him and the other prisoners? How did Paul know that none of the prisoners had escaped? But even if we don't have all the answers, we do know what happened.

The Jailer Converted (29-34)

Unwilling to believe his ears, the jailer called for the servants to bring a light, and he rushed into the jail. When he saw that the prisoners were all still there, he fell trembling before Paul and Silas. Various emotions must have surged through his heart. He must have felt relief that the prisoners were still there, gratitude for the part that the two missionaries had played in keeping the prisoners there, and concern for his own future.

His first question was, "What must I do to be saved?" (Acts 16:30). Commentators have struggled to understand the content of his question. It does not seem likely that he was concerned about being saved from punishment for allowing the prisoners to escape. He had been reassured by Paul that all the prisoners were still there. Nor, given his background, would he have asked it in the same sense as did those on Pentecost who had just heard Peter's sermon implicating them in the crucifixion of Jesus. His pagan background undoubtedly colored his understanding of what salvation involved. Yet some things he surely understood.

He may have heard the slave girl, who announced that Paul came to show the way of salvation. Some of this also may have come out in the scene before the magistrates. He certainly must have been impressed by the behavior of Paul and Silas as they responded to their mistreatment differently from other prisoners. He also knew that Paul and Silas were different because of the way they had conducted themselves during and after the earthquake. He may not have been absolutely sure of what Paul and Silas had to offer, but whatever it was, he knew that he wanted it.

Paul had a better understanding of what the jailer had in mind than does any modern commentator. Thus, from the answer that Paul gave, we gain a clearer understanding of what the man asked. "Believe in the Lord Jesus, and you will be saved—you and your household," came Paul's response (Acts 16:31). There was certainly no reason to exclude the jailer's family and servants from these blessings. They were offered salvation on the same terms—that they believe, repent, and be baptized. And then he spoke the word of the Lord to him and his household. Paul's words led the jailer to do two things. First of all, he tended to the wounds of Paul and Silas. This marked a change in his behavior, for a few hours earlier, when the two men had been brought to the jail, he had made no attempt to care for them. The next thing that happened was that he and his family were baptized. Chrysostom, a great preacher of the fourth century, observed that the jailer "washed and was washed. He washed them from their stripes, and he himself was washed from his sins." The baptismal service was then followed by a joyous meal.

Paul and Silas Released (35-40)

The new day brought a new situation for the two missionaries. The magistrates, concluding that Paul and Silas had suffered enough, sent word to the jailer to release them and send them on their way out of town. They must have reasoned that the sooner the two got out of town the sooner things would return to normal.

But Paul was not willing to let them off that easily. He insisted that the magistrates personally come and release them. Paul was not seeking to humiliate the officials out of a desire for personal revenge. Instead, he was defending a legal right. As a Roman citizen, he had been illegally beaten and then thrown into jail without a trial. If this illegal treatment passed unchallenged, it meant that Paul might very well encounter trouble from the same source should he ever return to Philippi. Further, his stand would provide some protection against persecution of other Christians who later might be in similar situations.

When this was reported back to the magistrates, they lost no time in getting down to the prison. If Paul's claim that he was a Roman citizen was true, they could be in for considerable trouble from the Roman government. They publicly escorted the two men from the prison. After they had granted Paul and Silas their release, they asked the two to leave town to avoid further disturbances. They probably had no legal basis for this request, but Paul seemed quite willing to move on. He may have felt that the church there was already strong enough that he could leave it, especially since it seems that Luke remained there. After a final meeting with the Christians at the home of Lydia, they headed westward along the Egnatian Way.

SECOND MISSIONARY JOURNEY

CHAPTER SEVENTEEN

Through Macedonia and Into Greece
Acts 17

The Missionaries in Thessalonica (17:1-9)

Paul and Silas had been able, in a short time, to establish a church in Philippi. Though they might have remained there longer, they decided the time had come for them to move on. Their continued presence there would probably have incited more controversy, which would not have benefited the church. Luke and possibly Timothy were left behind to minister to the young church.

Preaching in the Synagogue (1-4)

Paul and Silas followed the Egnatian Way westward. Scholars disagree about whether Timothy accompanied them to Thessalonica or whether he rejoined them in Berea (Acts 17:14). They came first to Amphipolis, the capital of the first Roman district of Macedonia, located about thirty miles from Philippi. Apparently, there was no Jewish synagogue in the city, for the missionaries did not stop to evangelize there. Instead, they passed on through, coming next to Apollonia, about twenty-seven miles westward. But they did not stop there either. Thessalonica was their destination because there was a synagogue there.

Thessalonica, founded in 316 B.C. by a general of Philip of Macedon, soon became one of the most important cities of the area. It was located on the Egnatian Way and on the Thermaic Gulf, giving it a good outlet to the Aegean Sea. The Romans had made it a free city and granted it tax concession, all of which contributed to its prosperity. Today, the city is sometimes called Salonika and, after Athens, is the largest city in modern Greece.

For three sabbaths, Paul visited the synagogue and was permitted to teach, reasoning with them from the Scriptures. Paul's method was to show that the Old Testament Scriptures taught that the Messiah would have to suffer and die. The line of prophecies that predicted a suffering-servant Messiah had not been understood by the Jews. When Jesus attempted to share this idea with the apostles, even they had some problems with it (Matthew 16:21-23). After convincing at least some of his hearers that the Old Testament prophesied this kind of a Messiah, he went on to show that Jesus, and Jesus alone, satisfied these requirements. Some of the Jews were convinced by this line of reasoning, but many more of the "God-fearing Greeks," either proselytes or Gentile attenders of the synagogue, and several "prominent women" were persuaded by Paul (Acts 17:4). These may either have been women of some wealth or wives of some of the city's leading citizens. We are told that they joined Paul and Silas, which may indicate that the missionaries were forced to withdraw from the synagogue and meet in another location.

Opposition by the Jews (5-9)

As had happened so often in the past, the most serious opposition came to Paul from the Jews. They were jealous because Paul had drawn away so many from the synagogue. Unable to answer his arguments, they turned to violence to save their cause. Unfortunately, the resorting to such violence is not unknown in disputes today. The Jews had no intention of becoming involved directly in the violence. They might suffer some injuries themselves if they did. Instead, they went to the marketplace and hired some "bad characters" (Acts 17:5—"lewd fellows of the baser sort," the King James Version puts it) to do their dirty work. These ruffians had no qualms about stirring up a riot if the price was right. Within a short time, they had the city in an uproar.

Then they went searching for Paul and Silas. They went straight to the house of Jason, who had become a believer. But Paul and Silas were not there. Either they were working in some other part of the city or, hearing about the mob, had wisely sought refuge somewhere else. Angered because they did not find the two missionaries, the mob turned on Jason. Other than this mention of Jason, we know little else about him. Although the name is Greek, it was a name that Jews had come to use. One of the high priests during the Syrian period had borne this name, serving from 174-171 B.C. It is likely that he was one of the members of the synagogue who had become a Christian.

Jason and some other Christians in his house were seized and dragged before the city officials. Luke calls these men *politarchs,* a term not found in other Grecian writings. This has led some critics to assert that Luke was in error. However, archaeologists have now found inscriptions that contain this title in several Macedonian towns. Apparently, it was a title used only in Macedonia. Thus Luke's historical accuracy is again vindicated.

It was not enough for the accusers to bring Jason and his friends before the town officials. They had to bring charges against them that they had violated some law. To charge that they brought a new religion would hardly serve as a serious accusation. Grecian society was tolerant enough by this time that such a charge would not have been taken seriously.

The charge they hit upon was sedition. First of all, they charged Jason with harboring men who had "caused trouble all over the world" (Acts 17:6, 7). The King James Version translates the Greek more literally: "These that have turned the world upside down. . . ." Paul and Silas, although not in the court, were accused of defying Caesar's decree by claiming that Jesus was king (Acts 16:7). Because the title "king" had a bad connotation in Roman history, the emperors never used this title of themselves. But out in the provinces, the people who were not Romans undoubtedly did use it in reference to the emperors.

The charges made by these Jews in Thessalonica against Paul and Silas were similar to the charges that the Sanhedrin had brought against Jesus. In order to find a charge that would stand before Pilate, they had to accuse Jesus of making himself a king. Pilate knew very well that the charge was false, but caved in under pressure from the Jewish leaders. The Jewish agitators in Thessalonica may have supposed that the city officials would also succumb to such pressure. The mob, when they heard these charges, responded angrily, just as the Jews had hoped they would, adding to the pressure on the officials. But the officials were not so readily pressured as were the officials in Philippi. Instead of bringing any kind of judgment against Jason or the two missionaries, they only required Jason to post a bond that required Paul and Silas to leave town or at least to cease teaching.

Paul and Silas in Berea (17:10-15)

We don't know where Paul and Silas were while all this was going on. They may have been in another part of the city or even in hiding in the home of one of the Christians. If they were in hiding, it was not an act of cowardice on their part. Nothing

179

would have been gained had they themselves stood before the officials. Indeed, their presence might have stirred the crowd to an uncontrollable frenzy.

The Noble Bereans (10-12)

As soon as night came, the brothers sent Paul and Silas to Berea. During their short stay in Thessalonica, the missionaries had established a church that could stand on its own without their guidance. Had they remained, they almost certainly would have been involved in further strife. Berea may have been selected as their destination because the Christians in Thessalonica had friends or relatives there. On the other hand, Paul may have chosen it because it was close enough that he could return to Thessalonica when the situation calmed down.

Berea (the modern Verria) was located on the Egnatian Way about forty-five miles south and west of Thessalonica. Not only was it readily accessible to a traveler from Thessalonica, it also had a synagogue. As soon as he arrived in town, Paul made his way to the synagogue. His reception there was quite different from the reception he had received in Thessalonica and in some of the cities in Galatia. We are told that "the Bereans were of more noble character than the Thessalonians" (Acts 17:11). Instead of surrendering to their prejudices, they eagerly listened to what Paul had to say and then turned to the Scriptures to see whether or not it was true. For this reason, many Sunday-school classes call themselves "Bereans." We wish that the many Sunday-school classes that bear the name Berean would be as diligent in their study of the Scriptures as were these ancient Bereans. The open-mindedness of the Jews in Berea led many of them to become believers. One of these converts was named Sopater (Acts 20:4). They were joined by many prominent Greek women and Greek men, who had probably been proselytes to the Jewish faith. Even the Jews who did not become believers created no controversy.

Jewish Opposition Again (13-15)

Even though the Berean Jews did not cause any problems, word soon got back to Thessalonica about the work of Paul and Silas. Not content to stir up trouble in Thessalonica, they hurried to Berea and tried the same tactics again. They were talented rabble-rousers, for their tactics worked again. Or at least, they worked to the extent that once again Paul was forced to leave town to keep the peace. Some of the brothers accompanied Paul to the coast where they caught a ship to Athens. But Paul did not abandon the believers in Berea. Silas and Timothy, who apparently had rejoined them, remained behind to teach and preach. The brothers brought Paul to Athens, where they left him.

Paul in Athens (17:16-34)

Paul had not intended to remain in Athens alone for any length of time. The men who had brought him to Athens were told to send Silas and Timothy as soon as possible. We don't know how much time lapsed before they were able to join him.

Paul in the Marketplace (16-18)

When Paul arrived in Athens, he did not come as a tourist to take in the sights of the intellectual capital of the ancient world. The Parthenon and the other magnificent temples that covered the Acropolis and lined the streets were then in their full splendor, unravaged by time. Viewing these brought him not joy but pain, for in them he saw not the architectural genius of the Greeks but their religious depravity. Paul was certainly no stranger to idolatry. In every city he visited, he must have seen pagan temples and pagan worship. But the situation in Athens seems especially to have plagued him. Perhaps because of Athens' reputation as a great intellectual center, Paul had hoped that its citizens would have avoided the grosser aspects of paganism. Paul had to learn, as we do today, that intellectual brilliance and religious and moral purity do not automatically travel hand in hand.

After all he had been through during the past several weeks, few people would have faulted Paul if he had relaxed and taken a few days' vacation in Athens. But Paul's spirit was too tormented to enjoy the beautiful city about him. Others might see beautiful statues and breathtaking temples, but Paul saw men lost in darkness and damned. Such a situation would not allow Paul to rest.

Since there was a synagogue in Athens, Paul went there and reasoned with the Jews and with the God-fearing Greeks, as he had done in so many places in the past. But he did not confine his witnessing to the synagogue. He was soon in the marketplace speaking to anyone who would listen. Before long, he attracted the attention of the Epicurean and Stoic philosophers. These philosophers enjoyed nothing better than to gather in the marketplace and engage in learned discussions. They especially enjoyed

181

discussing the new and the novel (Acts 17:21), and the message Paul brought certainly must have struck them as novel.

Epicurus, who founded the group that bore his name, had lived in the late fourth and early third century B.C. He taught that the gods, if they existed at all, were not involved in the activities of man. His system is thoroughly materialistic, holding that man at his death returned to the atoms of which he was composed. He also taught that man's chief goal in life was to seek pleasure and avoid pain. Epicurus himself did not eagerly advocate seeking sexual or other physical pleasures. Instead, he urged his disciples to search for a life of tranquility. Unfortunately, with some of his later disciples, his high principles degenerated into a hedonistic approach to life that had as its motto "Eat, drink, and be merry, for tomorrow we die." We scarcely need to be reminded that such a philosophy has numerous modern counterparts.

The Stoics took their name from the Greek word for portico, where their founder, Zeno, often taught. Zeno was a contemporary of Epicurus, and the two schools of philosophy, though different in many ways, developed side by side. Zeno taught that man ought to try to live logically and in harmony with nature. Stoics strongly emphasized the importance of doing one's duty. This commitment to reason and duty often led men to live lives of austerity and high ethical standards.

Disciples of these two schools of philosophy, though differing greatly in their daily lives, at least agreed on one thing: the message Paul brought was different. Some accused him of being a "babbler" (Acts 17:18). The word literally means a "seed picker" and was applied to birds that hopped about picking up tidbits from the street and gutter. Later, it was applied to persons who developed their philosophy by taking a bit from one school and a bit from another and combining them and pretending it was something new. To some of these Athenians, Paul was just another itinerant philosopher passing through town. Others, who apparently had listened more closely, accused him of advocating foreign gods because he spoke about Jesus and the resurrection.

Paul's words had piqued the interest of the Athenians enough that they wanted to hear more. Hence, they brought him before a session of the Areopagus. This group, which had taken its name from the Areopagus (Mars' Hill in the King James Version) where it had formerly met, had at one time enjoyed great influence in Athens. But as Athens declined politically, the power of the

Areopagus had wained. In Paul's day, it had jurisdiction over murder cases and public morals and perhaps education. It must be pointed out that Paul was not on trial before this tribunal. These men had little else to do to occupy their time; so they requested that Paul come before them to present his teaching. This was not a hostile group as he had faced so many times in the past, but one that was, if not friendly, at least open to new ideas.

Paul's Sermon Before the Areopagus (22-32)

Most men would have been overwhelmed at the invitation to speak before such a learned and august body, but Paul welcomed the opportunity with enthusiasm. The King James Version leads us to believe that Paul presented his sermon on the top of Mars' hill, a rough, rocky little prominence rising to the west of and below the Acropolis. However, this does not seem a very likely place for the meeting. The Areopagus ordinarily met in the Royal Portico in the city marketplace, and it is reasonable to suppose that this is where Paul presented his message.

Paul's sermon before these learned Athenians was a masterpiece. He gauged his audience well and spoke to their needs. Because he knew that the doctrine he was bringing would sound strange and new, he began with something that would be familiar to the Athenians. Unlike the Jewish audiences that he had spoken to so often in the past, he knew that he could not appeal to the Old Testament as an authority. Instead, he quoted from one of the Grecian poets. Paul was bold in his presentation, and yet he was not offensive. He knew that the Athenians were accustomed to a frank and open sharing of different ideas without becoming offended or succumbing to anger. His approach was rational because his audience was expert at logical discussion. He argued that the true God was a universal God, not just a God of a select group. This point of view the Athenians, unlike the Jews, would appreciate. Paul concluded his message by setting forth the doctrine of divine judgment. Any message to lost sinners that does not include this reminder is incomplete. True, the gospel is good news, but the full meaning of that good news is lost unless it is painted against the somber background of the Judgment.

Paul opened his sermon by noting that the people of Athens were quite religious. This may not have been a compliment; the word can mean superstitious, and the King James Version so translates it (Acts 17:22). In the ancient world, Athens did have a reputation of being a religious city, a reputation enhanced by its many temples and shrines; so Paul may have been doing nothing more than recognizing this in his introduction.

As Paul had walked around the city, he had noticed among the many idols an altar to an unknown god. Apparently the Athenians, lest they unwittingly offend one of the gods by ignoring him, had built a shrine to his honor. It is the kind of precaution we might expect a deeply religious but pagan people to take. Paul used this reference as a means of catching the attention of his audience and leading them into the sermon that he wanted them to hear. He had come to tell them about the god that they had been worshiping in ignorance. Paul was not implying that in their ignorance they were actually worshiping the one true God. Rather, he was using their ignorant piety as a means of introducing them to the one true God. Paul did what every preacher should do: begin with his hearers where they are and attempt to lead them to where they ought to be.

Paul's first point was that the true God was the creator of the world and everything in it. Such a beginning would have been unnecessary for a Jewish audience because the Old Testament taught this great truth. But the Greeks, with their hazy and often contradictory myths about creation, certainly needed to hear it. Since God had created the world, it was logical to understand that He was Lord, the ruler of everything. While the Greeks held that Zeus was the head of their pantheon, Zeus fell far short of being the absolute ruler that Paul set forth. The lesser gods and demigods were in almost constant revolt against Zeus and his authority, hardly the picture of an absolute ruler.

Further, the true God, since He had created the universe, could not be confined to man-made temples. This was a lesson that even the Jews had not completely learned. They believed that, in some sense, Jehovah could be confined to the temple in Jerusalem. Stephen had angered his Jewish hearers when he had said that "the Most High does not live in houses made by men" (Acts 7:48). God did not live in physical temples, nor, for that matter, did He need the things that man could give Him, such as animal sacrifices. Some in Paul's audience might very readily have agreed with this point. While most Athenians still went through the ceremonies involved in the worship of their various gods, many did this more as a civic duty than as an act of worship. Paul further strengthened his argument by pointing out that God has given even life and breath to man. Since He is the very source of life, He could hardly be dependent upon men's lives for His support.

Paul next affirmed the unity of the human race. The Greeks felt themselves innately superior to all other peoples, referring to them as barbarians as an indication of their contempt for them. The Athenians, in turn, felt themselves superior to all other Greeks. In a similar fashion, the Jews had divided all of mankind into two classes: themselves, whom God had specially called, and everyone else, whom they termed Gentiles, an expression of condescension. We moderns do not have a monopoly on racial prejudice. It is as old as the human race!

Grecian mythology provided several versions of the origin of man. But Paul swept all these aside: "From one man he made every nation of men" (Acts 17:26). All men sprang from Adam. They may differ in language, in skin complexion, and in customs; yet they all have one Father, and thus they must all be brothers. We have been a long time learning this truth, and even yet it is far from being universally accepted.

Commentators differ about the exact meaning of the latter part of Acts 17:26. Some argue that it deals with the separation of the races, that God has rigidly fixed the boundaries between them. If it was God's original intent to keep the various races rigidly segregated, then intermarriages across the centuries have long since thwarted this goal. Others take it in a geographical sense. God assigned each race or nation its own place on the face of the earth. But mass migrations, either willing or forced, long ago obliterated these lines. It is true that God did, at least for a period in history, assign the Israelites to the promised land. But their disobedience caused Him to withdraw this promise. Still others understand this in a more general sense that God has intervened in the history of the nations to direct their destinies. This latter view seems the least fraught with difficulties, and it certainly accords with other Scriptures that teach that God has a continuing interest in the ongoing historical process.

God's concern with the affairs of mankind was not the result of some mere whimsy. It stemmed, instead, from His purpose for man. It was God's will that all men diligently seek after Him. The entrance of sin into the world shattered the close relations that man shared with God at the creation. God immediately put into effect His plan to bridge the gulf that sin had opened. He also put in the heart of every man a deep longing for God that would not be satisfied with anything less than a return to the sweet communion that God and man had once known.

Through the centuries, man has sought God. He sought the one true God through many gods—polytheism. He has sought Him by making God the sum total of everything—pantheism. In his arrogant sophistication, he has denied that God even exists—atheism, or that He can ever be known—agnosticism. When his own misguided efforts to find God have failed, he has often given his unbridled passions full reign in his life—hedonism. When all of these efforts have failed, and they always do, man has descended into the depths of degradation and despair. When a person sinks to these depths, even the yearning for God is quenched. Or as Paul wrote, "You were dead in your transgressions and sins." Man was "separate from Christ, excluded from citizenship in Israel and foreigners to the covenants of the promise, without hope and without God in the world" (Ephesians 2:1,12).

Man's efforts to find God have again and again failed, not because God has been unavailable, but because man has insisted on seeking God in his own selfish ways. Man should have been able to see the hand of God in the starry heavens and the towering mountains. In writing to the Romans, Paul asserted that nature alone provided evidence enough that man had no excuse for being ignorant of God (Romans 1:18-20). Even some Grecian poets had recognized man's unique relationship with God. Paul apparently paraphrased one of them in stating that in God "we live and move and have our being." Another poet asserted, "We are his offspring" (Acts 17:28). The point of this argument is that on every hand, God is close to man and so intricately involved in his nature that the human race has no excuse for not knowing God.

Paul's next argument logically followed from this. If man is a child of God, is it not absurd to suppose that God could be worshiped through idols of stone and wood made of human hands? Centuries before, Isaiah had pointed out the utter folly of worshiping idols (Isaiah 44:9-17). If idolatry is so irrational, as Paul clearly pointed out, why has it been so widespread? Almost every culture in almost every age has developed some form of idolatry. Perhaps one reason that idolatry has been so universally practiced stems from the fact that one dimension of man is physical. He is, after all, a physical being living in a physical world. Though he is also a spiritual being, he becomes so preoccupied with the physical that he is soon blinded in his spiritual dimension. All that he is able to see or understand is the physical, and so when he turns to worship, he can worship only that which he can see with his physical eyes. Jesus reminded the woman at the well that "God is spirit, and his worshipers must worship in spirit and in truth" (John 4:23, 24). Yet many are so bogged down in the physical that they never reach this level of worship.

We may protest that we today are not guilty of idolatry. And, of course, if we think of idolatry only in terms of images of stone, wood, or metal, our protests may be valid. But if we are honest, we have to acknowledge that we do practice idolatry, but on a more sophisticated level. An idol is anything that we allow to occupy the place that rightly belongs to God and Jesus Christ. In our more candid moments, we may admit that we have allowed many things to come between us and our Lord. It may be fame, money, pride, or even a church building—anything that keeps us from serving our Lord as faithfully as we should.

Since Jehovah God is our Creator and our Lord, He has a right to make certain demands of us. This is Paul's next point. In the past, God in His wonderful grace had not called men to a strict accounting. He had been willing to make allowances for their ignorance. This parallels Paul's statement to the pagans in Lystra: "In the past, he let all nations go their own way" (Acts 14:16). He expressed a similar view in Romans 3:25: "In his forbearance he had left the sins committed beforehand unpunished."

But now, Paul insisted, God has commanded that all men everywhere repent, not just the Jews alone, but everyone. We are reminded of John the Baptist's call, "Repent, for the kingdom of heaven is near" (Matthew 3:2). This ringing cry carried all over Judea, and many responded to it. But now, Paul asserted, here is an even more demanding reason to repent—the Day of Judgment is at hand. The concept of the Day of the Lord or a Day of Judgment was familiar to the Jews, for the Old Testament had sounded this note on many occasions. The Greeks, on the other hand, were not familiar with the concept, in part, at least, because they had managed to keep their morality and their religion separated. This judgment would come by the man God had appointed, even Jesus Christ.

No doubt, Paul's mention of a Day of Judgment brought cynical sneers from his sophisticated audience. Luke tells us that they sneered at the mention of the resurrection. The resurrection is crucial to Paul's argument, because the proof of the testimony about the judgment is guaranteed by the resurrection. Without the resurrection, little else matters. Without the Easter message, the Day of Judgment is anything but good news.

Some, like their sophisticated modern counterparts, were put off by the message of the resurrection and turned away to pursue other novel ideas. However, Paul's words about the Judgment and the resurrection struck a responsive note in the hearts of others, and they desired to hear more.

Results of Paul's Sermon (33, 34)

Paul's message had been designed to lead cultured pagans to an understanding of God and of the coming judgment, and to introduce them to Jesus Christ. Unlike Peter's sermon on Pentecost, its immediate aim had not been to make converts. This would require additional teaching. Luke gives us no information about this additional teaching. It may have occurred over a period of several days or even several weeks. We occasionally hear people say that Paul failed at Athens. Obviously this was not the case. One of the members of the Areopagus, Dionysius, became a believer, as did a woman named Damaris, and several others. A few of the men became "followers of Paul" (Acts 17:34—literally, the word for *became followers* means "became bound"). One writer says they were "glued" to Paul.

During the New Testament period, we hear nothing further from the Christians in Athens, and, so far as we know, Paul never again returned to the city. A tradition states that Dionysius was the first bishop of the church in Athens, but it is a late tradition. Many have wondered why the gospel was not more widely received in Athens. There are no ready answers, but across the centuries, the intellectual communities have not been the most fertile ground for the gospel. Intellectual pride and a sense of self-sufficiency insulate these people from a sense of need that a flagrant sinner might experience. Paul recognized this when he wrote in 1 Corinthians 1:20, 21; "Where is the wise man? Where is the scholar? Where is the philosopher of this age? Has not God made foolish the wisdom of the world? For since in the widsom of God the world through its widsom did not know him, God was pleased through the foolishness of what was preached to save those who believe." But just because it is difficult to win the sophisticated intellectuals, it does not mean that we should not try to reach them with the gospel.

CHAPTER EIGHTEEN
Completing the Second Missionary Journey
Acts 18

Paul in Corinth (18:1-17)

Luke does not tell us how long Paul remained in Athens, but it may very well have been a month or more. When the converts in Athens were strong enough to stand on their own, Paul made plans to leave. He had intended to wait for Silas and Timothy in Athens, but for some reason they were delayed, and Paul moved on to Corinth without them, leaving word for his companions to join him there.

Corinth was located on the isthmus that joined the Peloponnesus with the rest of Greece. It thus sat astride the main highway that ran north and south through Greece. It was also the connecting route between the Ionian and the Aegean Seas. To avoid the long voyage around the southern tip of the Peloponnesus, which could be quite hazardous, especially in the winter, small ships were actually pulled out of the water and transported across the narrow isthmus and put back into the water on the other side. Attempts were made to construct a canal across the isthmus in ancient times, but it was only in the last century that such a project was completed. Now ships can sail from the Corinthian Gulf to the Saronic Gulf.

Corinth had been an important city throughout much of the history of Greece. The city had been destroyed by the Romans in 146 B.C., and many of its buildings had been dismantled and shipped to Rome. But a hundred years later, Julius Caesar refounded the city. As a result of its strategic location, the city soon prospered and attracted people from all over the Empire. Its cosmopolitan population, along with its wealth, gained it a reputation for corruption and worldliness unrivaled in the ancient world. Indeed, the very name *Corinthian* came to be applied to a person of voluptuous tastes and low morals. Towering above the city was Acrocorinth, where stood the temple of Aphrodite, the goddess of love. It is said that a thousand priestesses, sacred prostitutes, plied their trade there.

It was to such a city that Paul chose to go. The need for the gospel was certainly great, but the obstacles seemed overwhelming. Paul's letters to the church at Corinth reflect the struggle that the church had to make against the corruption of the society around it. In 1 Corinthians 6:9-11 Paul wrote: "Do not be deceived: Neither the sexually immoral nor idolaters nor adulterers nor male prostitutes nor homosexual offenders nor thieves nor the greedy nor drunkards nor slanderers nor swindlers will inherit the kingdom of God. And that is what some of you were."

Paul Makes Friends in Corinth (1-3)

When Paul left Athens, he was not under any threat of persecution or of political pressure, unlike his recent experiences in Macedonia. Corinth lay some fifty miles to the south and west of Athens, a trip of two or three days. In spite of its reputation for licentiousness, Corinth offered some advantages as a center for evangelism. It had a large and varied population, and as a major trade center, it offered contact with many people who were rootless and looking for the security and hope that Christianity could offer.

It did not take Paul long to make friends in this busy environment. In order to earn his living while he awaited his fellow missionaries to join him, Paul turned to his trade of tentmaking. It was a common practice for Jewish young men who turned to scholarly pursuits also to learn to work with their hands at a trade. This practice certainly stood Paul in good stead on more than one occasion, enabling him to carry on his preaching and teaching ministry without being a burden to the people. (See Acts 20:34; 1 Thessalonians 2:9; 2 Thessalonians 3:8.) While in the practice of his trade, he met two Jews, Aquila and his wife, Priscilla, who were also tentmakers. They had only recently arrived in Corinth, having been forced to leave Rome by a decree of Emperor Caludius that expelled Jews. This decree must have been issued in A.D. 49 or 50. The Roman historian Suetonius reports rioting in Rome at the "instigation of one Chrestos." Some scholars understand this to refer to the followers of Christ, whose appearance in Rome caused violence among the Jews, just as it had in the provinces. Some even go so far as to claim that Aquila and Priscilla were already Christians when Paul first met them. Of course, we have no definite proof of this. It is interesting to note that although they later became faithful co-laborers with Paul, no mention is made of their conversion, lending some support to the speculation. This Jewish couple provided Paul a place to stay and companionship until Silas and Timothy arrived.

Paul Meets Opposition in Corinth (4-17)

When the Sabbath came, Paul was in the synagogue, preaching and teaching as usual. After a few weeks, Silas and Timothy arrived from Macedonia. Upon their arrival, Paul was able to give his time entirely to preaching Christ to the Jews in Corinth. The evidence points to the fact that Paul's two companions brought a gift of money from the churches, which freed him from the necessity of working at tentmaking. Silas and Timothy also brought good news from Thessalonica, where the brethren were faced with threats and persecution. In the face of these pressures, they had been steadfast (1 Thessalonians 3:6). This encouraging word led to Paul's writing his first letter to the church at Thessalonica.

This encouraging news came at a most needed time, for Paul was soon embroiled in a bitter controversy with the Jews in the synagogue. The New International Version says they "became abusive" (Acts 18:6), but the Greek states that "they blasphemed." This was more than just an attack against Paul, which in its most abusive form would hardly be blasphemy. Paul had preached to the Jews that Jesus was the Christ. Apparently, the Jews had turned their attacks against our Lord, which would be blasphemy.

When it became evident to Paul that the Jews would no longer listen, he shook out his clothes as a dramatic gesture against them. This reminds us of a similar incident at Pisidian Antioch on the first missionary journey when Paul and Barnabas shook the dust from their feet in protest against the Jews' rejection of the gospel. Paul made it clear that he had fulfilled his obligation to them, and that their blood would be on their own heads. Paul understood that his ministry was first to the Jew, but when that door was closed, then he was obligated to go to the Gentile. That time had come in Corinth (Acts 18:6).

When Paul left the synagogue, he did not have far to go. He found a place to continue his ministry right next door in the home of Titus Justus. His name indicates that he was a Roman, perhaps a member of one of the Roman families that Julius Caesar had settled in Corinth. He is also described as a worshiper of God, perhaps indicating that he had worshiped in the synagogue with the Jews.

When Paul began teaching there, the Jews must have found the close proximity of this house to their synagogue especially galling. Anyone attending the synagogue would have to be aware of Paul's work and its growing success. One can't avoid thinking of somewhat similar situations that arise when churches split in our own times.

Not only did Paul carry on his ministry within earshot of the synagogue, his preaching also led the ruler of the synagogue, Crispus, along with his family, to become believers. But the message soon reached out beyond the Jewish community, and the Gentiles began to respond in growing numbers.

The growth of the congregation and the potential for hostility from the synagogue next door may have led Paul to believe that the time had come for him to move on. But if Paul had any inclinations in this direction, these were soon removed. One night, the Lord appeared to him and reassured him. He was to continue to speak out boldly. Christ had many people in the city, and He would protect Paul as he attempted to reach them with the gospel. On at least two other occasions Paul had similar reassuring visions: once in Jerusalem (Acts 23:11) and again on the voyage to Rome (Acts 27:23, 24). With this kind of reassurance from the Lord, Paul was able to continue his ministry in Corinth, but not entirely free from conflict. There is a lesson in this for us. While our Lord has promised to be with us when we are busy working for Him, He has not promised to spare us from all conflict or pain.

With the church located right on their own doorstep, the synagogue leaders could not avoid the fact that Christians were becoming more numerous. When the Jews could stand it no longer, they began their attack on Paul. This time, they did not resort to physical violence, nor did they stir up ruffians to do their dirty work. Instead, they followed the legal route and brought him to Gallio, the proconsul of Achaia. The place of judgment was a raised platform called the "bema." In the ruins of ancient Corinth, one today can see the bema where we can be almost certain the apostle Paul stood at this trial. If they could get a legal pronouncement against Paul and the Christians by Gallio, then Christianity would be hampered in all of Achaia, which at that time encompassed the whole southern part of the Grecian peninsula.

Gallio was a brother of the famous Roman philosopher, Seneca. He had gained a reputation of being personable and competent. An inscription dates his arrival in Corinth in July, A.D. 51. This information allows us to date Paul's stay in Corinth with some precision, although we cannot say exactly when during his year-and-a-half stay he appeared before the proconsul.

The charge that they brought against Paul was that he was leading people to worship God in ways contrary to the law. Judaism had been recognized as a legal religion by the Romans. Christianity, in the early days, was probably considered by the Romans to be but a sect of the Jews. If the Jews could convince Gallio that Christianity was a different religion, then it would no longer enjoy its legal status. We can be sure that the Jews made their case eloquently. Then it was Paul's turn to plead his defense, but Gallio intervened even before Paul had a chance to speak. Gallio certainly was not versed in the Old Testament, and he must have found the Jewish arguments confusing. But out of all the discussion, one thing seemed clear to him. Paul and the Christians had not violated any Roman laws. Their teachings might conflict with the teachings of the Old Testament as the Jews understood them, but this was of no concern to a Roman magistrate. The Jews would have to settle such disputes among themselves. It would appear that the Jews did not accept very graciously his dismissal of the charges against Paul and continued to try to argue their case. Disgusted with their behavior, Gallio had them ejected from before the judgment seat.

The ejection of the Jews from the court led to further violence. Some in the crowd, perhaps in an outburst of anti-Jewish sentiment, fell upon Sosthenes, the synagogue ruler who had succeeded Crispus, and beat him up. Luke tells us that Gallio showed no concern about what happened in his court. Perhaps he was disgusted by the public agitation the Jews had caused and was willing to let their spokesman suffer for his impertinence. He may also have felt that allowing the Gentile population to vent some of its anti-Jewish feelings would be good politics. Some believe that Sosthenes, the target of this violence, later became a Christian. A Sosthenes is mentioned as being with Paul when he wrote his first epistle to the church in Corinth (1 Corinthians 1:1).

Paul's Return to Antioch (15:18-23)

In a few short verses, Luke tells of Paul's return to Antioch. Since this trip involved no outstanding incidents, Luke chose not to burden us with any details about it.

Paul Sails for Syria (18-21)

In a vision, Paul had been assured by the Lord that no harm would befall him while he was in Corinth. The Lord's promise had been carried out in the trial before Gallio. Thus encouraged, Paul remained for "some time" in the city (Acts 18:18). Whether this period was a part of the year-and-a-half's stay mentioned in Acts 18:11 or in addition to it, we cannot say for certain. In any event, he stayed long enough that the Jews could not claim that they had run him out of town. With the church prospering and its critics silenced, at least temporarily, Paul concluded that it was time for him to return to the home base in Antioch.

He did not start on this trip alone, but took Priscilla and Aquila with him. They departed from Corinth by its eastern port, Cenchrea, built on the Saronic Gulf. At Cenchrea, Paul had his hair cut as the fulfillment of a vow. This vow may have been an expression of God's care for him while he was in Corinth. This may have been some form of a Nazirite vow that was completed when he left Corinth. Some commentators have been troubled by this act, looking upon it as an unwarranted concession to Judaism. But this seems to have been no more than an expression of thanksgiving expressed in a traditional Jewish fashion. Becoming a Christian did not mean then and does not mean now that one must abandon everything in his previous culture. God requires us to give up only those things that interfere with our obedience to Him.

The first stop on the voyage was Ephesus, the most important city in the Roman province of Asia. It was located a few miles inland on the Cayster River and on a major highway that ran eastward through Asia Minor. Thus the city's commercial importance was insured. It was also the center for the worship of the goddess Artemis, a matter that became quite important during Paul's later visit to the city.

Paul lost no time in visiting the synagogue in Ephesus. As was his usual practice, he used this visit as an opportunity to present Christ to the Jews. When he prepared to leave, they asked him to remain longer, but he insisted that he must continue his journey.

194

However, he did promise to visit them later "if it is God's will" (Acts 18:21). For Paul, this was not a polite expression he injected just to make conversation. He knew from an earlier experience when he had desired to come to Ephesus that such an action was not possible unless God did indeed will it. But even though he had to continue his journey, he did not leave the Jews in Ephesus without some guidance. Priscilla and Aquila remained with them and carried on an effective ministry until Paul was able to return some time later.

Paul's Stay in Antioch (22, 23)

Paul's destination was Antioch of Syria, but he landed instead at Caesarea. Perhaps the only ship that he could get from Ephesus was going to Caesarea, or unfavorable winds may have blown them off course. The harbor at Caesarea had been built by Herod the Great and had soon become Palestine's chief port.

While there, Paul "went up and greeted the church" (Acts 18:22). This may have been the church at Caesarea, but most commentators believe that it was the church at Jerusalem. This seems a reasonable assumption, since Paul's other missionary journeys ended with a visit to Jerusalem. In addition, the expression *went up* is commonly used of a trip to Jerusalem (e.g. Luke 1:42; John 2:13; 5:1; Galatians 1:17; 2:1).

After visiting Jerusalem, Paul then journeyed to Antioch. Many think that this trip was made over land rather than by sea. If so, it was a trip of nearly four hundred miles and probably took three weeks or more to complete. So far as we are told, Paul made this part of his journey alone. After spending some time—perhaps several weeks—at the home church, Paul became restless again. And so he set out to visit the churches in Galatia and Phrygia that he had started on his first journey and that he and Silas had visited on their second journey.

Paul used this opportunity to strengthen the disciples in the churches. Undoubtedly, they had grown during his absence, and the new members especially needed attention. But the Galatian churches had other problems. Paul's letter to the Galatians indicates that the Judaizers had been at work among the churches, trying to bring them back into bondage to the law. The tone of this letter indicates that Paul was determined to meet this problem head on; so we can understand why he wanted to spend some time with these churches.

195

Apollos, an Eloquent Preacher (18:24-28)

As a prelude to describing Paul's return to Ephesus, Luke introduced his readers to Apollos. He had arrived in Ephesus after Paul had left, and soon began an effective ministry there. Later on, he also carried out a ministry in Corinth.

Apollos Introduced (24-26)

Apollos (perhaps a shortened form of Apollonius) was a native of Alexandria, a product of the large Jewish community there. He is called a "learned man" (Acts 18:24—the King James Version says he was an "eloquent man"). In the ancient world, learning and eloquence were so closely linked together that both terms are appropriate. Apollos also had a thorough knowledge of the Scriptures, in this case the Old Testament. The Greek translation of the Old Testament that we call the Septuagint was made in Alexandria, and it is likely that Apollos was a student of this translation.

Apollos had become a Christian, apparently, before he came to Ephesus. It is likely that Christianity was carried to Alexandria soon after Pentecost by some from Egypt who heard Peter's sermon. There are some early traditions about the church in Egypt, and we know that by the end of the second century, Alexandria had become one of the strongest churches in the Roman Empire. Yet Apollos' instruction in the Lord had been incomplete. Though he taught accurately about the Lord, he knew only John's baptism. We have no explanation of how this may have happened. Yet a dozen men at Ephesus had a similar problem (Acts 19:1-7).

This raises an interesting question. The King James Version states that he was "fervent in the spirit" (Acts 18:25), which literally translated the Greek. The New International Version says only that "he spoke with great fervor." The problem is this. Does the mention that he was fervent in the spirit mean that he had received the Holy Spirit even though he had not experienced Christian baptism? If so, why was his case different from the dozen who had to be rebaptized before they could receive the Holy Spirit? The easiest way out of this problem is to hold that the mention of the spirit does not refer to the Holy Spirit but to the enthusiasm that Apollos had as he spoke.

Apollos' knowledge of Scripture, along with his eloquence, soon won him the opportunity to speak in the synagogue. There, Priscilla and Aquila heard him. Realizing that he was preaching a defective gospel, they took him aside and, according to the King

James Version, taught "him the way of God more perfectly" (Acts 18:26). Priscilla and Aquila wisely chose to do their teaching privately. It would have been humiliating to Apollos had they attempted to correct him in public. We could very well take a lesson from this couple and learn that tact is a Christian virtue. It is a mark of Apollos' humility that he, a learned scholar, was willing to take instruction from persons who made their living with their hands. Although Luke does not mention it, it seems reasonable to suppose that at the conclusion of his instruction, Apollos was baptized. At least, the baptism of the dozen mentioned in the next chapter would point to such a conclusion.

Apollos in Achaia (27, 28)

After some time, Apollos chose to move to Achaia, the southern part of Greece that included Corinth. Some manuscripts indicate that he was invited to come to Corinth by some Corinthians who had come to know him in Ephesus. While this may have been the case, the manuscript evidence is not very strong in support of this view. The Christians at Ephesus were willing for him to go to Achaia and even wrote a letter of introduction to the Christians there. This letter from the brothers in Ephesus indicates that Paul's brief visit and the work of Priscilla and Aquila had borne fruit, resulting in the planting of a church.

Apollos proved to be a great blessing to the church at Corinth. In some persons, an increase in knowledge leads to a decline in zeal, but not so with Apollos. With a better understanding of the faith, he was better prepared to refute the Jews in public discussion. The thrust of his argument was to show from the Scriptures that Jesus was the Messiah predicted in the Old Testament. Because these discussions were held in public, a wider audience would become aware of the differences between Judaism and Christianity. This would encourage the Christians and to make the faith they proclaimed more acceptable to the Gentiles.

Apollos was a major factor in the rapid growth of the Corinthian church, as is evidenced in Paul's words in 1 Corinthians (1 Corinthians 1:12; 3:4-7). It is true that Paul names one of the divisive parties in the church after Apollos, but this seems to have been only an illustration and not a suggestion that Apollos had created the division. In 1 Corinthians 16:12, Paul reports that he urged Apollos to return to Corinth, something he would not likely have done if Apollos had caused division in the church.

CHAPTER NINETEEN

Paul's Ministry in Ephesus

Acts 19

Paul Begins His Ministry in Ephesus (19:1-10)

The nineteenth chapter of Acts tells of Paul's ministry in Ephesus, a ministry that proved to be quite fruitful. And because it was so fruitful, it involved Paul in a great deal of controversy. Paul's earlier controversies had arisen with the Jews, but this time it was with the pagan worshipers of the goddess Artemis. Paul's disputes with the Jews had been theological in nature. In Ephesus, Paul's problems with the pagans arose, not over theology, but over money. The silversmiths in Ephesus were unhappy with Paul because his preaching caused men and women to turn from worshiping Artemis and quit buying the silver images that had proved a source of handsome profits.

Ephesus had a long history. It may have had its beginnings as early as the twelfth century B.C. About 560 B.C., it was conquered by Croesus, the famous king of Lydia. He dedicated the city to the goddess Artemis. Within a few years, the city fell to Cyrus the Great of Persia. In 334 B.C., Ephesus became a part of the empire of Alexander the Great. According to one tradition, the great temple to Artemis had burned the very night that Alexander had been born. After the city came under his control, he offered to rebuild the temple, an offer that the priests refused. They feared that if Alexander made such a gift, he would seek to control the temple. The priests tactfully suggested that their reason was that it was inappropriate for one god to build a temple for another god.

It took the Ephesians over two centuries to restore the temple. But their patience and persistence paid off, for when it was completed, it was soon recognized as one of the seven wonders of the ancient world. And for good reason. It measured 420 feet in length and 240 feet in width. The roof, supported by 117 columns, was 60 feet high. The temple contained an image of Artemis, who, as the goddess of fertility, was often depicted as having many breasts. Acts 19:35 informs us that the people believed the image "fell from heaven," which may indicate that a meteorite had been placed in the temple as an object of worship.

The famous temple was devastated in A.D. 262 by raiding Goths. It was rebuilt on a smaller scale, but it was destroyed again in the fourth century after Christianity gained the ascendancy in the Roman Empire. Later, some of the stones from the temple were used to build a church in Ephesus, the Church of Saint John, and the famous basilica, Sancta Sophia, in Constantinople. Traditions tell us that the apostle John spent some of his later years in Ephesus.

Paul Discovers Some Defective Disciples (1-7)

After Apollos had arrived in Corinth, Paul left Galatia and Phrygia and made his way to Ephesus through the interior. Some modern translations, for *interior* (Acts 19:1), have *upper country,* which indicates that Paul took the route that crossed the high tablelands of the interior rather than another route that followed the Lycus and Meander River valleys, passing through Colossae, Hierapolis, and Laodicea. From Antioch of Pisidia, this would have been a journey of more than 250 miles and would have taken two weeks or more.

Upon his arrival in Ephesus, Paul was almost immediately faced with an unusual situation. He met about a dozen disciples who had not received the Holy Spirit. Even worse, they had not even heard about the Holy Spirit. Upon questioning them further, Paul learned that they had received John's baptism, not Christian baptism. In discussing the matter with them, he pointed out that John's baptism was a baptism of repentance that looked forward to the coming of Jesus. These men were quite receptive to Paul's teaching and readily submitted to being baptized again, this time in the name of Jesus. After their baptism, Paul placed his hands upon them, and they received the Holy Spirit and began to speak in tongues, a phenomenon that had been experienced at Pentecost and in the household of Cornelius.

The problem surrounding these men was rather similar to that of Apollos when he first came to Ephesus (Acts 18:25, 26). In that case, it was Priscilla and Aquila who instructed him in the way of the Lord. In both cases, the problem was solved by additional instruction. How many of our present problems in the church might be solved if the knowledgeable could learn to provide instruction lovingly to those who need it—and if those who need it could learn to receive such instruction humbly. In both of these cases, the problem was solved without any further repercussions.

But these two cases have raised a number of provocative questions that attract the interest of scholars to this day. First of all, were these twelve men Christians? Luke calls them "disciples" (Acts 19:1), a term often but not exclusively used to identify Christians. We also wonder why Priscilla and Aquila did not instruct them as they had Apollos. Some feel that they had already left Ephesus and were in Rome or at least headed in that direction. If Priscilla and Aquila had already left, why did not the elders of the congregation handle the problem? It seems apparent that when Paul arrived, the congregation was still quite small in number and had not yet selected leaders.

Commentators have raised other questions. How could they have listened to the preaching of John and not known of the Holy Spirit, for John mentioned the coming of the Spirit? Or had they been baptized by Apollos before he had been fully instructed? Yet another question has been raised: if those receiving John's baptism needed to be rebaptized, what about the twelve apostles? Yet we read nothing about their being rebaptized. We could ask other questions too, but most of them, like those above, would have to remain unanswered. In such matters, it is better to leave some questions unanswered than to resort to speculation. None of us should presume to be wise beyond that which is written.

Paul Speaks in the Synagogue (8-10)

After this incident, Paul went to the synagogue. When he first arrived in Ephesus on his earlier visit, he had gone into the synagogue. At that time, the Jews had urged him to remain longer and continue his teaching. When he had left, he had promised to return. Now he was back, not as a stranger, but to fulfill his promise. For three months, he continued to teach about the "kingdom of God" (Acts 19:8). Then history began to repeat itself. Some accepted the truth, but many hardened their hearts and began to speak out strongly against the Way (the term sometimes applied to Christianity). This is an excellent illustration of how people respond differently to the message of salvation. The difference is not in the message, but in the people who receive it. The same sun rays that melt the wax will harden the clay.

When the opposition in the synagogue became so strong that Paul could no longer carry on a fruitful ministry, he left. At least the Jews in Ephesus allowed him to continue his teaching in the synagogue longer than they did in other places. Further, they did not resort to violence, either legal or physical, when he left. But Paul's ministry in Ephesus was not ending; it was just beginning. Taking the believers with him, he held daily discussions in the lecture hall of Tyrannus, which Paul probably rented for this purpose.

Paul was able to carry on this ministry for two years, longer even than he stayed in Corinth. This ministry proved to be a victorious one, for people from all over the province of Asia, both Greeks and Jews, heard the gospel (Acts 19:10). It is entirely likely that during this period, disciples went out into the surrounding cities and preached, starting churches there. Later on, when John wrote in Revelation to the seven churches in Asia, he may very well have been writing to churches that were started during this period.

Paul's Continuing Ministry in Ephesus (19:11-22)

After informing us that Paul stayed two years in Ephesus carrying on his effective ministry, Luke proceeded to give us some reason for, and examples of, this ministry.

His Miraculous Ministry (11, 12)

On previous occasions Paul's preaching had been accompanied by miracles (Acts 14:3, 8-10; 16:18; 2 Corinthians 12:12), but the miracles in Ephesus were unusual. Luke tells us that they were "extraordinary" (Acts 19:11), perhaps in number and certainly in the way they were performed. Articles of clothing that Paul had either worn or touched became the media for the healing. These would be carried to persons who were sick or who were demon possessed, and they were made whole. We are reminded of the occasion when the woman with a flow of blood sought healing by touching Jesus' garment (Matthew 9:20-22). We must realize that no power resides in the garment. The power of healing came from God. He only used the garment as a channel for His power.

One important purpose of New Testament miracles was to provide credentials for God's spokesmen. In Ephesus, where the practitioners of Eastern magic were prevalent, unusual miracles were needed to capture the attention of the people. On radio and television, we occasionally hear contemporary evangelists promise to send to their listeners handkerchiefs or other items that have been specially blessed and are thus supposed to have miraculous curative powers. These evangelists probably take their cue from this passage. It is worth noting that they often suggest that requests for their wares be accompanied by monetary offerings. Needless to say, no such suggestions were made by Paul.

Paul and the Sons of Sceva (13-16)

Luke next related another unusual miracle associated with Paul's ministry in Ephesus. A band of wandering Jewish exorcists came to Ephesus and prepared to ply their trade there. Such vagabonds were common in the first and second centuries. They are mentioned by both Josephus and Justin Martyr. It is likely that these exorcists either watched Paul cast out demons or had heard about his powers. Since it was obvious that his power was greater than theirs, they decided that they would employ what they took to be more powerful magic than their own. These exorcists are identified as the seven sons of Sceva, "a Jewish chief priest" (Acts 19:14). Several suggestions have been made about the identity of Sceva. No such name has been found in the list of Jewish high priests. However, it is possible that he did belong to one of the twenty-four priestly courses. Or these men may have falsely claimed that their father was a high priest in order to enhance their reputation. If so, they were neither the first nor the last to use false credentials to gain wider acceptance.

When these charlatans tried to use the name of Jesus in an exorcism, what follows was as humorous as it was tragic. The demon in the man informed them immediately that they and the powers they claimed were unknown to him: "Jesus I know, and I know about Paul, but who are you?" (Acts 19:15). The poor man, demonstrating such great strength as was common for demon-possessed persons (the Gadarene demoniac, for example), immediately leaped upon the seven sons of Sceva and administered such a beating that they fled naked and bleeding. We suspect that these rascals did not remain long in Ephesus.

Sorcerers Reached by the Gospel (17-20)

News of such a dramatic incident no doubt spread rapidly all over the city with predictable results. No one else would attempt to invoke the name of Jesus to practice magic, and everywhere the

203

name of Jesus was held in high esteem. This incident, as bizarre as it was, proved to be the catalyst that led many to Christ. Many practitioners of black magic openly confessed their involvement in it, and they probably also admitted that many of their claims for its power were fraudulent. Their change of heart was no passing fad, for they brought their scrolls of sorcery and burned them, perhaps in some kind of a public ceremony.

The action of these ex-sorcerers could well serve as an example of us today. By destroying the tools of their evil trade, they helped remove some of the temptations to lapse back into it. By destroying these scrolls, they also made sure that no one else would be tempted by them. The value of the destroyed scrolls was fifty thousand pieces of silver. (These were probably drachmas, coins about the size of a quarter and representing a worker's pay for a day.) Thus, a considerable amount of money was involved, indicating just how extensive the practice of black magic was in Ephesus. Yet this amount of money is nothing compared to the amount of money invested today in the occult, black magic, astrology, and Satan worship.

Such a public and dramatic gesture by the former occultists would not go unnoticed even in such a large and busy city as Ephesus. As the word spread, the word of the Lord also spread, and many converts were won as a result. This summary report, typical of Luke's narrative, concludes his account of this incident and prepares us for the next episode.

Timothy and Erastus Sent to Achaia (21, 22)

The growth of the word of the Lord in Ephesus was most gratifying. But the very success of his work there probably began to make Paul restless. He was the pioneer, the trailblazer, and with so many other new fields beckoning, he was not content to remain in Ephesus when he felt that the church was strong enough that he could leave it in the care of someone else. He decided first to go to Jerusalem. The King James reads, "Paul purposed in the spirit" (Acts 19:21), which translates the Greek more accurately. This reading would leave open the possibility that he was led by the Holy Spirit in this decision.

Paul's reason for wanting to go to Jerusalem was to deliver a collection for the benefit of the Christians there. The collection would be gathered in Achaia and Macedonia, which is why he wanted to pass through those areas before he went to Jerusalem

(1 Corinthians 16:1, 2). But Paul's horizons were more distant than either Jerusalem or Greece. "I must visit Rome also"—how that sentiment must have burned in his heart! Some day that longing would be fulfilled, but little did he know that he would arrive there in chains as a prisoner.

To prepare the churches in Achaia and Macedonia for his coming, he sent Timothy and Erastus on ahead. Timothy we have already met on Paul's second missionary journey. Some identify Erastus with the Erastus mentioned in Romans 16:23, who is the director of public works in Corinth. The name was quite common in the Roman world, however, and no positive identification can be made. After they had left, Paul remained a while longer in Asia. Some scholars believe that Paul wrote his first letter to the church at Corinth during this period. Paul's reference to Timothy in 1 Corinthians 16:10, 11 seems to substantiate this belief. As it turned out, this delay proved to be quite dangerous to him and it very well could have been fatal.

The Riot in Ephesus (19:23-41)

In Ephesus, Paul did not encounter the serious problems with the Jews that he had in many other places. True, he had been forced to leave the synagogue, but the Jews had not threatened him or stirred up violence against him. But Paul was to experience violence from another quarter.

Paul's plan was to remain in Ephesus until Pentecost (1 Corinthians 16:8). This reference places Paul in Ephesus during the middle of the spring. During this time of the year, the Ephesians had a special festival in honor of Artemis. Naturally, the silversmiths would enjoy enhanced sales of their products during this festival. But because so many had accepted the gospel, sales were off, and the silversmiths turned their disappointment and anger against the Christians.

The silversmiths made "shrines" (Acts 19:24). We don't know just what these shrines were; they may have been models of the famous temple of Artemis. While archaeologists have found no examples of these at Ephesus, they have found such shrines made of terra cotta or marble. These models often contain an image of Artemis, who was usually depicted as a many-breasted figure with her arms extended. Devotees of this cult, after having the shrine blessed at the temple, would carry it home, where it would be used in acts of household worship.

Demetrius voiced the concern over lost sales that the other silversmiths felt. In so doing, he aroused them to take some kind of action against the Christians. Paul, whom he accused of leading astray large numbers of people, was the chief target of his attack. Demetrius may have exaggerated the numbers of people Paul had influenced, but he understood very well a major thrust of Paul's message—"man-made gods are no gods at all" (Acts 19:26).

Demetrius' words fell on receptive ears, stirring his fellow workers to anger. Like teenagers at a pep rally, they began to shout, "Great is Artemis of the Ephesians!" (Acts 19:28). As the craftsmen moved through the city streets, chanting their cries, others began to join them. The result was a confusing uproar. Whether the mob deliberately sought out Paul's companions, Gaius and Aristarchus, or whether they chanced upon them, we are not told. We don't know when these two men joined Paul in his work at Ephesus. Several persons in the New Testament bear the name Gaius, and the one here bearing that name cannot be identified with certainty. Aristarchus was from Thessalonica (Acts 20:4). He later accompanied Paul on other journeys. In any event, the mob moved into the theater, which was used not only for theatrical productions but for town meetings and even trials. The theater, which had seats for about 25,000 people, was situated at the end of a wide marble street that ran through the city to the harbor. The mob would have come down this street to the theater.

When Paul learned what had happened to his companions, he quickly rushed to the theater and was prepared to appear before the mob. His intention was probably to speak to the crowd to defend himself. Paul was unwilling to allow his companions to be endangered in his stead. The disciples wisely restrained him, for they knew that his appearance would only serve to inflame the mob further. And that is exactly what it was—an aroused mob that was more likely to be moved by its emotions than by Paul's logic. Even some of the officials of the province, called "Asiarchs," sent a message, joining in this plea to keep Paul from entering the theater (Acts 19:31). These officials traveled about the province of Asia, and their presence in Ephesus at this time lends support to the view that this was the time of special celebration for the goddess Artemis. Though these Asiarchs were not Christians, they were friends of Paul. When or how Paul made their acquaintance, we are not told.

Confusion reigned in the theater. The verb tense indicates that the mob "kept on shouting." Some people shouted one thing, some another. The majority of the people who had rushed into the theater had no idea even why they were there. Unfortunately, mobs haven't changed much over the centuries. At this point, some of the Jews pushed Alexander forward and some tried to silence the crowd so that he could speak. There is nothing to indicate that he was a Christian Jew; so it is not quite clear why he became involved. The general populace probably did not distinguish between Jews and Christians, and since Jews were known to be opposed to idolatry, the crowd may have been accusing them of discouraging people from buying the shrines of Artemis. If this is the case, the idea was to put Alexander forward in order to explain the difference between Jews and Christians and thus relieve the Jews of any responsibility for the problem.

If that was the plan, it didn't work. As soon as the mob saw that he was a Jew, they went into a renewed frenzy. They may have identified Alexander as a Jew by his appearance, his clothing, or he may have been well known in the community. As it turned out, his appearance gave the Ephesians an opportunity to voice their prejudice against Jews. For two hours, they continued to shout, "Great is Artemis of the Ephesians!" Such a prolonged frenzy may have seemed almost unbelievable to most of us a few years ago, but violent street demonstrations in recent years have shown that even our own country is not entirely free of such mindless passions.

After two hours, the crowd had probably shouted themselves hoarse, and the city clerk was able to quiet them down. The word that is translated "city clerk" (Acts 19:35) is sometimes translated "scribe." However, in many Grecian cities, he was the chief administrative officer, not just a secretary. He was responsible for maintaining correspondence with the Roman government, for publishing Roman decrees, and for presiding over the town meetings. Once the official got the people's attention, he first reassured them that they had nothing to fear from the Christians or anyone else. The reputation of Ephesus as the "guardian of the temple of the great Artemis" (Acts 19:35) was not endangered by Paul and his friends. Everyone knew that the temple contained the image of Artemis that had fallen from the sky. No other temple could make such a claim. Since this was the case, their outburst was uncalled for.

Then the city clerk reminded them that there were courts available to hear their case. It is apparent that he was familiar with Paul and his work. He knew that Paul was not a temple-robber, nor had he blasphemed against Artemis or the temple. Since Paul had broken no laws, Demetrius and his fellow artisans could bring him before the civil court if they felt they had a just cause. There the cause could be heard before the Romans, represented by proconsuls. Or if they chose not to go that route, they could get a hearing before a lawful assembly.

The city clerk, who seems to have had a sincere desire to insure that Paul got justice, revealed yet another concern that may have troubled him even more. The word of this riot would undoubtedly get back to Rome. In fact, the clerk himself was probably required to report it. Rome took a dim view of such riots and might, as a result of this tumult, take stern action against the city. The crowd by this time was physically and emotionally exhausted, and this, along with the clerk's words of warning, seemed to have brought them to their senses. At least, there was no protest when the clerk dismissed them.

CHAPTER TWENTY

The Third Missionary Journey

Acts 20

Through Greece and Back to Troas (20:1-16)

After the riot at Ephesus, Paul made plans to leave town. As he had several times in the past, he deemed it wiser to move on and defuse the tense situation that had developed. Had he remained in Ephesus, his presence would have continued to have been the center of ongoing controversy. Such a controversial atmosphere would have made it difficult if not impossible to carry on his work.

To Macedonia, Achaia, and Back to Troas (1-6)

In six brief verses Luke gives us a sketchy summary of Paul's trip that we have come to call his third missionary journey. Although Luke gives us only the barest outlines of this trip, we can fill in some of the details from Paul's letters.

Even before the riot, Paul had planned to leave and travel through Macedonia and eventually return to Jerusalem. To that end, he had sent Timothy and Erastus on ahead to prepare the way for his coming (Acts 19:21, 22). The riot seems only to have hastened Paul's departure. After some final words of encouragement for the brothers at Ephesus, he started on his trip.

At some point during his stay in Ephesus, Paul had written his first letter to the Corinthians. The occasion for this letter was the disturbing news Paul had received about some of the problems that had developed in the church at Corinth (1 Corinthians 1:10, 11). Since it was sent directly to Corinth, it would arrive before Timothy; so Paul mentioned in the letter that Timothy was coming (1 Corinthians 4:17).

Paul probably traveled over land on the first part of this trip, going from Ephesus to Troas. There he took a ship across to Macedonia, where he visited the churches in Philippi, Thessalonica,

THIRD MISSIONARY JOURNEY

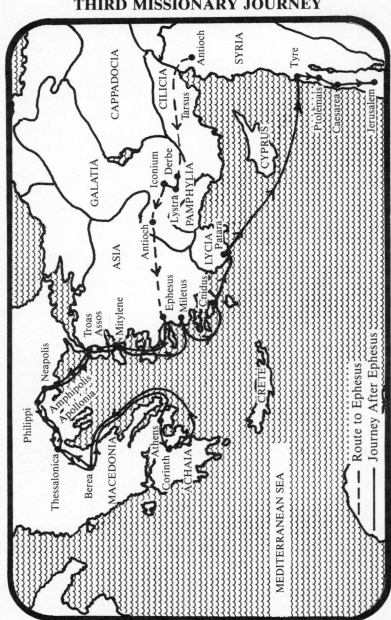

MEDITERRANEAN SEA

Route to Ephesus

Journey After Ephesus

and Berea. Once more we turn to Paul's writings, 2 Corinthians in this case, to fill in some of the details of this trip. It seems evident that Paul had some problems along the way, for in 2 Corinthians 7:5 he wrote, "For when we came into Macedonia, this body of ours had no rest, but we were harassed at every turn—conflicts on the outside, fears within."

The "conflicts on the outside" may have been references to threats or even physical persecution he suffered along the way. The "fears within" may have stemmed from his concern about the situation in Corinth. Before leaving Ephesus, Paul had sent Titus ahead to Corinth to assess the situation. Titus was to return to meet Paul in Troas, but did not arrive at the appointed time. Paul, after waiting awhile, went on into Macedonia. In Macedonia, perhaps in either Philippi or Thessalonica, Titus met Paul, and his report served to reassure Paul, at least in part (2 Corinthians 7:6, 7). But the report was not entirely optimistic. Some in Corinth had been questioning Paul's authority. This led him to pen 2 Corinthians, which he sent back to Corinth by Titus and two other brothers, possibly Timothy and Luke (2 Corinthians 8:17-19, 22, 23). The attitudes of some in Corinth toward Paul may have caused him to tarry longer in Macedonia until his letter had time to produce some changes among his critics.

After this delay, Paul finally arrived in Greece, where he remained three months. While there, he was able to put to rest some of the criticisms that had been leveled at him. He was also able to take a collection, which he planned to take back to Jerusalem for the relief of the saints there. During this stay in Corinth, Paul wrote his letter to the church at Rome. His plan was to take the collection on to Jerusalem and then visit Rome on his way to Spain (Romans 15:24, 25). But the best laid-plans, even Paul's, "gang aft a-gley." Paul did eventually get to visit Rome, but not exactly as he had planned, and so far as we know, he never did visit Spain. His original plan was to sail directly from Corinth to Palestine, but this plan had to be changed. Some of the Jews got word of his plan and hatched a plot to assassinate him along the way and possibly steal the collection. But Paul thwarted their plans by returning overland back through Macedonia.

Paul sent seven men on ahead to Troas, where he planned to meet them. These men—Sopater, son of Pyrrhus from Berea, Aristarchus and Secundus from Thessalonica, Gaius from Derbe, Timothy, and Tychicus and Trophimus from Asia—represented several of the churches where the collection had been taken. Their presence on the trip would assure the contributing churches that their money was used for its designated purpose. In the name of good stewardship, modern churches would be well advised to follow a similar practice.

Paul was possibly accompanied by Titus, and Luke joined them in Philippi (this is one of the "we passages" in which Luke reveals his presence). At Philippi, they took a ship across to Troas, where the others awaited. Luke gives us a clue about the time of the year, stating that they left Philippi after the "Feast of Unleavened Bread" (Acts 20:6—the Greek says "days of unleavened bread," which accurately reflects the fact that during the seven days after the Passover, unleavened bread was used). This note indicates that his trip through Macedonia to Corinth and back through Macedonia took almost a year.

Paul at Troas (7-12)

The voyage from Neapolis (the port city for Philippi) to Troas took five days, whereas an earlier voyage in the opposite direction had taken only two days (Acts 16:11). Since it was early spring, it is likely that they faced some rough weather and contrary winds that slowed their trip. After arriving at Troas, they remained seven days there. Luke does not give us any information about what they did during that time, but, knowing Paul, we can be quite sure that he was busy preaching and teaching. This passage seems to indicate that a congregation was already in existence there. If such was the case, the presence of Paul and his companions would provide an excellent opportunity for a revival or an evangelistic meeting.

This congregation met "on the first day of the week" for the purpose of breaking bread (Acts 20:7). No small amount of scholarly ink has been used in trying to determine just exactly what this expression means. Literally, the Greek says that they met on the "first of the sabbaths." Some feel that Luke was using the Jewish method of counting, which meant that the first day began at sundown on Saturday. In which case, the church began its meeting on Saturday evening and continued past midnight. It is more likely, however, that Luke was using the Roman method of counting time, because this was a Gentile church. If this was the situation, then the meeting began on Sunday evening and continued past midnight until early Monday morning.

Whether or not the regular meeting on the first day of the week had become the established practice this early in the history of the church, we simply cannot say. This is the first reference to it, although Paul in writing to the Corinthian church hints that this was the practice when he advised them to set aside their money on the first day of the week (1 Corinthians 16:2). Although references in the first century to the church's meeting on the first day of the week are scanty, it is evident that the practice was well established in the second century. Even though we do not have a "thus saith the Lord" for meeting on the first day of the week, there is certainly more evidence for meeting on the first day than for meeting on any other day.

The purpose for their meeting was to "break bread." While this expression can refer to a common meal, it is obvious that in the church, it came to refer to the Lord's Supper. (See Acts 2:42.) In fact, in the early church, Christians often ate a common meal together (called the "*agape* feast" or "love feast"), after which they shared in the Lord's Supper. They probably met at night because many of the Christians were slaves and the only time they had free were the late evening and early morning.

Our Lord did not give Christians a specific command that they were to observe the Lord's Supper on the first day of each week. Instead, He extended a gracious invitation for believers to share in this memorial feast. Paul, in writing to the Corinthians, gave some brief instructions about how it should be observed (1 Corinthians 11:20-34). He stated: "Whenever you eat this bread and drink this cup, you proclaim the Lord's death until he comes" (1 Corinthians 11:26). But because we are invited rather than commanded does not mean that we can take a casual attitude about our gathering at His table. We obey a command out of fear or perhaps out of respect. An invitation we accept out of love, a far more compelling force than fear.

Some denominations observe monthly or quarterly Communion rather than weekly Communion. This practice has its basis in custom and habit instead of Scriptural precedent. It is argued by some that frequent observance of the Lord's Supper will cause it to become common. It is interesting to note that those who observe weekly Communion never complain that it has become less meaningful because of its frequency. Indeed, just the opposite seems to be the case. Those accustomed to weekly Communion feel a real emptiness when on occasion they are forced to miss it.

One might just as readily argue that frequent prayer makes it less meaningful or that one's affection for his or her spouse would be more meaningful if he only on rare occasions said, "I love you."

The church at Troas met for the purpose of breaking bread, not for a song service, a sermon, or to take a collection. This would seem to suggest that as important as those things may be, the Lord's Supper ought to occupy the central place in our worship services. It affords worshipers an opportunity to look back to the cross and Jesus' suffering, to witness to the world that He is coming again, to examine their hearts to purge them of the sins that so readily burden them, to look upward to Him to renew their covenant with Him. When one approaches the holy table with this attitude, the Lord's Supper can never be a perfunctory ceremony observed only as a habit.

The meeting was prolonged as Paul preached to them, talking until midnight. Westerners might feel uncomfortable in such a service, conditioned as we are to twenty-minute sermons. But people from other cultures, who are not slaves to the clock, could identify with this experience very readily. The people must have sensed that this would be the last time they would see Paul, and they were reluctant to pronounce the benediction. The term used to describe Paul's speaking is not the word usually used to mean "preach." Rather, the word means "to discuss, to dispute, to answer questions." It would appear, then, that it was more an open discussion than a formal worship service.

Luke injects an interesting note that there were many lamps in the upstairs room where they met (Acts 20:8). These little lamps were quite common in that period. They were usually nothing more than a small, closed bowl with a handle on one side and an opening for a wick on the other. The fuel was usually olive oil. These lamps did not provide much light, and they were smoky, but it was the best they had. Luke's reason for mentioning the lamps may have been to suggest that the room was stuffy. This would help explain what happened next.

A young man named Eutychus was sitting in a window, perhaps because the room was crowded. While windows in those days had shutters, they did not have glass in them. Apparently the shutters were open; so there was nothing to protect anyone sitting in the window. The hour was late, the room was stuffy, and perhaps Eutychus had put in a hard day's work. It is not surprising that slumber overtook him and he fell into a deep sleep. All at once, he lost his balance, and before anyone could grab him, he fell to the ground, three stories below.

This brought Paul's discourse to a rapid halt. As soon as people realized what had happened, many must have rushed down the stairs to learn Eutychus' fate. Such a fall was certain to bring serious injury if not death. Their worst fears were realized as he was "picked up dead" (Acts 20:9). Paul also made his way down the stairs and pushed his way through the onlookers surrounding the inert body which had been laid out on the ground. Paul wasted no time in meeting the need. He stretched his body across the young man and put his arms around him. This reminds us of the actions of Elijah and Elisha in similar situations (1 Kings 17:21-23; 2 Kings 4:34-37). Then he turned to the crowd to reassure them and silence their wailing: "Don't be alarmed! He's alive!" Luke tells us nothing more about the miracle, but he doesn't need to. The youth who had been killed by the fall was now alive and as good as ever.

After this amazing incident, the people returned to their meeting, where they "broke bread"—observed the Lord's Supper. What a Communion service this must have been with rejoicing, praise, thanksgiving, and soul-searching all combined. Their excitement sustained them so that Paul talked until the break of day. Luke closed his account of this incident with a reference to the young man, noting that the people were greatly comforted.

Arrival at Miletus (13-16)

At daybreak, Paul's party boarded the ship that was to carry them down the coast. Paul, apparently to take advantage of this last opportunity to teach the Christians at Troas, remained behind. Then he walked across the peninsula to meet his companions at Assos, no mean feat for one who had spent the whole night talking. The ship put in at Assos, where Paul was reunited with his fellow travelers. The next day, they sailed to the island of Chios; on the day following, they crossed over to Samos; and the third day, they arrived at Miletus, bypassing Ephesus. Paul knew that if he spent any time at Ephesus, he would not be able to reach Jerusalem in time for Pentecost.

Paul's Last Meeting With the Ephesian Elders (20:17-35)

Paul's most pressing concern at this time seems to have been his desire to reach Jerusalem in time for Pentecost. This feast attracted Jews of the dispersion from many lands, and it is likely that Paul saw this as an opportunity to preach to a large and varied audience.

Paul's Manner of Life Among the Ephesians (17-22)

Paul might have chosen to bypass Ephesus lest he once again arouse the anger of Demetrius, the silversmith. A second such disturbance would likely affect the church adversely. Yet he longed desperately to see once more the leaders with whom he had labored for so long. Since the ship planned to stay in Miletus for more than a day, this allowed him to send to Ephesus for the elders. Since Ephesus was thirty miles or more from Miletus, it would have taken at least a day for the messengers to travel there and another day for the elders to return.

Once the elders arrived, Paul delivered a hortatory message, the gist of which Luke preserved for us. Since this was a personal speech delivered to a small group of close friends, it does not follow a neat, logical outline. It must have been filled with deep emotions, and it is likely that Paul was interrupted several times by the elders.

He began by reminding them of his manner of life when he lived among them. The tone of Paul's comments suggests that some within the church had been critical of him; so Paul felt a need to defend his ministry there. Since the elders were quite familiar with his work, Paul had only to remind them of it without going into great detail. He had served with humility and with deep emotional involvement—"with tears" (Acts 20:19). He mentioned also the effort of the Jews, who threatened him and tried to undermine his work. In Acts, only one such incident is mentioned—the occasion when Alexander tried to speak against him in the theater. But in writing to the church at Corinth shortly after leaving Ephesus, he mentions being "in danger from my own countrymen" (2 Corinthians 11:26), leading us to believe that he had to live under almost constant threats from the Jews.

In his preaching and teaching ministry, Paul did not hesitate to proclaim the truth that his hearers needed, although at times they may not have wanted to hear it. He had carried on this ministry both in public and in the privacy of the people's homes. He set an excellent example for us today. There is a great need for the public proclamation of the truth, but often one's best teaching takes place in the home or in some other private setting. Nor was Paul a

216

respecter of persons, proclaiming the need for repentance and faith in Christ to both Jews and Greeks.

Paul's Immediate Plans (22-24)

After this introduction, Paul conveyed to the elders his immediate plans to go to Jerusalem. He said that he was "compelled by the Spirit" to make this trip (Acts 20:22). *Spirit* is capitalized in the New International Version, indicating that the translators believed that the Holy Spirit compelled him to go. However, the King James Version and the New American Standard Bible do not capitalize it, showing that these translators believe that the trip to Jerusalem was something Paul had purposed to do, not something that he was compelled to do. This may be the better interpretation, for later on at Caesarea Paul was warned by the prophet Agabus not to go to Jerusalem, lest he be taken by the Jews and turned over to the Gentiles. Agabus stated that the Holy Spirit had given him this warning, and as a result Paul's friends tried to persuade him not to go. But neither the prophetic words or the pleadings of friends had any effect on Paul. Apparently, his mind was made up.

Along the way, the Holy Spirit, speaking either directly to Paul or through prophets, warned that he would suffer hardships if he went to Jerusalem (Acts 20:23). Yet these warnings had no effect on him. He had no other desire than to spend his life, sacrificially if need be, for the cause of Christ. When Christ had called Paul, He had given him the task of evangelizing the Gentiles. Paul was determined to complete that mission even if it cost him his life. For nearly two thousand years, Paul's example has called men and women into similar sacrificial commitments.

Paul's Warning to the Elders (25-31)

Paul was convinced that the elders would never see him again. He may have come to this conclusion because he believed that his trip to Jerusalem would lead to his imprisonment and death, or because he planned to work in other areas such as Rome and Spain. Interestingly, some of Paul's comments in 1 Timothy and 2 Timothy indicate that he did visit Macedonia, Troas, Miletus, and possibly Ephesus after his release from his first Roman imprisonment (1 Timothy 1:3; 4:13; 2 Timothy 4:13, 20).

Paul's conviction that he would never see these beloved leaders again lent urgency to his admonitions. He reminded them that he

217

had not hesitated to declare the whole will of God to them, and, thus, if the people had failed to respond, he would not be guilty of their blood. His statement reminds us of the responsibility of the watchman, who has an obligation to warn the wicked (Ezekiel 3:16-21).

The leaders have an obligation first of all to guard themselves. A careless shepherd leads to an endangered flock. Leaders are subject to special temptations. Their positions of prominence can make them vulnerable to pride. The examples they set can cause envious people to try to trap them into sin. The extra burdens that they carry can be physically and spiritually exhausting. We can be sure that Satan has reserved most of his fiery darts for them.

When leaders have learned to guard themselves, then they are ready to guard others. The Ephesian leaders had been made overseers of the flock by the Holy Spirit in order to protect it from the ravages of the wild animals that would attack it. Just how the Holy Spirit had made them overseers, we are not told, but it seems likely that the Holy Spirit had acted through the inspired teachings of Paul to lead to their selection and training. In Acts 20:17, these men had been called elders; now they are called overseers or, in some translations, bishops. It is obvious that these are but different terms for the same office. In the centuries that followed, a distinction arose between the office of elder and the office of bishop, leading to the elevation of the bishop over the elders. This eventually led to the development of the hierarchy that is characteristic of the Roman Catholic Church.

Paul urged the elders to be shepherds of God's church, which our Lord bought with His own blood. Most of us are modern urbanites, quite unacquainted with the work of a shepherd. Thus, we miss the full impact of Paul's statement. A shepherd leads, he does not drive his flock. He leads the flock to verdant pastures and thirst-quenching water. He seeks the lost, the wandering ones. He binds up the wounds of the injured. He provides security when the elements or enemies threaten. And, not least, he is willing to lay down his life for his sheep.

Paul next turned to specific warnings. Always lurking in the shadows are the wolves who wait for the opportune moment to attack ferociously or to sneak in, cleverly disguised in sheep's clothing. Jesus used similar words to describe these enemies (Matthew 7:15). Paul may have had some particular false teachers in mind, such as the Judaizers, whose teachings were even at that very time disrupting many churches. However, with prophetic vision, he may have seen beyond the immediate situation. A generation later, the Ephesian church was assaulted by false teachers, among them the Nicolaitans. The church was able to resist them, in part, perhaps, because of Paul's warning. (See Revelation 2:2, 6.) Yet this church was guilty of leaving its first love (Revelation 2:4).

Unfortunately, the danger is not always from the outside. Paul warned that even some of the elders themselves would become false teachers and seduce members of their flock to follow them. The pages of church history are replete with the names of leaders who have espoused false doctrines or built ecclesiastical power structures for their own selfish motives. For this reason, every congregation must exercise care in choosing its leaders, and it must maintain constant vigilance to insure that those who are chosen remain faithful to their calling.

Once more Paul turned to the example of his own life. For the period he had lived and worked among them—approximately three years—he had labored night and day to warn them and guard them. His warnings were not those of a solemn judge who hurls his dictums from the aloofness of the elevated bench. Rather, he admonished daily with tears, sharing in their defeats, suffering in their disappointments, not only sympathizing, but empathizing.

Paul's Closing Words and Departure (32-38)

Since he would no longer be able to work among them, he committed them to God. That commitment would be carried out through the ministry of the word of His grace. Because the writings that we now know as the New Testament were only then being penned, they could not yet refer to the Scriptures for guidance. Yet they had etched deeply in their memories the preached word of grace, which would suffice until it was available in written form.

The word of grace was able to build them up. Paul used this same figure, which depicts the church as a building, in Ephesians 2:22, as did Peter in 1 Peter 2:5. Individual Christians were the stones that make up this building. They are laid upon the cornerstone, which is Christ Jesus. This process can be accomplished only through the word of grace. But the building can grow only when the Bible is studied. The neglect of Bible study has often prevented the construction to continue as it should.

The end result was that they would receive an inheritance, a term that Paul used several times in his writings to refer to eternal life. To that purpose they were sanctified, that is, set apart. Sanctification is not some mysterious process by which one achieves sinless perfection. It is, instead, the process whereby one is dedicated or set apart to God. It is an ongoing process that will be completed only when the saints have gained their eternal inheritance.

The ancient world, like our own, was quite familiar with teachers and leaders who used their positions to grow rich. In Paul's world, gold, silver, and clothing were the most widely accepted measures of wealth and symbols of status. Paul had not acquired these at the expense of the Ephesians; he had not even coveted them. Paul had a right to expect the church at Ephesus to support him, a point that Paul made in 1 Corinthians 9:11-14. Yet Paul chose not to insist upon this right. Instead, he worked with his own hands to provide for the needs of himself and his companions. Paul worked hard, presumably at his trade of tentmaking. In this way, he set an example of how the able ought to support the weak.

To provide further support for his position, Paul then quoted the words of Jesus: "It is more blessed to give than to receive" (Acts 20:35). These words are not recorded in any of the Gospel accounts. Whether these words of Jesus came to Paul by direct revelation or whether he learned them from Peter or one of the other apostles, we are not told. Certainly these words are most appropriate in this context. A selfish, egocentric person may question the truth of these words, but one who has given freely and generously understands them quite well.

Luke gave us only the gist of Paul's message to the elders. His speech must have gone on for some time. Then it was over, and Paul was ready to say his final farewells. It was an emotionally moving scene for everyone involved. They knelt down and prayed together. Then they wept, and they embraced him and kissed him. Tears were shed because Paul was leaving them, but the flow of tears must have been greater because they believed that they would never see him again.

CHAPTER TWENTY-ONE

Jerusalem at Last

Acts 21

Paul's Trip to Jerusalem (21:1-16)

Paul's determination to visit Jerusalem was unwavering. He had received warnings along the way that such a visit could be dangerous, and he himself was fully aware of these dangers. He wanted to visit Jerusalem to deliver to the poor saints there the collection that he had gathered. But there was no compelling reason why Paul had to deliver this gift personally. The men accompanying him were certainly quite capable of doing this. A more pressing reason seems to have been his desire to vindicate his work among the Gentiles. Perhaps he still believed that if he could just present his position to the religious authorities in Jerusalem, they would then understand what he was doing. At the very least, he hoped to convince some of the Judaizers within the church that it was God's will for him to work among the Gentiles.

From Miletus to Tyre (1-6)

Paul's departure from the Ephesian elders was not easy. The strong bonds of fellowship that had been built during Paul's stay with them could not be painlessly severed. For that reason, Luke used strong language to describe this departure—"After we had torn ourselves away from them . . ." (Acts 21:1).

Putting out to sea, they sailed to Cos, a small island off the Southwest coast of Asia Minor. Centuries earlier, Hippocrates had founded a medical school there. The fact that his personal physician had attended this school led Emperor Claudius to grant Cos immunity from taxes. The next day, the ship sailed to Rhodes. From Rhodes, the missionaries sailed across to Patara on the coast of Lycia on the mainland of Asia Minor.

At Patara, the party took passage on a ship that was sailing to Phoenicia. The vessel that they had been on was probably a

221

coastal vessel that stopped at numerous ports along the coast. Since Paul was in a hurry to get to Jerusalem by Pentecost, he now chose a ship that would sail more directly to Palestine.

Leaving Patara, the ship sailed south of Cyprus and landed at Tyre. While the ship was being unloaded, Paul and his party had an opportunity to visit the church there. We have no information about when the church there was formed. We know that during the persecution that followed the death of Stephen, some of the Christians fled to Phoenicia (Acts 11:19). Some of these may have formed a nucleus for a church. The seven days it took the ship to unload and take on a new cargo gave Paul an extended opportunity to visit with the disciples there.

The disciples in Tyre had a message for Paul. "Through the Spirit," Luke says, they "urged" him not to go to Jerusalem (Acts 21:4). Does that mean the Holy Spirit forbade Paul to go to Jerusalem, and yet Paul disobeyed this command? This hardly seems likely, given Paul's total commitment to the will of the Lord. A better explanation is that the Holy Spirit indicated to the disciples in Tyre that Paul would be persecuted if he went to Jerusalem. These disciples in their love for Paul and their concern for his safety urged him not to make the trip.

When the time came to leave, Paul was accompanied out of the city by the men, their wives, and their children. There on the beach, the group knelt in prayer. No doubt they prayed for the continued safe journey of Paul and his party. They also must have prayed that Paul would be kept from harm after he arrived in Jerusalem. We wonder what the sailors and other onlookers must have thought about this public prayer meeting. Sometimes a public demonstration of piety can have a profound impact on unbelievers. Once the final good-bye had been said, the party boarded the ship for the last leg of their voyage to Palestine.

From Tyre to Caesarea (7-9)

The next stop along the way was Ptolemais, also known as Accho or Akka. It was located about eight miles north of Mount Carmel. Its natural harbor made it an important port in Palestine. There, as at Tyre, Paul found Christian brothers.

The next day, Paul reached Caesarea, about forty miles south of Ptolemais. There they stayed in the home of Philip the evangelist. Philip was one of the seven who had been chosen to serve at the tables in Jerusalem (Acts 6:1-6). His work in Samaria and his winning the Ethiopian eunuch had earned for him the title of evangelist. Philip had preached in many of the coastal towns south of Caesarea several years earlier (Acts 8:40) and apparently had settled there to make Caesarea the base for his evangelistic activities. Caesarea had also been the home of Cornelius when Peter came to his house to preach to him.

Luke adds a bit of interesting information that Philip had four "unmarried daughters" (literally, "virgin daughters") who propesied (Acts 21:9). Since Luke gives us no further information about them, we have no idea about their place or function in the church. Some have seized upon this verse to argue for the existence of a special office of prophet or prophetess in the New Testament church. Others have used this verse along with some of Paul's statements to argue that virginity was superior to the married state. We doubt that this verse can carry such a burden. We are not told whether these sisters did their prophesying in the public worship service of the church at Caesarea or whether they prophesied only in private. It is worth noting that the Holy Spirit had not given them any message about Paul's planned visit to Jerusalem. Such a warning awaited the arrival of Agabus.

Paul's Visit in Caesarea (10-16)

Paul remained in Caesarea several days, perhaps as much as a week. During this period, the prophet Agabus came down from Judea. This is probably the same Agabus who is mentioned in Acts 11:28. It is entirely possible that word of Paul's arrival in Caesarea had been sent to Jerusalem. As a result, Agabus was dispatched to warn Paul of the dangers in coming to Jerusalem.

Agabus dramatized his prophecy as did some of the Old Testament prophets. We think immediately of Isaiah (Isaiah 20:2-4), Jeremiah (Jeremiah 13:1-11), and Ezekiel (Ezekiel 4:1-6). Taking Paul's belt (usually referred to as a girdle, this was a sash or piece of cloth tied tightly about the waist), Agabus tied his own hands and feet with it. Then he delivered his message: "If you go to Jerusalem, you will be bound like this and handed over to the Gentiles" (Acts 21:1, author's paraphrase). Nor was this a warning to be taken lightly, for Agabus spoke by the Holy Spirit.

When the people heard this, they pleaded with Paul not to go to Jerusalem. Paul's fellow travelers, including Luke, had heard this warning before, and they also raised their voices against his going. But Paul, in spite of the object lesson and in spite of the pleading, was adamant. He insisted that he was not only willing to be bound but to die for the Lord, if necessary. Paul was a stubborn man. Of course, he had to be to undertake and continue on his various missionary enterprises. Persons who flinch in the face of hardship or dangers do not last long as missionaries. Faced with this kind of determination, Paul's friends gave up. All they could say was "The Lord's will be done" (Acts 21:14). Their conclusion does not necessarily mean that they now agreed with Paul that it was God's will that he go to Jerusalem. Rather, it sounds more like a note of grim resignation upon their realization that nothing was going to change Paul. It is certainly open to question whether Paul really was carrying out the will of God in going to Jerusalem, especially in the light of all the warnings that God had sent along the way. But even if we question his wisdom, we must admire his courage.

Since the decision was made, there was nothing left to do but to get ready for the trip. The verb used may mean getting pack horses ready, which may indicate that they rode horses up to Jerusalem, a distance of about sixty-five miles. Several of the disciples accompanied Paul along the way. This was a common practice in those days. It not only provided protection; it also provided fellowship. Paul was brought to the house of Mnason, an old disciple, and possibly an old friend of Paul. Since he was from Cyprus, it is possible that he was a convert of Paul and Barnabas on their first missionary journey. His home may have been on the outskirts of Jerusalem, or possibly even in the city.

Paul Arrives at Jerusalem (21:17-26)

With Paul's arrival in Jerusalem, what we often refer to as the third missionary journey came to an end. Several years had elapsed since Paul's last visit to Jerusalem. Many things had changed in those years, but one thing had not changed—the Jewish hostility toward Paul.

Paul's Greeting of James and the Elders (17-19)

A warm reception from the brothers awaited Paul in Jerusalem. The next day, Paul and his companions went to visit James and the elders. This was James, the brother of the Lord, who had played such an important part in the Jerusalem Conference some years earlier (Acts 15). It cannot have been the apostle James, because he had been martyred earlier by Herod (Acts 12:2). Although he was a recognized leader in the Jerusalem church, we are

224

not told what office he held. It seems apparent that he was not an elder, for he is distinguished from the elders. In Galatians 1:19, Paul indicates that he was an apostle, not one of the Twelve, to be sure, but a special apostle. This meeting allowed Paul the opportunity to give a detailed report of his activities among the churches in Asia, Macedonia, and Greece. Since much of his work had been among the Gentiles, it would be of special interest to the leaders of the Jerusalem church.

Charges Against Paul (20, 21)

Their response was not long in coming. They began to praise God (Acts 21:20), and the verb here indicates that they continued to praise God. They rejoiced that so many of the Gentiles had accepted Christ. They probably also rejoiced because the Lord had moved them to send such a generous offering to Jerusalem.

But the leaders of the Jerusalem church had a problem. "Many thousands" (literally, "myriads" or "tens of thousands") had become Christians (Acts 21:20). Yet, at the same time, they held on to many of their Jewish ways. These converts were disturbed because they had heard that Paul was telling Jewish converts who lived among Gentiles that they no longer had to conform to the Mosaic law, including the circumcision of their sons. Of course, Paul had never taught anything like this. Paul understood that the decision of the Jerusalem Conference, that converts did not have to live by the law of Moses, applied only to Gentiles who became Christians. Anyone who suggested otherwise had either misunderstood what Paul had taught or had deliberately misrepresented what he had taught. Unfortunately, even Christians will sometimes distort other persons' positions in order to win an argument. Apparently, that is what happened in this case. Since most of us have had experiences like this, it behooves us to make sure that we know the other person's position before we broadcast it to others. We ought to avoid hearsay information, especially when we can gain it firsthand from the people involved.

Dealing with the Charges (22-26)

James and the other Jewish leaders proposed a way to meet the criticism. They might have sought out each person who was disturbed by Paul's actions and tried to explain to them that the information they had heard about Paul was wrong. But this would have been time consuming. They suggested, instead, an act

225

that would make it clear to all that Paul had not been urging Jewish Christians to abandon their customs. They asked Paul to sponsor four men who had taken a Nazirite vow. We do not know the circumstances under which these men took this vow. Ordinarily, the Nazirite vow was for thirty days, although it could be longer. During the period of the vow, the Nazirite was to drink no wine or eat the fruit of the vine, nor was he to touch a dead body. At the end of the period, he presented an offering in the temple and his head was shorn.

The church leaders wanted Paul to pay the expenses for the sacrifices of these four men, a practice that was common when a person taking the vow was poor. In order to be able to do this, Paul had to purify himself by taking some kind of a vow. We are told nothing about the vow that Paul was asked to take, but it may have required him to observe the provisions of the Nazirite vow along with these men until their vow was completed. The church leaders felt that if the Jewish Christians observed Paul involved in this fashion, they would be reassured that he was not urging fellow Jews to turn away from keeping the law.

Paul's action in this situation has caused some commentators no end of problems. They feel that his participation in this rite contradicted his position that salvation is by faith apart from the works of the law. But Paul was not guilty of any inconsistency in this situation. Earlier, he himself had entered into some kind of a vow that may very well have been a form of the Nazirite vow (Acts 18:18). It is well to point out that Paul did not view his actions as a form of salvation by works. Rather, he was following a principle of expediency that he had laid down for his own ministry. "Though I am free and belong to no man," he wrote to the Corinthians (1 Corinthians 9:19, 20), "I make myself a slave to everyone, to win as many as possible. To the Jews, I became like a Jew, to win the Jews." In this same passage in 1 Corinthians, Paul went on to explain that to those outside the law, he would act as one outside the law. However, this was not to be taken to mean that he would do anything unlawful to God, for he was under Christ's law. And so we can be certain that Paul in this action was not compromising any teaching essential to the gospel.

We today are often faced with similar situations. Missionaries who work with persons who have come out of paganism often meet such situations. But we don't have to visit a foreign country to be involved in the same kind of things. Living among a population that increasingly represents diverse religions and cultures, we are not that far from a foreign mission field. For example, should one attend the wedding of a Buddhist friend, knowing that the ceremony will involve Buddhist rites? Could a Protestant attend a Catholic wedding? Such questions should not trouble us if we understand the principle that Paul had laid down and which he was following in this situation in Jerusalem.

A Christian should never participate in an activity that compromises his Christian convictions or goes contrary to the Word of God. This means that one should never be involved in any activity that is itself immoral. Granted these limitations, a Christian can make many concessions to the beliefs and cultural practices of others. In so doing, he must recognize that many things that have been incorporated into his own culture may seem upsetting to others. For example, how would Paul have viewed some of the beliefs and practices associated with our observance of Christmas and Easter? Many of these came to us from pagan sources, and Christians of the first century might have had serious reservations about some of them.

In asking Paul to involve himself with these four men, the leaders of the Jerusalem church made it clear that this was a special situation. They had no intention of requiring Gentile Christians to follow the same practice. The only requirements laid upon them were that they were to abstain from meat offered to idols, from eating blood, from the meat of animals that had been strangled, and from sexual immorality, the prohibitions that had been set forth at the Jerusalem Conference (Acts 15:29).

Having agreed to this arrangement, apparently without any serious objections, Paul purified himself along with the men. Then he went to the temple to notify the priests of the date upon which the men's vows would be fulfilled. Since the men themselves were considered ceremonially unclean during the period of their vow, they could not go into the temple, and so Paul had to make these arrangements for them.

Paul Arrested (21:27-40)

Paul had been willing to make concessions to the Jewish Christians to allay their suspicions of him that he had been teaching Jews to abandon the law of Moses. While it was not Paul's idea, he went along with the suggestion of James that he be responsible for the four who had taken the Nazirite vow. All went

227

well at first, when Paul took the men and purified himself at the temple. But then a chance incident almost proved fatal.

Paul Seized by the Crowd (27-29)

When the seven-day period required for the fulfillment of the men's vows was almost completed, Paul was sighted by some Jews from Asia who probably had come to Jerusalem for Pentecost. It is likely that these Jews were from Ephesus, for they had earlier seen and recognized Trophimus, who was an Ephesian. Since Paul had labored in Ephesus for many months, they had had an opportunity to get to know him well. Further, the Jews in Ephesus had been especially antagonistic against Paul. Not only had they refused to accept the gospel when Paul had preached to them, they had publicly maligned the Way (Acts 19:9). Seeing Paul in Jerusalem only served to arouse old antagonisms.

They began to shout to attract attention, and since there was probably a crowd in the temple at the time, it was not long before an angry mob had gathered about Paul. The Jews of Asia knew exactly what would arouse their fellow Jews. They charged that Paul had turned people away from the law; but worse, he had brought Greeks into the temple area. This latter charge was calculated to arouse them to a frenzy. During the feast periods, the Jews tended to be more volatile than usual. Histories of this period tell of several bloody uprisings among the Jews, several of which occurred at the time of the great feasts.

The Jews were especially concerned to maintain the sanctity of the temple. Surrounding the actual temple was the court of priests, which most of the time only priests could enter. (See the map of the temple area on page 40.) Surrounding this was the court of Israel, which was open only to Jewish men. The court of women surrounded the court of Israel. As its name indicates, Jewish women could enter this court. The women's court was surrounded with a balustrade to separate it from the court of the Gentiles. Gentiles were excluded from the three inner courts, and at the entrances to the women's courts were signs in both Greek and Latin, warning any Gentile who might try to enter. Two of these inscriptions have been discovered, one in the nineteenth century and the other in 1935. These inscriptions decreed death for any Gentile who dared violate this prohibition. Though the Romans ordinarily denied the Jews the right to exercise capital punishment, they did permit the death penalty against anyone guilty of violating this prohibition. Thus Paul was in a dangerous situation if they proved the charges. Even his Roman citizenship would not protect him.

The basis for their charge that Paul had desecrated the temple was that some of them had earlier seen Trophimus, a Gentile, in Jerusalem with Paul. They had assumed that Paul had brought him into the temple. Knowing the viciousness of these Asian Jews, it is entirely possible that once they had seen Paul in Jerusalem, they had kept him under surveillance, hoping that they might catch him in a situation that would give them a basis for bringing charges against him. Of course, the charge that Paul had brought a Gentile into the restricted area of the temple was not true, but mobs aroused to an angry pitch are not inclined to be too careful about getting all the facts before they go on a rampage.

Paul Rescued by Roman Soldiers (30-36)

Word spread rapidly through the crowded city streets, and soon an angry mob had assembled about Paul. The Jews who were from Asia might have remembered the mob scene in Ephesus and deliberately used the same tactics in Jerusalem. Seizing Paul, they dragged him out of the temple area, probably into the court of the Gentiles. The Levites, who worked in the temple area and watched over it, quickly closed the gates so that the strife would not take place within the sacred precincts.

The mob immediately set upon Paul, determined to kill him without the benefit of a trial or even a hearing. Probably the only thing that saved his life was that the mob was without a leader and the turmoil was so great that no one knew exactly what was going on. Word soon reached the Roman commander about the trouble. The commander was headquartered in the Tower of Antonia, a large tower built by Herod in the northwest corner of the temple area. Its strategic location allowed the Romans to observe activities in the temple area, a fact that angered the Jews, but they could do nothing about it. Taking some men with him, the commander rushed down into the temple area. Seeing the Roman soldiers advancing upon them with drawn swords, the mob quit beating on Paul and backed away. Mobs are usually a cowardly bunch, who find courage only in situations where they greatly outnumber a weaker victim.

Arriving on the scene, the commander arrested Paul and ordered him to be bound in chains. Since Paul was the center of the turmoil, the commander supposed that he was the cause of the trouble. In any event, he arrested Paul and put him in protective custody, where the Jews could not get to him.

Then the commander began his inquiry into the cause of the riot. He may have questioned Paul first, but the angry mob probably interrupted, some saying one thing and some another. Unable to get the facts from the mob in that noisy situation, he ordered Paul taken into the tower for further questioning. But the sight of Paul being taken away from them aroused the mob to further action. In spite of the soldiers, the mob pressed so forcefully upon them that Paul had to be carried to the steps of the tower. Their shouts of "Away with him!" (Acts 21:36) remind us of the mob almost thirty years earlier that had cried out for the blood of Jesus (John 19:15).

Paul Permitted to Speak to the Crowd (37-40)

As they reached the top of the stairs and were about to enter the fortress, Paul spoke to the commander. The commander was surprised that Paul spoke Greek. He had taken Paul for an Egyptian who a short time before had attempted to lead an insurrection against the Romans. Josephus writes about an Egyptian who led 30,000 men to the top of the Mount of Olives. He had promised his followers that the wall of Jerusalem would fall and his men could then descend upon and defeat the Romans. Felix, the governor, sent out Roman troops who quickly dispersed the rebels, killing about 400 of them. The Egyptian leader had escaped. It may be that the Roman commander thought that Paul was this Egyptian, returning to stir up more trouble.

The fact that Paul spoke such fluent Greek made it obvious that he was not an Egyptian insurrectionist. Then Paul identified himself—a Jew from Tarsus. Paul's words so impressed the commander that he gave him permission to address the crowd. He probably hoped that Paul could satisfy the crowd and bring an end to the unpleasant affair. Paul stood on the steps and motioned to the crowd, signifying that he wanted to speak. It must have been several minutes before the crowd became quiet. Paul began his speech in the Aramaic language. (The King James Version says that he spoke in the Hebrew language, but this is not likely. Hebrew was spoken only by the scholars, and thus the crowd would not have been able to understand it. Aramaic was akin to Hebrew and was the language spoken by the people.)

CHAPTER TWENTY-TWO

Paul's Defense
Before the Temple Mob

Acts 22

Paul's Speech in the Temple Area (22:1-22)

It is interesting that Paul, in making his defense before the angry mob in the temple, completely ignored the charges that had been made against him. The charge that Paul had brought a Gentile into the temple area closed to them and thus had defiled the temple could have readily been answered. It was a trumped up charge without a shred of evidence to support it. If Paul had been guilty of the charge, where was the Gentile that he had supposedly brought into the temple?

Yet Paul chose not to follow this line of reasoning. Instead, he used it as an opportunity to try to preach to his fellow countrymen. Even though he had scarcely had time to catch his breath from the beating the mob had given him, his first thoughts were to try to reach his people with the gospel. On another occasion, he had expressed his deep passion for them: "I have great sorrow and unceasing anguish in my heart. For I could wish that I myself were cursed and cut off from Christ for the sake of my brothers, those of my own race, the people of Israel" (Romans 9:2-4).

Paul, the Persecutor of Christians (1-5)

Given the opportunity to speak to the angry mob, Paul sought a way to gain rapport with them. The first thing that he did was to speak to them in Aramaic. Then he addressed them respectfully as brothers and fathers, reminding us of the introduction Stephen used under rather similar circumstances a quarter of a century earlier. Our word *apology* comes from the Greek word that is here translated "defense" (Acts 22:1). But Paul had no intention of apologizing for his life or actions. The word was often used to describe one's actions in a carefully-planned legal defense in a court of law. This was what Paul had in mind.

231

When the crowd heard him speak in Aramaic, they became very quiet and gave him their attention. This is a normal response when one hears another, supposedly an enemy or a foreigner, speak his own tongue. Paul's first line of defense was to identify himself to his audience. He was a Jew. That certainly would have received a positive response among the crowd. He had been born in Tarsus, a major city in the Roman Empire that may have had a population of a half a million. In other words, Paul was no simple rustic from a remote country village. This fact, we can be sure, was not lost on his audience.

He had been "brought up" in Jerusalem (Acts 22:3), another positive mark as far as his audience was concerned. We are not quite sure what Paul had in mind by this statement. Did he mean that he had spent his childhood there, or did he mean that he had come to Jerusalem in order to receive fuller instruction in the law? Either way, his listeners were bound to be pleased.

He had studied under Gamaliel, a highly respected Jewish teacher who had died only a half-dozen years earlier. Gamaliel had been involved in the trial of the apostles (Acts 5:33-39) and had urged restraint in dealing with them. Two things had resulted from his study under this respected teacher: he was thoroughly trained in the law of the fathers, a fact to which some of his Jewish opponents would readily attest. He was also just as zealous for God as any of them. His intensive study of the law had not dampened his zeal but had inflamed it, a result not always evident among scholars.

As evidence of his zeal, Paul pointed out that he had been a persecutor of those who followed the Way, Christians, that is. Since this activity had occurred nearly twenty-five years earlier, not many in the crowd would have known this; they needed this reminder. Nor was Paul's involvement in persecuting Christians a minor one. He was responsible for throwing men and women into prison and even for the execution of some of them. He had readily given his assent to the stoning of Stephen. The high priest and the council could testify to his acts of persecution. They had, after all, provided him letters giving him the authority to go to Damascus and seek out and persecute Christians there.

Paul's Account of His Conversion (6-20)

Luke has preserved for us three accounts of Paul's conversion (Acts 9, 22, and 26). Each of the accounts provides us some details that the others may have omitted. Carrying the letters that gave him the authority to arrest Christians, Paul had hurried toward Damascus. At noon, as he approached the city, a bright light, brighter than the noonday sun, had enveloped him. Falling to the ground, he had heard a voice calling his name, "Saul! Saul! Why do you persecute me?" (Acts 22:7). Paul must have related this in such a dramatic fashion that he held his listener's attention.

The account here and in Acts 9:5 are similar, except in this chapter the Lord identifies himself as "Jesus of Nazareth." This could have been an addition by Paul so that his audience would know exactly who it was. Paul's companions saw the light and heard the sound but did not understand the voice. Paul was then instructed to go into Damascus where he would be instructed about what he should do. Blinded by the brilliant light, his companions had to lead him into the city.

Paul did not give all of the details of his experience in Damascus. For example, he did not tell of his going without food or water for three days. Nor did he tell of Ananias' vision directing him to go to Paul. Paul was giving an abbreviated account of his conversion experience and these details were not essential for his purpose. In mentioning Ananias' visit to him, he did, however, state that he was "a devout observer of the law and highly respected by all the Jews living there" (Acts 22:12). This would reassure his listeners. He didn't mention, however, that Ananias was a Christian. This probably would have immediately alienated his audience if he had mentioned it.

Once Paul had recovered his sight, Ananias relayed to him the message that he had received in his vision. God had chosen Paul to know His will, to see the Righteous One, and to hear His words. Then he was to become a witness to all men of all that he had seen and heard. Even though he did state that he was to become a witness to all men, apparently the Jews listening to Paul did not catch the full implication of what he had said. To them, "all men" simply meant all Jews and did not include Gentiles.

Next, Paul was instructed to arise and be baptized and wash away his sins. In his speech, Paul did not stop and explain baptism for his hearers. It is generally held that the Jews at that time practiced baptism for those who became proselytes to the Jewish faith. We also know that the Essenes performed baptism as a ceremonial washing for sin. Some in Paul's audience may also have known about John's baptism.

In his discourse, Paul then moved from Damascus to Jerusalem, relating a vision he had while praying in the temple. The Lord had warned him to leave Jerusalem at once, for there were those who wanted to kill him. Paul protested, however, insisting that the Jews in Jerusalem knew of his zeal for the law and his actions against Christians. Somehow, he believed that his defense of the law and his persecution of Christians would protect him from the Jews. But the Lord knew better and ordered him to leave Jerusalem and go to the Gentiles.

The Response to Paul's Speech (21, 22)

Up to this point, the Jews had listened to Paul's speech quietly, but one word—*Gentiles*—instantly changed this. Their pent-up anger exploded in a noisy outburst. Whatever else Paul may have wanted to say was lost in their outcry: "Rid the earth of him! He's not fit to live!" (Acts 22:22). We find their behavior shocking. We pride ourselves on being more tolerant, willing to permit others to express their points of view even when they are diametrically opposed to our own. But actually, our supposed tolerance may be indifference. Our own faith may be so shallow that we scarcely feel it worth defending, much less becoming violent about it.

The tragedy of this situation was that their prejudice against the Gentiles, or even any mention of them, prevented them from hearing the rest of Paul's message. Had he been allowed to continue, there is no doubt that he would have conveyed to them the good news of the gospel, the good news that God has offered salvation to all men. Prejudice of any kind exacts a high price, but none higher than the price that these Jews paid.

Paul and His Roman Captors (22:23-30)

The crowd's violent outburst must have caught the Roman commander completely by surprise. Since Paul was speaking in Aramaic, he may not have understood what he was saying. But even if he couldn't understand the words, Paul's manner and tone of voice certainly did not call for such a violent response. It is little wonder that the Jews had a reputation for being a violent people, difficult to rule.

Paul Removed to the Barracks (23-25)

The Jews continued their outburst for some time. To their shouts, they added threatening actions. They took off their cloaks

234

and probably hurled them to the ground. We cannot be certain just what this signified. It may have been a gesture of disgust and outrage. Or they may have been taking off their cloaks in preparation for violent action such as throwing stones, as the Jews had done in the case of Stephen. Then they began to throw dust into the air or perhaps at Paul. Had stones been available, they would probably have used them instead.

Realizing that Paul and his troops were endangered by the mob, the commander ordered Paul to be taken into the barracks. He wisely chose to avoid a confrontation that was certain to be bloody and also difficult to explain to his superiors. Once the commander, his troops, and Paul were safely inside the fortification, he ordered Paul to be flogged. Paul was no stranger to beatings. He had received thirty-nine lashes from the Jews on five different occasions and three times he had been beaten with rods (2 Corinthians 11:24, 25). But flogging was worse than any of these. The instrument used had a short wooden handle, to which was attached from three to nine leather thongs. Pieces of wood, leather, or bone were attached to these thongs so that each blow would rip and tear the skin and flesh. Usually two men, one on each side, administered the flogging. Death often resulted from a severe flogging.

In Paul's case, the purpose of the flogging was to beat the truth out of him. The commander could not understand why Paul's very presence aroused such antagonism among the Jews. He had got no coherent answers from the mob; so he was determined to get them from Paul. Paul was taken out and tied to a post in preparation for flogging. But before the soldiers began their terrible work, Paul appealed to the centurion who was to preside over the beating. Paul's mention that he was a Roman citizen immediately got the attention of the officer. Shocked and disturbed by Paul's claim, he hastened to the commander for further instructions.

The commander lost no time in responding to this information. He knew that he would be in serious trouble if he beat a Roman citizen without a trial. "Tell me, are you a Roman citizen?" he asked of Paul (Acts 22:27). It is apparent from his question that he was skeptical. Paul hardly appeared the part of a Roman citizen. His beating by the mob left him bruised and bleeding, and probably his clothes were torn. Further, the commander knew that he spoke Aramaic, an unlikely skill for a Roman.

Paul's reply that he was a Roman citizen removed some of the commander's skepticism. Of course, Paul could have been lying in order to escape a beating. But while Paul did not carry around with him proof of his citizenship, his claim could readily be checked against the citizenship list of Tarsus. A prisoner was not likely to make a false claim, for this was punishable by death.

A lingering doubt may have led to the commander's response. "I had to pay a big price for my citizenship" (Acts 22:28). Certainly it did not seem likely that Paul, at least as he appeared in his present condition, could have purchased his citizenship. He had been born a citizen. We do not know how Paul gained his citizenship. Perhaps his father or his grandfather had either purchased it or gained it through military service, in which event, this privilege would pass on to his descendants.

This brief exchange brought an immediate response from Paul's captors. Those who had been prepared to beat the truth out of him withdrew immediately, and the commander himself experienced serious concern. Putting Paul in chains and giving the order to have him tortured without ascertaining his citizenship was a serious offense. He realized that if word got to Rome, he might be in considerable trouble. This may explain why later on he went to such lengths to assure Paul's safety.

Paul Before the Sanhedrin (30)

Paul was immediately released from his chains, but he spent the night in the barracks in protective custody. The commander was in a dilemma. He had not been able to learn anything from the crowd that would allow him to make formal charges against Paul. Certainly there was nothing in Paul's brief speech before he was interrupted that would provide a basis for charges. His efforts to interrogate Paul under the threat of the scourge had ended abruptly when Paul had announced his citizenship.

The commander's solution was to convene the Sanhedrin and bring Paul before that group. This seemed the best way out of his dilemma. He could not legally hold Paul without formal charges. Yet to release him might lead to another riot or his assassination, neither of which would have looked good on his record. The next day, he brought Paul down to a session of the Jewish high court.

CHAPTER TWENTY-THREE

In Jeopardy in Jerusalem

Acts 23

Paul Before the Sanhedrin (23:1-11)

Acts 23 opens with Paul standing before the Sanhedrin prepared to speak. This was not a trial, but a hearing to determine what charges, if any, might be laid against Paul. It is likely that there were some preliminaries before Paul was given the opportunity to speak. Luke chose to omit these details from his account. Probably, the commander had begun by asking the Sanhedrin to present their charges. Since the Sanhedrin's charges would be vague and meaningless to the commander, he then turned to Paul for his answer.

Confrontation With the High Priest (1-5)

Paul offered no apologies as he looked the members of the Sanhedrin squarely in the eye and made his reply. Perhaps he was looking for men he might recognize. Although nearly a quarter of a century had passed since he had stood with them against Stephen, it is possible that he knew some of the men. He addressed them as "brothers" (Acts 23:1—in the Greek, it is "men, brothers"). Such a familiar address, though respectful, was hardly the one appropriate for addressing such an august body. This may be a further indication that this was not a formal meeting of the Sanhedrin but an informal hearing in the tower of Antonia. Paul made no apologies for standing before them. He had lived these past twenty-five years "in all good conscience." Whether Paul intended to shock the Sanhedrin or not, his words had that effect.

In what sense had Paul lived "in all good conscience"? First of all, Paul did not intend to suggest that he had lived without sin. Indeed, he readily acknowledged that he was a sinner. The conscience is a monitor that tells us to do what our mind tells us is right. Sometimes, however, our mind makes a decision about the rightness or wrongness of a situation without all the facts, or it approaches the facts with a bias. As a result, our judgment about what is right or wrong is in error. In urging us to an erroneous judgment, our conscience can lead us far astray. This was the situation in which Paul had found himself. Trained as a Pharisee, his judgment had told him that Stephen and other Christians were wrong and deserved to die. At the urging of his conscience, Paul had given his consent to the murder of Stephen. But he was quite wrong in so doing. Paul's judgment told him that Christians in Damascus should be sought out and imprisoned. In obedience to his conscience, then, he set out to do exactly that.

Later, after Paul had become a Christian, his judgment told him that he should honor Christ. Following his conscience, he did just that. Further, revelation from God informed him that he should take the gospel to the Gentiles. Once more, Paul had followed his conscience. This time, he was right in following his conscience.

One's conscience is not a safe guide for conduct. Not only can it be led astray by false information or wrong judgments, it can become seared so that it no longer serves as an alert watchman. One can destroy a nerve ending by burning it or by pricking it with a pin. So mistreated, the nerve ending no longer sends its message of warning to the brain. In a similar fashion, one can destroy his conscience by repeatedly disregarding its messages. So treated, a conscience loses its sensitivity and no longer performs its proper function. (See 1 Timothy 4:2; Titus 1:15.)

The high priest purported to be outraged by Paul's response and ordered one of the guards to strike him in the mouth. Nothing better demonstrates his arrogance and cruelty than this act. He was upset by being called out to preside over such a session, and he was further angered because Paul was not in the least intimidated by the whole proceedings. Ananias was accustomed to having people come before him cringing, bowing, and scraping. But Paul stood before him and spoke with calm assurance. Paul was accountable only to God and did not have to ingratiate himself to this human court.

Paul's response was quick in coming. "God will strike you, you whitewashed wall!" (Acts 23:3). Some have been shocked by the force of his reply. After all, they say, when Jesus stood before this court, He didn't speak out against His persecutors, but He was

238

"as a lamb dumb before his shearers." We need to realize, however, that Paul was not concerned at that moment in defending himself. He was quite willing to suffer and die for his faith if necessary. He was, rather, defending a principle. His concern was that the gospel get a fair and honest hearing, a hearing that would not be prejudiced by the arrogant actions of the high priest. As a defender of the faith, Paul had every right to challenge the illegal actions of Ananias.

We need also to realize that Jesus did not always behave as a meek lamb. The money changers scurrying from the temple to escape His wrath would hardly have characterized Him as meek! And He used language quite similar to Paul's in denouncing the hypocrisy of the Pharisees. "You are like whitewashed tombs," Jesus said, "which look beautiful on the outside but on the inside are full of dead men's bones" (Matthew 23:27). Both Paul and Jesus used this expression to point up the hypocrisy of the persons they were denouncing.

Something else is worth noting in Paul's reply. Knowingly or otherwise, Paul's condemnation of the high priest was prophetic. Ananias was one of the worst high priests who ever occupied the office. He had a reputation for being greedy, cheating both the people and the lower priests under him. He was also accused by the people of being a collaborator with the Romans. When the Jews rebelled against Rome in A.D. 66, he was sought out and assassinated by Jewish patriots.

Those standing near Paul were shocked at his boldness. Though their rebuke came as a question, it was a rebuke nevertheless. "You dare to insult God's high priest?" (Acts 23:4). Paul's response that he did not know that Ananias was the high priest has led to several different interpretations. Some hold that since this was not a formal meeting of the Sanhedrin and Ananias was not wearing his formal regalia, Paul really did not know who he was. This hardly seems likely because in the course of the meeting, it would soon have become obvious that Ananias was presiding. Others feel that Paul spoke rashly in condemning the high priest and was offering a kind of an apology. Another view is that Paul spoke sarcastically. The high priest's behavior in ordering Paul struck was so contrary to proper behavior that no one would recognize that he was the high priest.

Regardless of what Paul intended to imply in his response, he was quick to affirm his respect for the office of high priest. This respect was based upon the teachings of Scripture, probably Exodus 22:28. In referring to this passage, which would certainly have been familiar to the Jewish leaders, Paul was indicating that he had not abandoned his belief in the Mosaic law.

The Sanhedrin Divided (6-10)

At this point in his hearing, Paul took a different tack. Either from his experience with the Sanhedrin twenty-five years earlier or from comments he had heard during the meeting, he realized that some members of the council were Pharisees and some were Sadducees. He identified himself as a Pharisee. In what sense was he a Pharisee? Certainly not in the sense that he was a hypocrite or a narrow legalist. He did share with the Pharisees their reverence for the Scriptures and their concern for obeying the teachings of the Scriptures. These attitudes would not bring him into conflict with his Christian faith. He could have argued that in becoming a Christian, he was simply carrying out the teachings of the Scriptures in a higher and nobler sense than that in which the Pharisees had understood these teachings.

The most significant point of agreement that he shared with the Pharisees was the belief in the resurrection of the dead. Paul also knew that the Sadducees rejected any such belief. While Paul may not have anticipated the outcome of his injecting this doctrine into the discussion, he certainly knew that it would be controversial. Since it was obvious that he was not going to get a fair hearing from the Sanhedrin, he chose to divert the pressure from himself by raising the issue. This tactic worked because immediately, a dispute broke out between the two parties. The Pharisees, as a result of Paul's statement, looked more favorably upon him, while the Sadducees despised him all the more.

The differences between the Sadducees and the Pharisees went beyond their disagreement over the question of the resurrection of the dead. The Sadducees also rejected a belief in angels and spirits. Beyond these doctrinal differences lay other matters that seriously divided the two groups. The Sadducees were the political rulers and usually worked with the hated Romans. Further, the Sadducees lived quite worldly lives, paying little attention to the minutia of the law that so held the attention of the Pharisees.

Before long, the whole assembly was in an uproar. Some of the "teachers of the law" (literally, "scribes"—Acts 23:9) came to Paul's defense. When it came to the matter of the resurrection and the belief in angels and spirits, the Pharisees agreed with Paul. This turn of events gives us a clue about the intensity of the feelings between the Sadducees and the Pharisees. So bitter were they against one another that they could not even remain united against Paul, whom they considered a common enemy. So far as we know, Paul had said nothing before this assembly about angels. However, we need to understand that Luke has given us only a summary of the meeting. Paul may actually have mentioned something about angels. Or they may have had reference to Paul's speech the day before on the steps of the Tower of Antonia. In that speech, Paul had mentioned the appearance of the Lord to him both on the road to Damascus and later in Jerusalem.

If the Sadducees and Pharisees had been given time to prepare their case against Paul (as they had in the case of Jesus' trial), they might have agreed to bury their differences and present a common front against Paul. But the hurried call of the Roman commander for a hearing did not leave them time to get their act together. These factional differences continued to plague the Jews. A decade later, even when they were in a life-and-death struggle in a rebellion against Rome, they often dissipated their strength in fighting among themselves.

As the verbal strife turned to physical shoving and pulling, Paul was caught in the middle with one group trying to attack him and the other trying to defend him. The commander, apparently watching the situation from above, began to fear for Paul's life. Seeing the danger, he quickly sent soldiers down into the room to rescue him and bring him back into the safety of the barracks.

Reassurance From the Lord (11)

The commander had called the Sanhedrin together for a hearing in order to have a basis for charges against Paul. But the hearing had ended in a brawl, and the commander knew no more about Paul than he had before. It was obvious to him, however, that Paul's life was endangered by the antagonism of the Jews. He had little choice but to lodge Paul in the Tower for his own safety.

That night, as Paul lay in his cell, wondering what his fate might be, the Lord stood beside him. "Take courage!" Jesus told him. "As you have testified about me in Jerusalem, so you must also testify in Rome" (Acts 23:11). Paul needed these words, not because he feared for his life, but because he was perplexed about how all these things would turn out. For a long time, Paul had wanted to carry the gospel to Rome, but he had been thwarted in this. Here he received the assurance of the Lord that he would indeed see Rome. In spite of the cuts and bruises he had suffered from the mob and from the Sanhedrin, he must have slept well the rest of that night. The Lord did not tell him all the things that he would have to suffer before he reached Rome—imprisonment, further hearings, shipwreck. All of us can be thankful that the Lord does not reveal to us the many things the future holds in store for us. He knows that that would be a burden heavier than most of us would want to try to bear.

The Plot to Kill Paul (23:12-22)

If the Jews were anything, they were persistent. It is difficult for us to imagine just how bitter they were in their feelings toward Paul, especially over a theological matter. Perhaps our problem is that most of us today don't take theology all that seriously. Some of these Jews were not content just to sit around and complain about the situation. They decided to take matters into their own hands. More than forty of them agreed to an oath (literally, the Greek reads that they "cursed themselves" or "put themselves under a curse"—Acts 23:12). They pledged neither to eat nor drink until they had killed Paul. This aspect of their oath indicated that they intended to accomplish their purpose within a matter of hours.

The Plot Hatched (12-15)

With forty men fanatically committed to Paul's death, the plotters had a good chance of success. They needed only a way to get close enough to Paul to carry out their deed, but at this point, they required help. For this reason, they went to the "chief priests and elders" (Acts 23:14) with their scheme. It seems reasonable to suppose that these leaders were all Sadducees, since the Pharisees had sought to protect Paul. The fact that these men were even willing to listen to this plot, which was both immoral and illegal, tells us something about the character of Jewish leadership at that point in history. It is little wonder that within a decade, they had brought the wrath of the Romans down upon the whole nation.

The plot was simple enough. They needed only a way to get Paul out of the barracks and out of the Tower of Antonia. The leaders were to ask the commander to bring Paul to their chambers for another hearing. This request would seem reasonable

242

enough to the commander. Then, as Paul was being brought to the hearing, he would be attacked along the way. The Sanhedrin met in a part of the city some distance from the Tower; so Paul would have to be brought through narrow and twisting streets to get him there. There were several places along the route that would have afforded excellent spots for an ambush. Even if the Roman soldiers surrounded him, they could not protect him completely. Of course, in any such attack, the Romans could be expected to give a good account of themselves, but these assassins were quite willing to accept casualties in their efforts to get at Paul.

It sounded like a perfect deal for the leaders. Here was their chance to get rid of Paul without being directly involved. Their hands would not hold the bloody daggers, and they could plead innocence if they were ever questioned later. Thus, they gave their consent to the plot.

The Plot Detected (16-22)

The plot required absolute secrecy, and this is where the scheme went awry. In some fashion, Paul's nephew learned of the plot and immediately brought this word to Paul. Although Paul was in the protective custody of the Romans, he was not officially charged with any crime; so he was free to have visitors. This reference to Paul's sister raises some interesting questions. This is the only clear reference we have to his family, leading to the assumption that he had been rejected by them.

It is assumed by some that Paul's sister lived in Jerusalem, but that is only an assumption. Is it possible that his nephew was in Jerusalem as a student as Paul had been many years before? Or is it possible that he had come to observe Pentecost and had remained because of Paul's imprisonment? To these questions and others we have no answers, only speculations. The Greek word applied to Paul's nephew usually means a young man from twenty to forty years old; so he was not a young boy.

As soon as the young man had explained the situation to his uncle, Paul called one of the centurions and asked that his nephew be taken to the commander. Realizing now that Paul was a Roman citizen, the centurion immediately did as he was asked. The commander took the young man by the hand to reassure him and led him aside to insure privacy. The commander seemed to sense the importance of the situation and gave it his serious attention.

Paul's nephew related to the commander what he had earlier told Paul. The Jews, that is, some of the Jewish leaders, had conceived a plot to assassinate Paul. After what the commander had just seen of these men, he had no trouble believing the story. These men had, even in judicial proceedings, shown a remarkable lack of restraint and fairness. Under these conditions, the warning not to give in to their request to bring Paul before the Sanhedrin was unnecessary. The commander knew very well what kind of people he was dealing with. After the commander had heard the young man's story, he dismissed him with a warning to tell no one about the situation. The commander may already have had in mind what he would do, but he wisely chose not to reveal any of his plans to Paul's nephew. His life would certainly have been endangered had the plotters learned of his visit to the prison. The less he knew of the Romans' plans, the better off he would be.

One might raise an interesting question at this point. The Lord had already informed Paul that He would stand by his side and protect him and that he would have the opportunity to witness in Rome. Why did Paul bother to take any precautions to protect his life? Even though the Lord had promised to protect Paul, this did not necessarily mean that He would use miraculous measures to do so. It is reasonable to believe that the Lord used human agencies—Paul's nephew and the Roman commander—to help accomplish His ultimate purpose. God does not have to use extraordinary means to accomplish His will when ordinary means will serve the same purpose. Just because God wills something does not mean that human responsibility ends.

Paul Transferred to Caesarea (23:23-35)

The commander may have been negligent in giving permission for Paul to be scourged without checking to find out whether he was a Roman citizen. But once he learned who Paul was, he certainly could not have been charged with negligence in protecting him. With the decisiveness that came from military experience, he quickly made plans to meet the problem.

The Commander's Plan (23, 24)

It did not take the commander long to weigh his options. He could have given in to the Jews' request, realizing that Paul would probably be murdered. This might have been the easy way out. It was the way Pilate took when Jesus was on trial before him. But

244

the man's sense of duty would not permit this. He might also have kept Paul under arrest until he had more information about him. But this would have allowed the Jews the opportunity to plan other assassination attempts. The best solution was to get Paul out of town as soon as possible. This had the added advantage of relieving the commander of any further responsibility in the situation.

Two centurions, each commanding a hundred men, were assigned to the task. In addition, seventy horsemen and two hundred spearmen were also assigned to the task force. This constituted a small army, a rather formidable force just to protect one man. But the commander was taking no chances. He knew the Jews well enough to suspect that the conspiracy against Paul might be extensive. By acting quickly and by using an overwhelming force, he believed that he might thwart any attempt against Paul's life. This group was to leave at the third hour, that is, nine at night, after it was completely dark. Operating at night, the Romans would have the added advantage of secrecy, since it would have been impossible to hide the operations of so many soldiers during the daylight hours. One wonders how the soldiers may have felt about being called out on a night operation like this, especially after having been on duty all day.

The Commander's Letter to Governor Felix (25-30)

The commander, Claudius Lysias, sent a letter to Felix, the governor, giving an explanation of the situation. In the letter, Lysias put his own actions in the best possible light and also cleverly passed the buck to the governor. Lysias presented himself as having saved the life of a Roman citizen from a Jewish mob. He omitted the fact that at the time of the rescue, he did not know that Paul was a Roman citizen. Nor did he tell Felix that he had given permission for Paul to be scourged without even trying to find out whether he was a Roman citizen.

Lysias did accurately report the legal situation. The Jews brought no charges against Paul that were worthy of death or even imprisonment. The Jews' charges had to do with religion and their own law, matters about which Lysias knew little. Still, he knew enough about what they were charging to know that none of the accusations had any standing in the eyes of Roman law. Then he told of the plot against Paul's life, which was the real reason for sending Paul to Felix. He concluded by stating that he had ordered his accusers to present their case before Felix. Actually, this latter statement was not true at the time he wrote the letter, but by the time Felix received the letter, Lysias would have given the order to the accusers.

Paul Taken to Caesarea (31-35)

During the night, the soldiers took Paul as far as Antipatris. This town was more than thirty miles from Jerusalem, and the road led through rough, mountainous terrain. Even under daylight conditions, this would not have been an easy march. Fortunately, Paul was provided a mount, either a horse or a donkey; so he didn't have to walk (Acts 23:24). If the Jews had planned an attack against the Romans, the most likely place would have been along this road. From Antipatris on to Caesarea, the road ran through the coastal plain and thus was level. There the cavalry could provide adequate protection for Paul, and the foot soldiers returned to Jerusalem.

Once the troops arrived in Caesarea, they delivered Paul and the letter to Felix. Having read the letter, Felix inquired about what province Paul was from. This may have been a routine question to determine whether Felix had jurisdiction over Paul. Since Paul was from Tarsus in Cilicia, Felix could handle the case. Paul was then lodged in Herod's palace until his accusers arrived for the trial. This large palace had been built by Herod the Great in about 10 B.C. and was later taken over by the Romans as the residence and administrative center for the governor. Paul was kept in one of the prison cells in this complex.

CHAPTER TWENTY-FOUR

On Trial in Caesarea

Acts 24

Paul's Case Presented Before the Governor (24:1-21)

Paul was back in Caesarea, a city he had passed through only a few days earlier as he made his way up to Jerusalem. The prophecy that Agabus had uttered in Caesarea that Paul would be seized by the Jews and turned over to the Romans had literally been fulfilled. Felix had assured Paul that his rights as a Roman citizen would be respected and that he would get a trial. But even though Paul did get his hearing, the wheels of justice ground slowly, and Paul stayed in jail in Caesarea for two years.

The Case Against Paul (1-9)

We can imagine the disappointment of the Jews when they learned that Paul had escaped their plot and was now safely lodged in prison in Caesarea. Apparently, Lysias informed them of this situation and also informed them that any trial of Paul would be held there, not in Jerusalem. It would take them a day or two to get ready to make the trip and the trip itself would take two or three days, depending on whether they walked or rode horseback. Thus, after five days (Acts 24:1), Ananias along with some of the elders and Tertullus, a lawyer, arrived in Caesarea and prepared to plead their case against Paul. The fact that the high priest himself made his trip and lent his prestige to the arguments against Paul indicates how serious he thought Paul's offenses were.

Tertullus is called a lawyer. This word may also be translated "orator." These men were noted for their eloquence and were often employed in court cases with the hope that their sophisticated manner and eloquence would be persuasive with the judges. Some have argued that since Tertullus is a Roman name, he must have been a Roman, employed because he could plead the case in

Latin before the Roman governor. However, there is no indication that Latin was used in the trial, nor was there any necessity to do so, because it seems obvious that Felix spoke Greek as well as Latin.

Tertullus opened his case with a few statements of fulsome praise of Felix. This was in keeping with the usual rhetorical practices of the time. Both Tertullus and Felix knew that his words were flattery, either lies or half-truths. For example, the "long period of peace" that he mentioned (Acts 24:2) was only partially true. Felix had put down several bands of robbers, but he had done so with such a heavy hand that he had aroused new antagonisms. Tacitus, a Roman historian, wrote that "with savagery and lust he exercised the powers of a king with the disposition of a slave." His corrupt nature was evidenced by his effort to extract a bribe for Paul's release. Even the Romans finally came to recognize his evil ways and removed him from office two years after this.

Once Tertullus had concluded his flattering introduction, he turned to the charges against Paul. He had a weak case, and he obviously knew it, but with the skill of a trained lawyer, he tried to make the best of it. While Luke gives us only the gist of the case he presented, three distinct charges emerge.

First of all, Paul was accused of being a disturber of the peace "all over the world" (Acts 24:5), that is, the Roman Empire. A clever lawyer could point to disturbances in Antioch of Pisidia, Lystra, Philippi, Thessalonica, Corinth, and Ephesus (Acts 13:50, 51; 14:19; 16:16-24; 17:5-9; 18:12-17; and 19:23-41) that seemed to follow wherever Paul went. Of course, a shrewd lawyer trying to make a case would conveniently leave out the fact that angry Jews had caused nearly all of these disturbances by attacking Paul.

The second charge was that he was a "ringleader of the Nazarene sect" (Acts 24:5). The word translated "ringleader" means one who is a military leader or commander. This term was hardly appropriate when applied to Paul since he was a missionary and preacher, not the leader of the church. James or Peter might more accurately be described by this term. This charge, if it could be made to stick, would be a serious one. The Romans had experienced considerable trouble with rebel bands in Palestine. Lysias, who may have had some personal experience fighting some of these groups, at first mistook Paul for an Egyptian who had led a group of renegades in a bloody uprising against the Romans. The Romans, who were sticklers for law and order, would be quick to act against anyone who seemed to pose a threat to their rule.

Interestingly, this is the only time in the Scriptures that the term Nazarene is applied to Christians. It is used several times in the Gospels in reference to Jesus (cf. Mark 16:6; Matthew 2:24). Judaism was recognized as a legal religion by the Romans. If Tertullus could convince Felix that Paul was not really a Jew but the leader of an illegal sect, then he could be charged with violating the Roman laws governing religions.

The third charge against Paul was that he had tried to desecrate the temple. Originally, the Asian Jews had charged that Paul had actually brought Trophimus, a Gentile, into the temple, a clear case of desecration. Since this charge was false and could not be proved, Tertullus only charged him with attempting to desecrate the temple. According to Tertullus' account, the Jews arrested Paul as he was about to carry out this act. Of course, this was not really the case. The Jewish mob had pounced upon Paul and would have killed him had not the Romans come to his rescue.

In the New International Version, the latter part of verse 6, verse 7, and part of verse 8 are omitted from Acts 24 because they are not contained in the better manuscripts. The footnote carries these words: "and wanted to judge him according to our law. But the commander, Lysias, came and with the use of much force snatched him from our hands and ordered his accusers to come before you." If these omitted verses were actually the words of Tertullus, he was certainly guilty of some perverted reasoning. He cleverly shifted the blame for the riot in the temple from the Jews who were about to lynch Paul to Lysias, who is accused of police brutality.

The Jewish leaders who had come to Caesarea to press charges against Paul agreed with the testimony of Tertullus. They certainly must have known that the statements he had made were not true. But people who would be willing to collaborate in the assassination of Paul would have few qualms about committing perjury against him. With such corrupt religious leaders heading their nation, it is little wonder that the Jews were at that point in history plunging headlong toward destruction that saw its culmination in the destruction of Jerusalem in A.D. 70. The words of the ancient prophet, "Like people, like priest," were never more true (Hosea 4:9).

Paul's Response to the Charges (10-21)

The Jews undoubtedly brought detailed testimony to substantiate their charges. Luke has given us only a brief summary of their testimony. Once this testimony had been completed, Felix motioned for Paul to begin his defense. Paul had had no advanced warning about the charges that the Jews might bring against him. With no time to prepare his defense, no battery of consultants to aid him, and no eloquent speaker to plead his case, Paul had to take the stand. But more important than any of these to his defense, Paul had the assurance that the Lord was standing by him. In addition to the Lord's general promise to all Christians that He would give them "words and wisdom" when they were on trial (Luke 21:14, 15), Paul had the specific assurance from the Lord that he would eventually see Rome.

Paul opened his defense by a statement of fact about Felix, not a bit of eloquent flattery. Paul could honestly state that he was glad to make his defense before Felix because the governor had had many years of experience in dealing with the Jewish people. He knew that they were a stubborn, aggressive people to deal with. He also had become acquainted with their devious ways. Paul knew that he had a better chance of a fair trial under such a person.

Paul met the first charge head-on. He had gone up to Jerusalem only twelve days before. Paul's chronology presents some difficulty, but he probably meant that only twelve days had elapsed from the time that he had left Caesarea to go up to Jerusalem and his arrest and return to Caesarea. He did not include the five days he had spent in prison in Caesarea awaiting his trial. Paul's point was that during that time he had not engaged in any public disputes either in the temple or in the synagogues. He challenged anyone to prove that he had. The Jews had no witnesses to support their charges in this matter, and Paul wanted to make that point very clear to Felix. He did not even mention the charge that he had stirred up trouble "all over the world." No proof had been presented for this charge, and, besides, such activities, even if they had occurred, were beyond the jurisdiction of Felix. Paul concentrated on the charge that he had been a troublemaker in Jerusalem.

Paul did admit that he was a follower of the Way, which Tertullus had contemptuously referred to as the "Nazarene sect." Paul might very well have reminded Felix that the Sadducees and the Pharisees were also considered sects. Paul insisted that he believed everything that agrees with the Law and the Prophets, that is, the Old Testament Scriptures. What he did not mention was that he did not necessarily accept all of the interpretations that later generations had added on. Of course, this was Jesus' contention also, and it brought Him into frequent conflict with the Jewish teachers and leaders. What Paul did not state but certainly believed was that Christianity was the logical culmination of the teachings of the Scriptures.

A proper understanding of the Scriptures led to the hope in God of the resurrection of the righteous and the wicked. There had to be a touch of irony in Paul's statement that "these men" shared this belief (Acts 24:15). Paul may have intended the statement in a general sense that Jews generally held to a belief in the resurrection. Also, some of the Jewish leaders present at his trial may have been Pharisees, who did share this belief with Paul. But others were Sadducees, who denied this belief. Perhaps Paul was subtly suggesting that the Sadducees, who denied the resurrection, were really the heretics, not he.

Paul concluded this part of his defense by affirming that he had always strived to keep his conscience clear before God. This certainly should be the way one lives if he believes in the resurrection both of the righteous and the wicked. Do the worldly lives of many church members today reveal the fact that they really don't believe in such a resurrection?

After this statement, Paul turned his attention to the third charge, that he had tried to profane the temple. He stated that his purpose in coming to Jerusalem after many years' absence was to bring gifts to the poor and to make offerings. The gifts were the collection that he had made from the churches during his third missionary journey and which he and his companions had brought to Jerusalem. The offerings may have referred to any offerings he had intended to bring as a part of the Feast of Pentecost or specifically to the offerings he had presented on behalf of the four who had taken the Nazirite vow.

Paul had originally been charged with bringing a Gentile, Trophimus, into the part of the temple forbidden to Gentiles. But since this charge was completely groundless, Tertullus had not brought it up, preferring instead to make a more vague charge. Paul met this charge by pointing out that he had been ceremonially clean when he had gone into the temple. Further, there had been no crowd with him in the temple, nor had he created any disturbance. He insisted that the Jews from Asia, who had originally made the charge, should have been there to present it in person. Since they were not there, the implication by Paul was that there was no basis for their charge. Paul's present accusers were not eyewitnesses to the events in the temple that led to the charge against him; so their testimony was secondhanded. The only thing they could testify about was the court proceedings. But a violent disagreement had broken out between the Pharisees and the Sadducees before any decision was reached. Felix was aware of this of course, because of Lysias' letter, but Paul reminded him of it to show how flimsy were the charges against him.

Then Paul mentioned the thing that had precipitated the sharp dissension in the meeting of the Sanhedrin. Paul had raised the question whether he was being tried for his belief in the resurrection. This had immediately brought the Pharisees to Paul's defense and aroused the antagonism of the Sadducees. Since the resurrection was the bone of contention, Paul was challenging the Jews to prove that this doctrine was wrong and that his belief in it made him a troublemaker.

Felix Postpones His Decision (24:22-27)

Felix readily saw that the Jews had no case against Paul. The only way that justice could have been served was to have released Paul. But Felix, who already was unpopular with the Jews, did not wish to antagonize them further by freeing him. So he sought a way out of his dilemma.

The Trial Adjourned (22, 23)

Felix had more than a passing understanding of Christianity. His several years in Samaria and Judea had given him an opportunity to learn about the Way. As a governor, he had an interest in keeping abreast of the religion and political activities of the people. It was especially important that he be aware of religious activities about the Jews, because their religion and politics were so intertwined.

Instead of making a decision on the spot, Felix chose to postpone it, hoping that the Jews would go back to Jerusalem and forget the matter. We also know that he had another reason for not releasing Paul immediately. He hoped to extract a bribe from Paul. The pretext he gave for postponing his decision was that he wanted to await the arrival of Lysias. That this was a pretext is obvious, since so far as we know, Lysias never did come to Caesarea.

Paul was then turned over to a centurion, probably the head of the prison, for safekeeping. However, he was not thrown into the dungeon and treated like a common criminal. Perhaps Paul's Roman citizenship spared him this fate. He was given some freedom, which probably means that he was not chained to a guard. His friends were also allowed to visit him and minister to his needs. Prison accommodations and fare were hardly luxurious, and it is likely that Paul's friends brought him food and other items that would make his stay in jail less burdensome. Luke had accompanied Paul to Jerusalem, and we can be sure that he soon rejoined him in Caesarea. It is reasonable also to suppose that Philip and other brothers in Caesarea also visited him.

Private Hearing With Felix (24-26)

After "several days" (Acts 24:24)—perhaps after Paul's Jewish accusers had returned to Jerusalem—Felix sent for Paul to learn more about the Christian faith. Some texts indicate that this meeting was initiated by Drusilla. She was a Jewess, the younger daughter of Herod Agrippa I and a sister of Herod Agrippa II. When Drusilla, who was famous for her beauty, was fifteen, her brother arranged a marriage between her and the king of Edesa, a petty state in Syria. A few months later, Felix used a Cypriote magician to persuade her to leave her husband and become his wife, thus becoming his third wife.

Paul was not reluctant to use this opportunity to speak to the governor and his wife. Perhaps they had only an intellectual curiosity about Christianity, but Paul had no intentions of keeping his discussion on a strictly academic level. Paul may have been tempted to talk in glittering generalities about innocuous pleasantries, but he was not given to such compromises even when it might have led to his early release. Christianity deals with the great eternal truths, and among these are "righteousness, self-control and the judgment to come" (Acts 24:25). At some point, Paul had to confront these issues, and when he did, they were most painful to Felix.

Knowing what we do about the life of Felix, it should not surprise us that he felt more than slight discomfort at Paul's words. Like many people today, he had enough conscience left to feel convicted by the hearing of the Word. Yet he lacked the strength of character to do what he knew that he should do. Many pagan religions were simply systems designed to allow the devotee to appease the wrath of whatever gods he might worship. Morality was not a part of these religions. But since Jehovah God is a righteous God, those who would follow Him must display righteousness in their own lives.

Not only had the life of Felix lacked righteousness, it had also shown the lack of self-control. It is obvious that Felix was one who pursued his personal lusts without any particular concern for righteousness. One whose life is out of control has every reason to fear the coming judgment. Paul touched on the subject of the final judgment on several occasions in his preaching and his writings (Acts 17:31; Romans 2:16; 14:10, 12; 2 Corinthians 5:10; Ephesians 6:8).

Confronted by the claims of a righteous God, Felix was visibly moved by Paul's message. At such a point in one's life, he has but two choices. He may surrender to God's Word, or he may harden his heart against it. This latter action may take two forms. One may openly and even violently reject the Word, or he may attempt to postpone his decision. Felix took this second route. He promised to send for Paul at a more convenient time. How often we have heard sinners pursue this escape route! How could any time be more convenient than the present? Postponing a decision allows one to escape for the moment the demands of the gospel, but in the process, it also blunts the sensitive feelings of the conscience. If this course is followed often enough and long enough, the conscience becomes deadened to future appeals. Apparently, that is what happened to Felix. Although Felix frequently sent for Paul and talked with him, yet that convenient season never came. We are not told how Drusilla felt about the matter, but it would seem that she shared her husband's sentiments.

It would appear that the main reason Felix sought to talk with Paul was to elicit a bribe from him for his release (Acts 24:26). Of course, such a bribe would have been a violation of Roman law, but at the same time, such actions were common among public officials. Since the charges against Paul were insufficient to hold him according to the law, Felix would not have to answer to the Romans for releasing him. We wonder why Felix thought Paul would pay a bribe or, for that matter, where Paul would get the money to pay a bribe. Certainly there was nothing about Paul to suggest that he had any sizable sums of money at his disposal. Perhaps Felix thought Christians might be willing to raise money to have their leader set free.

Festus Succeeds Felix (27)

After two years, Felix was recalled by the Roman government. His brother, Pallas, who had enjoyed a prominent position in the Roman government, had fallen into disfavor with Nero, who was now the emperor. The Jews brought many charges of cruelty and corruption against Felix, and with his brother no longer in a position to defend him, Felix was recalled and banished to Gaul. In his effort to curry favor with the Jews, Felix kept Paul in prison even though he knew that he was innocent of any wrong-doing.

We have no word of Paul's activities during this two-year period. It is reasonable to suppose that he was granted some privileges. We can be sure that the church in Caesarea ministered to him, and we can also be certain that Paul helped strengthen the faith of Philip and the other Caesarean Christians. Other church leaders in Palestine, including some of the apostles, may also have visited him. Luke remained with Paul during this period, and many feel that he used this time to interview witnesses and gather other information that he would use in writing the Gospel of Luke. These two years may also have given him an opportunity to collect and edit the material that would become the book of Acts.

Felix was succeeded by Porcius Festus, who must have arrived in Palestine about A.D. 60 or 61. We know little about Festus, but from what little we know, it is apparent that he was a capable administrator. He sought to clear up all of the unfinished business and right some of the wrongs that Felix had left behind. Paul's case might not have appeared to him to have been all that important, but when he visited Jerusalem, the religious leaders quickly let him know that it was important as far as they were concerned. For this reason it was given a prominent position on Festus' agenda.

CHAPTER TWENTY-FIVE

On Trial Before Festus

Acts 25

A new administrator usually takes some time to examine and evaluate his situation before making any decisions. Among other things, he confers with as many people as he can, especially leaders with whom he will have to work. It was for this reason that Festus made a trip to Jerusalem and heard the pleas of the religious leaders.

Meeting With the Jewish Leaders (25:1-5)

Among the first things Festus did as governor was to make a courtesy call on the religious leaders in Jerusalem. This allowed him to become acquainted with the men who wielded a great deal of influence among the people. There certainly must have been several serious problems that they needed to discuss with the new governor. For example, a group of vicious bandits known as Sicarii had been ravaging the land, looting and murdering everywhere they went. But this was not the issue they brought up.

These religious leaders had long memories. Religious hatreds have a way of keeping memories inflamed. Their immediate concern was not the bandits or other problems that might seem equally pressing, but the apostle Paul, safely locked in prison in Caesarea. So desperate were they to get at Paul that they asked Festus to send for him at once and bring him to Jerusalem for trial. They may have supposed that Festus knew nothing about the case and would ignorantly accede to their wishes. Of course, their real purpose was not to bring Paul to Jerusalem for a trial but that they might have another chance to assassinate him. Festus had no inkling of their plot, but he was probably shrewd enough to see that their eagerness to get Paul to Jerusalem had ulterior motives. Perhaps the same zealous forty that had previously taken an oath to murder Paul were ready to take that oath again. But they did not allow for God, who had already promised that Paul would eventually reach Rome. God did not need a miracle to accomplish His purpose. A Roman governor would serve just as well.

Festus was quite willing to hear their charges against Paul, but it would be in Caesarea, not in Jerusalem. Festus had no desire to prolong his stay in Jerusalem, and a trial there would have required this. Further, he may have known that Paul was a Roman citizen and that, as a result, the Jewish Sanhedrin had no jurisdiction over him. The Jews had little choice but to accept Festus' decision. They might have aroused his suspicions had they protested too strongly. So several of them accompanied Festus back to Caesarea.

Another Trial at Caesarea (25:6-12)

By all rights, Paul should have been freed immediately after his first trial under Felix. But since Paul was not living under a constitution that prohibited double jeopardy, he had to face his accusers again. Luke did not provide a detailed account of the charges brought against Paul, but it is reasonable to assume that they were similar to those Tertullus had brought in the first hearing. Paul had been accused of being a rabble-rouser, of being a leader of a dangerous sect, and of desecrating the temple. These would certainly have been serious enough charges, had they been true, but just as at the first trial, there was no proof for them.

Once more, Paul was called upon to defend himself on short notice. But because he was innocent, he had no trouble presenting an adequate defense. Paul had not broken either the laws of the Jews or the laws of the Romans. Festus apparently was convinced that Paul was telling the truth and knew that the charges were trumped up. Yet he was also a shrewd politician and he did not want to start out his term of office by offending the Jews. Therefore, he turned to Paul and asked him if he would be willing to go to Jerusalem to stand trial. Paul knew of the previous plot against him; so even though he didn't have any direct evidence that the plot had been renewed, he knew the Jews well enough to suspect as much. But had Paul revealed his suspicions about the Jews' plans in their presence, he may very well have endangered the life of his nephew. He therefore chose another way to avoid Jerusalem. He appealed to Caesar, a right that he had as a Roman citizen.

This was not exactly the turn of events that Festus had anticipated. Quickly, he conferred with his council. This council was probably composed of advisors and lawyers who could provide him information on the finer points of the law. They did not have to discuss the matter at any great lengths before Festus saw that Paul's appeal gave the governor a perfect out. He knew Paul was innocent, and yet to release him would offend the Jews. However, by sending him on to Rome, he could be rid of the problem without angering the Jews. And so to Rome Paul would go!

Festus' Consultation With Agrippa (25:13-27)

Agrippa, often referred to as Agrippa II to distinguish him from his father, Agrippa I, was the great grandson of Herod the Great. Because he had found favor with both Emperor Claudius and Emperor Nero, he had been granted rule over an extensive territory. He had two sisters, Drusilla (the wife of Felix) and Bernice. Rumors persisted that he lived for several years in an incestuous relationship with Bernice. Like his father before him, he had the right to appoint the high priests. As a result, he had considerable knowledge of the inner workings of Jewish ecclesiastical politics. It was perhaps for this reason that Festus called on him for advice about Paul.

Paul's Case Explained (13-22)

As was appropriate, Agrippa (accompanied by Bernice) made a state call upon the new governor. The occasion of this visit provided Festus with a possible solution to a problem he faced. Paul had appealed to Caesar, and when Festus sent him on to Rome, he would need to have some explanation of the charges lodged against him. Even though he had heard the testimony of the Jewish leaders against Paul, he was certainly not clear in his own mind just exactly what laws Paul had violated. He felt, no doubt, that Agrippa, with his inside knowledge of the Jewish religion, would be able to provide some help.

Festus explained to Agrippa how that Paul had been left in prison by Felix. He also told how the chief priests and the elders wanted Paul executed. Festus had turned down this request because, as a Roman, Paul had a right to a fair trial. In court, the Jewish leaders had presented their case against Paul, but as far as Festus was concerned, they were not able to prove anything against Paul. Instead, they had argued about some of the finer points of their religion and about Jesus, who Paul had said was raised from the dead. Festus went on to tell Agrippa how he had asked Paul to stand trial in Jerusalem, but that Paul had refused, demanding instead that he be heard by Caesar.

Once he had received this explanation of the case, Agrippa expressed his willingness to hear Paul. Doubtless, Agrippa knew a good deal about Christianity. His father had been responsible for the execution of the apostle James, and he was old enough to have some understanding of the situation surrounding that event. It seems entirely likely that in his involvement with the religious officials in Jerusalem, he had heard about Paul. With all of this in his background, he was probably eager to hear Paul.

Agrippa's Help Sought (23-27)

Herod Agrippa, accompanied by his sister Bernice, had his opportunity to hear Paul the next day. The event was more than just an ordinary legal hearing. It was conducted with all the pomp and pageantry characteristic of that age. The word here translated "pomp" (Acts 25:23) is the Greek word *phantasias* and was used to describe a showy display. It sometimes conveyed the idea of a parade, and this may have been the case here. Along with Agrippa and Bernice were Festus, high ranking officers (the word is *chiliarchs,* the leaders of a thousand soldiers), and leading citizens of the city. Probably, some of the leaders of the local synagogues were included among the leading citizens. When this impressive group was finally assembled, Paul was brought in.

Festus then stated the occasion for the meeting. This information was not for the benefit of Agrippa, who had already been made aware of the facts in the case, but for the Gentiles who were present in the assembly. Festus was guilty of rhetorical exaggeration when he stated that all the Jews cried out for Paul's life. But the Sanhedrin had made such a demand, and this was interpreted as the voice of the people. Festus went on to acknowledge that Paul had done nothing worthy of death, but would be sent to Rome because he had appealed to Caesar. Festus' problem was that he needed some specific charges to bring against Paul when he sent him to Rome. Festus knew that Paul was not guilty of any punishable offense and should have been freed. The only reason he hadn't freed Paul was that he didn't want to alienate the Jews. If he sent Paul to Rome without any charges, Festus knew that he would be leaving himself open to charges of incompetency.

CHAPTER TWENTY-SIX

Paul's Defense Before Agrippa

Acts 26

Paul's Story of His Life (26:1-22)

In the previous chapter, Paul had already made his defense before Festus. Since this hearing was not a trial in the legal sense, Paul felt free to speak more directly to King Agrippa. The account Paul gave of his life in this chapter is similar to the account he gave before the mob at the temple, but the tone is different because of the different circumstances. Because of some differences in the two accounts, some have challenged Luke's credibility as a historian. But the differences in details can readily be accounted for by the differences in audiences and circumstances. The inclusion of details that were more pertinent in one situation than in another does not mean that Luke didn't get his facts straight.

Paul's Introduction (1-3)

The closing verses of Acts 25 indicate that this hearing was primarily to allow Festus to gain information that he might use in presenting official charges against Paul when he was sent to Rome. Festus, not being a Jew, had found himself at a loss in trying to understand some of the theological charges that had been raised against Paul. His hope was that Agrippa, since he was familiar with the Jewish religion, could make some sense out of the charges. Thus, the hearing was turned over to Agrippa.

Even as he began his defense, Paul realized that nothing he said would lead to his immediate release. He had already appealed to Caesar, and Festus had indicated that he would go to Rome to stand before Caesar. Thus freed of the necessity of arguing to gain his freedom, Paul could make his appeal both more personal and in greater detail than he had been able to on the steps of the Tower of Antonia in chapter 22. Paul opened his speech with a gesture of the hand that seemed to have been characteristic of speakers of that day. Then he spoke directly to King Agrippa, indicating that he appreciated this opportunity because he knew that the king had a good understanding of the Jewish religion. This was not empty flattery that often characterizes the opening of similar speeches, but a fact based upon Agrippa's life and interests. Paul indicated that his defense would be rather detailed and asked Agrippa's patience in hearing him out.

Paul's Early Life (4-8)

The manner of Paul's early life was no secret. The Jews had known of it since his childhood (or more precisely, his youth), both in Tarsus and in Jerusalem after he came there to study. We conclude that Paul's life both as a child and as a teenager was so outstanding that he had gained the attention of his fellow countrymen. He had lived as a Pharisee, the strictest of the Jewish sects. (Some scholars may hold that the Essenes were stricter than the Pharisees, but the strictest of the Essenes lived in separate communities such as Qumran near the Dead Sea and were not much involved in public life.) The Pharisees attempted to live by the strictest dietary laws and ritualistic practices. Since the Sadducees refused to live by such restraints, there was almost constant friction between the two sects.

The Jews could find no flaw in his earlier life, but they did take violent issue with what he had been teaching as a Christian. Paul insisted that he had not been teaching anything that was not contained in the law. The Jews had looked forward to the blessed hope given to the fathers. That hope included the fact that God would bless the Jews and through them bless the whole world. Although the Old Testament does not contain many specific references to the resurrection, yet it was Paul's contention that this was at the very heart of the hope of the fathers. The irony of the situation was that Paul was being prosecuted by the Jews precisely for advocating the resurrection, a central doctrine of the Jewish hope. Certainly there was nothing incredible about the fact that God is able to raise the dead. Why, then, should Paul be persecuted for advocating this doctrine?

Paul's Zeal in Persecuting Christians (9-11)

Paul understood what motivated the Jews. A quarter of a century earlier, he had stood where they were standing. He had felt it his duty to persecute Christians. He had actively carried out this persecution in Jerusalem. The eighth chapter of Acts gives us some of the details of this persecution. In trying to impress Agrippa with the dramatic change he had experienced, he stressed his own involvement at every point in this persecution: "I too was convinced that I ought to . . . oppose the name . . . what I did in Jerusalem. . . . I put many of the saints in prison, and . . . cast my vote against them. . . . have them punished, and I tried to force them to blaspheme. In my obsession . . . I even went to foreign cities to persecute them" (Acts 26:9-11). In so doing, he was also confessing his own sin in this disgraceful activity. One strong argument for the truthfulness of the Bible is that it does not attempt to whitewash the reputation of its heroes.

With the authority of the chief priests, he had imprisoned many saints and had been responsible for the deaths of others. Although the Bible mentions only the death of Stephen, there is no good reason to doubt that others were martyred in Jerusalem. Although the Romans had to grant permission to the Jews before they could carry out the death penalty, this probably was not too difficult to obtain, given the unstable political conditions in Palestine in that day. His mention that he had cast his vote against Christians has led some to believe that he was a member of the Sanhedrin. However, he may have been using this expression figuratively, indicating that he had approved of the death sentence for them.

Paul also mentioned that he had tried to cause many of them to blaspheme, probably by trying to make them deny Christ. Whether he relied on verbal persuasion to accomplish this or whether he may have resorted to torture, he did not say. But given Paul's frame of mind at that time, it is quite possible that he would not have hesitated to use torture to destroy the church. One of the tragic facts of history is that religion has been the source of a great deal of persecution. Unfortunately, that kind of fanaticism is not a thing of the past, but still exists in the present world.

Paul's "obsession" against the Christians led him to leave Jerusalem and go to other cities to seek out the saints. (Acts 26:11—other translations put this more strongly. The King James Version says, "Being exceedingly mad against them"; the Revised Standard says, "In raging fury against them.") These "foreign cities" were cities where the authority of the Sanhedrin would have been respected. The only one mentioned in Acts is Damascus.

Paul's Damascus Road Experience (12-14)

Of course, Paul's mission to Damascus was never completed. Before he reached that city, he was brought face to face with the Lord. For the benefit of Agrippa, Paul then repeated this experience, which had already been related in Luke's record in chapters 9 and 22. Some bits of information are added in this account that were not included in the earlier two. For example, we are told that the Lord addressed Saul in Aramaic and that He quoted the proverb, "It is hard for you to kick against the goads" (Acts 26:14). A goad was a long sharpened stick used to guide an ox or spur him on if he began to lag. A goad was used as a weapon by one of the judges, Shamgar, against the Philistines (Judges 3:31). If an ox kicked or rebelled against the goad, its sharp point only wounded him more deeply. This rustic proverb suggests that Paul, even as he carried out his persecutions against Christians, was beginning to have some reservations about his actions. This led him to strike out all the more violently against them, but such violence only made the pain in his heart deeper.

Paul's Commission (15-18)

Paul had cried out, asking the identity of the Lord. The Lord had identified himself as "Jesus, whom you are persecuting" (Acts 26:15). In relating the incident to Agrippa, Paul condensed the account, not telling how he was ordered to go into Damascus nor mentioning Ananias. Instead, he told of the Lord's commission to him as it was delivered by Ananias. Paul was to become a servant and a witness. The Lord promised to rescue him from his own people. The Lord had fulfilled this promise on numerous occasions, although Paul had not always escaped unharmed from these attacks by the Jews. The Lord also promised to protect him from the Gentiles, a promise that had also been amply fulfilled on many occasions.

Paul's mission was to open people's eyes, to turn them from darkness to light and from Satan to God. The Scriptures often relate darkness with evil and Satan (Ephesians 6:12). On the other hand, God is associated with light. Paul's commission here reminds us of similar commissions God had given to Isaiah (6:8-13; 42:6-9), to Jeremiah (1:8), and to Ezekiel (2:1-7). Those who received the message were promised forgiveness of sin and a place among the sanctified. This sanctification, Paul emphasized, came by faith.

Paul's Commitment (19-23)

The Lord's wish was Paul's command. With the same kind of dedication that drove him to try to destroy the church, Paul immediately turned to building it. For Paul, there was no place for a casual commitment, for an insipid lukewarmness. He had to be all out, one way or another. The Heavenly vision of the risen Lord had convinced him of the truth of the resurrection. Now he was ready to commit his life to proclaiming that good news.

Almost as soon as he had emerged from the waters of baptism, Paul had begun to preach the message of salvation in Damascus and then in Jerusalem. There is a textual problem with the phrase "in all Judea" (Acts 26:20). When Paul returned from Damascus to Jerusalem, we have no record that at that time he preached any place but Jerusalem. He did have an opportunity later to preach in places in Judea, and this may have been what he had in mind. But beyond the Jews, he also carried the gospel to the Gentiles. This was Paul's special calling, and it was this activity that especially aroused the antagonism of the Jews.

The offer of salvation was on the same terms for both Jews and Gentiles. First of all, they must repent, that is, express such a sorrow for their sins that they would not repeat them. They were then to turn to God. Paul's statement here (Acts 26:20) resembles Peter's sermon recorded in the second chapter of Acts. If the two messages were parallel, the turning to God would be equivalent to being baptized. But Paul's message did not stop with repentance and baptism. The sincerity of the converts' commitment was to be tested by their lives. This was the burden of the words of John the Baptist: "Produce fruit in keeping with repentance" (Matthew 3:8). We are also reminded of the words of Jesus: "By their fruit you will recognize them" (Matthew 7:16).

It was Paul's proclamation of this message that caused the Jews to want to kill him. It was not until this point in his message (Acts 26:21) that Paul finally revealed to Agrippa just why he had been arrested. He had proclaimed the message of hope; and worse (from the Jewish point of view), he had proclaimed it to Gentiles. For this reason and for no other, they sought his life. The mob had tried to kill him in the temple court; a band of assassins had plotted to kill him as he was being brought to trial; and the Jewish leaders tried to have him brought back from Caesarea to Jerusalem to have him assassinated. But God had protected him, and thus he was able to bring his testimony before Agrippa.

Regardless of the charges of the Jews, Paul insisted that he had never said anything other than what the prophets and Moses had already said. That message was that Christ would suffer and die to be raised from the dead. It was at this point that the Jews took issue with Paul. Paul had been led to understand that the Suffering Servant of Isaiah 53 was the promised Messiah, a connection that the Jews had not made even after several hundred years. They had also failed to understand that the Messiah would proclaim light both to His own people and to the Gentiles (Isaiah 42:1-6). We can be sure that Paul knew the Old Testament passages that had Messianic content and undoubtedly had quoted them many times in his discussions with the Jews in their synagogues and wherever else he had had an opportunity to speak. In speaking to Jews, he had the advantage of being able to start with these Old Testament passages and lead them to see that Jesus fulfilled them. In addressing a Gentile audience, he did not have this advantage. Yet the Gentiles were often more receptive than the Jews. Why? We can only conclude that the Jews' very familiarity with the Scriptures had closed their eyes to their fuller meaning. Unfortunately, this affliction is not unique to Jews, but certainly can be experienced by Christians as well.

The Effects of Paul's Story (26:24-32)

The Effect Upon Festus (24-27)

Festus sat through the presentation, probably only partially comprehending the full import of what Paul was saying. First of all, he was unfamiliar with the Hebrew Scriptures; so Paul's reference to Moses and the prophets would carry no meaning for him. Further, we don't know what language Paul used in speaking to Agrippa, but it would have been either Greek or Aramaic, either of which would have been a second language to Festus. Thus, whatever Paul said had to pass through both a cultural and a linguistic filter before it got to Festus. We should not then be surprised at his response to Paul.

Festus very shortly had recognized that Paul was a man of great learning. Yet he could not understand how a man so learned could so earnestly hold to views that seemed like theological hairsplitting, especially when holding those views had so alienated him from his own people. Festus could only conclude that all of Paul's studies had left him bereft of his wits—he was insane. How many times in the intervening centuries have other Christians heard this same charge! From the world's point of view one has to be mad to hold to his faith when facing the arena or the stake. One has to be mad to sacrifice his own possessions that others may be helped. One has to be mad to leave friends and family and journey to some distant and difficult land to carry the message of salvation to strangers. Mad? Only by the world's standards, and those standards are only temporary. In the words of the martyred missionary, Jim Elliot, "No man is a fool who gives up that which he cannot keep to gain that which he cannot lose."

Paul calmly denied the charge that he was mad. Certainly nothing about his conduct gave any basis for the charge. What Paul had proclaimed was "true and reasonable" (Acts 26:25). The word translated "reasonable" was often used by Greek writers to describe one who was level-headed and sensible, just the opposite of one who was mad. But Paul did not rely upon his own testimony to convince Festus. Instead, he appealed to Agrippa. Paul could assert with assurance that Agrippa knew about Christianity and at least its basic teachings. By this time, Christians were numerous enough in the king's realm that he certainly must have been aware of them. Though Christians had often been forced by their persecutors to meet secretly and out of the public's eye, there were still too many Christians for the movement to be totally hidden. Paul then aimed a question directly at Agrippa: "Do you believe the prophets?" (Acts 26:27). Paul did not wait for an answer but replied to his own question: "I know you do." Perhaps in the course of the hearing, something that Agrippa had said led Paul to believe that the king did believe in the Old Testament prophets. Of course, it was quite possible to believe in the prophets and still not understand or accept the fact that they pointed to Jesus as the Messiah. Apparently this was the case with Agrippa.

The Effects on Agrippa (28, 29)

King Agrippa was put in an uncomfortable position. If he denied that he believed the prophets, he would offend the pious Jews. If, on the other hand, he affirmed that he believed the prophets, then he would have to give a reason why he did not accept the teachings of the prophets: that Jesus was the Messiah. In his response, the king tried to avoid the dilemma by refusing to answer the question directly. His response has been variously interpreted. The New International Version turns it aside with a sneer: "Do you think that in such a short time you can persuade me to be a Christian?" The New American Standard Bible, however, portrays him as seriously considering Paul's appeal: "In a short time you will persuade me to become a Christian." We have no clue about his facial expression or the inflection of his voice when he made his reply. Had we been there and seen and heard him, we would better know the intent of his reply.

Regardless of Agrippa's intentions, Paul was not ready to give up. He made one last appeal to the king. Whether it took a short time or a long time, Paul was willing to try to persuade not only Agrippa but everyone who heard him to become a Christian. What started out to be a hearing of Paul's case, ends up with Paul's making an evangelistic appeal to his judges.

The Conclusion of the Hearing (30-32)

At this point, Agrippa arose, signaling that the hearing was over. Perhaps he was afraid to listen any further to Paul lest he be persuaded to become a Christian. Bernice and Festus accompanied him as he left the room. As they talked among themselves, they quickly concluded that the charges against Paul were baseless. He had done nothing worthy of imprisonment, much less death. Agrippa concluded that if Paul had not appealed to Caesar, he would have been set free. The truth is, Festus could have freed him had he so chosen. But Festus did not have to make this decision, which must have been a relief to him, for Festus would certainly have offended the Jews had he set Paul free. Festus, like Pilate many years before him, chose to allow an innocent man to suffer in order to save his own hide. But as it turned out, this was God's way of insuring that Paul would get to Rome.

CHAPTER TWENTY-SEVEN

Heading for Rome

Acts 27

From Caesarea to Crete (27:1-12)

F. F. Bruce calls Luke's account of the voyage and shipwreck "a small classic in its own right, as graphic a piece of descriptive writing as anything in the Bible." Luke describes the details so vividly that we can almost see the ship bobbing helplessly before the storm, hear the howl of the wind and the crashing of waves across the ship's deck, and feel the pitching of the deck beneath our feet.

This chapter of Acts also gives us some new insights into the character of Paul. In earlier chapters, we have seen Paul as a preacher, a teacher, and a theologian. We have seen him fearlessly face angry mobs and stand calmly before governors and kings. Here we see him as a practical man giving sound advice and encouragement in a difficult situation.

We may wonder why Luke wrote such a detailed account of this voyage. Paul had experienced difficult voyages before and had even been shipwrecked (2 Corinthians 11:25) prior to this trip. Perhaps the Holy Spirit, speaking through Luke, wanted us to see God's providential care of Paul in fulfilling His promise to see him safely to Rome.

Boarding the Ship at Caesarea (1, 2)

Acts 27:1 begins another of the "we passages" in Acts, indicating that Luke accompanied Paul on this trip. The last time that Luke had included himself in the narrative was in Acts 21:18, just before Paul's arrest in the temple. He gives us no clue about where he was or what he was doing during Paul's long imprisonment in Caesarea. It is reasonable to suppose that he was never far from Paul during this time, ministering to his needs and visiting in nearby churches. Many believe that he was doing research and

269

gathering material for the Gospel that bears his name. It is possible that he may even have begun to write it during this period.

Paul was detained in prison in Caesarea until transportation could be found to Rome. Not many ships would be sailing directly from Caesarea to Rome; so another route had to be found. When the time to depart had come, Paul and several other prisoners were placed under the control of a centurion named Julius. Whether these were persons who, as Paul, had appealed their cases to Caesar, or whether they were common prisoners already convicted and being sent to Rome to appear in the arena, we are not told. Some believe that Julius belonged to a special group of soldiers who served as couriers across the empire. According to this line of reasoning, he had accompanied Festus from Rome to Caesarea and remained with him as something of an honor guard until he was installed in office. Now he was returning to Rome, taking with him some prisoners.

The ship they boarded was from Adramyttium, a port in the Roman province of Asia (modern Asia Minor), not far from ancient Troas. This was probably not a large vessel, and it sailed along the coast of Syria and Asia Minor, never getting far out of the sight of land. Accompanying Paul and Luke was Aristarchus, a Christian from Thessalonica. He was previously mentioned in Acts 19:29. He, along with Gaius, was seized by the rioting mob in Ephesus. He also had been with Paul when he returned from his third missionary journey to Jerusalem (Acts 20:4). Aristarchus is mentioned in Philemon 24 and in Colossians 4:10, where he is described by Paul as "my fellow prisoner." Since these two epistles were written during Paul's imprisonment in Rome, it would seem that Aristarchus accompanied Paul all the way to Rome and shared his imprisonment with him or at least ministered to him during that period.

The Arrival at Crete (3-8)

After leaving Caesarea, the ship touched first at Sidon, some seventy miles up the coast. There, out of his kindness, Julius allowed Paul to go ashore (accompanied, no doubt, by a guard) and visit some of his friends. It is likely that these friends were members of the church at Sidon. While we have no direct reference to a church's having been established there, it may very well have been founded after the persecution following the death of Stephen (Acts 11:19).

When they set sail again, they were forced to sail east and north of Cyprus. The more direct route would have been to sail south of Cyprus, but the prevailing winds that time of the year were from the west and the northwest. Sailing around Cyprus as they did made their voyage longer, but they had a better chance of picking up favorable winds. Once they had passed Cyprus, they had to sail across a stretch of open water. By staying close to the coast of Cilicia and Pamphylia, they were able to take advantage of the land breezes and a favorable current that flows in a westward direction. This brought them to Myra in Lycia.

The ship Paul and his party were on was probably going to continue up the coast of Asia to Adramyttium. Had they stayed on this ship, they would probably have secured passage over to Neapolis. There they could have taken the Egnatian Way across Macedonia, crossed over the Adriatic, and then walked the Appian Way to Rome. However, if the party could find a ship going to Rome, the trip would take less time, and it certainly would have been less tiring on the centurion, his soldiers, and the prisoners. At Myra, they were able to find a grain ship from Alexandria on its way to Rome; so Julius arranged for himself, his soldiers, and the prisoners to take passage on this ship.

Rome imported much of her wheat from Egypt, and since the supply of grain was so vital to Rome, the fleet that provided this service was supervised by the government. Julius would have no difficulty securing passage on such a ship. Since the westerly winds made it difficult to sail directly to Rome from Alexandria, the ship had sailed north from Egypt, and then planned to work its way westward, passing south of Greece and coming to Sicily. Leaving Myra, the ship headed for Cnidus, a port at the southwest corner of Asia Minor. An unfavorable wind made slow going. Coming to Cnidus, they had a decision to make. They might have put in at the large harbort at Cnidus and waited for a more favorable wind, or they could push on, hoping that the wind would change even as they attempted to sail almost directly into it.

They chose the latter course, and as a result were forced to sail to the east of Crete. Then, sailing to the lee of the island, they made their way westward, coming to Fair Havens.

Paul's Warning (9-12)

At this point, those in charge of the ship had to make some difficult decisions. The season was late, after the Fast, Luke tells us. This was the Day of Atonement, an important Jewish feast that came in late September or in October. Thus, they were well into the dangerous sailing period. The ship might have wintered at Fair Havens, but the harbor was small, and the nearest town was two hours' walk away. Thus the pilot and the owner of the ship preferred to try to reach Phoenix to the west and winter there. Paul's counsel was to remain at Fair Havens for the winter. Whether he spoke through the leading of the Holy Spirit or whether he spoke out of his long experience in that part of the Mediterranean we are not told. The centurion, because he was the ranking officer on board, chose to reject Paul's advice and follow the advice of the shipowner. He was not long in regretting this decision.

Caught in a Storm (27:13-26)

The decision to leave Fair Havens and seek shelter for the winter in Phoenix was a fateful one. Little did those aboard the ship realize what was in store for them. In seeking to trade safety for convenience, they lost the ship and, but for the grace of God, would have lost their lives. This serves as a sharp reminder that our decisions also have consequences. Just as those ancient travelers ran into difficulties when they rejected sound advice, so may we also. Let us remember this when we are tempted to trade the safety of God's fold for the temporary conveniences or pleasures of the world.

Driven by the Storm (13-20)

Once they had made their decision, good fortune seemed to smile upon them. A gentle south wind began to blow, which would have made sailing around Cape Matala and westward and northward to Phoenix an easy day's sail. The comparative calm of the sea after the previous storm must have reassured them that they had made the right decision. But they were scarcely out of the harbor before the situation dramatically changed. In similar fashion, temptations come in a pleasant form to entice us to pursue bad advice. With a suddenness that was characteristic of the Mediterranean that time of the year, the gentle south wind became a tempestuous wind from the northeast, known by the sailors as Euraquilo.

Once the storm struck, the ship was helpless before it. There was no way that they could make Phoenix, and they were driven south and west. Their route took them to the south of the small island of Cauda. While they were in the lee of that island, they were able to make the lifeboat secure. This was a small open boat that in calm weather was usually towed behind the ship. The storm had struck so swiftly that they had not been able to bring it on board. The storm had probably swamped the boat, and so it was with great difficulty that they were able to bring it aboard. Luke used the pronoun "we" (Acts 27:16), indicating that perhaps he himself had acquired some blisters and sore muscles in the process.

Even with the lifeboat securely on board, their problems were not over by any means. Once they had passed the island of Cauda, the ship was again helplessly driven by the storm. To strengthen the hull of the ship, ropes were passed under it and tightened, thus giving added support to the timbers being pounded by the growing waves. Their next worry was the sandbars of Syrtis. We now know this as the gulf of Sidra off the coast of Libya. In places in this gulf, the water is shallow and filled with treacherous and shifting sandbars. A ship caught on one of these sandbars would quickly be broken to pieces by the storm. Among ancient sailors, this body of water had the reputation of being the graveyard of the Mediterranean. To try to keep the ship from being driven in that direction, the sailors lowered the sea anchor. By slowing the speed of the ship, they hoped that the storm would abate before they reached the dreaded Syrtis.

But this effort still did not protect the ship from a severe battering by the high winds. They next sought to lighten the ship by throwing overboard anything that could be spared. This apparently was some of the heavy cargo on the top deck, but not the grain cargo, which was finally jettisoned just before the ship ran aground (Acts 27:38). When even this did not improve the situation, some of the ship's tackle was thrown overboard. The storm continued, and the heavy clouds kept the sun and stars obscured. Sailors in those days lacked even the simplest navigational instruments such as the magnetic compass or sextant; and so their navigation depended entirely upon their use of the heavenly bodies. Since they did not know where they were nor in what direction they were being driven, they were completely at the mercy of the storm. As a result, they gave up all hope of being saved. Luke uses "we" in this passage, indicating that he shared the pessimism expressed by the other passengers (Acts 27:20).

Paul's Words of Encouragement (21-26)

During the battle against the storm, the sailors and passengers had gone without food for a long time. They had certainly had some food during this time, but with the ship pitching and tossing, the preparation of regular meals would have been impossible. Such a violent storm could also have brought on seasickness and would leave many without appetites. In this desperate situation, Paul arose to speak. He reminded them of his advice not to sail from Crete. This was not an attempt to say, "I told you so." Paul's purpose in recalling his earlier advice was so that they would believe what he was about to tell them now. His words would enhance his credibility as an expert. And what he was about to tell them was such good news that in their present hopeless condition he needed all the credibility he could find.

His first words were for them to take courage. They needed this. They were physically weakened by the lack of food, and the continuing storm had sapped their morale. They needed to be encouraged so that they could act effectively when the time came for action. The first piece of good news was that not one of the 276 aboard the ship (Acts 27:37) would be lost. Only the ship and its cargo would be destroyed. This was not a wild, hopelessly optimistic statement. It was based on the most solid of all assurances. Almighty God, who made the wind and the waves, had through an angel who appeared during the night, given Paul these assurances. Much earlier, God had promised Paul that he would stand before Caesar in Rome. In this difficult situation, God had reaffirmed His promise. In the quarter of a century that Paul had served God, his many experiences of God's loving watch care had left no doubt that God would also see him through this trial. Not only would God save Paul, but out of His grace, He would also spare all those who sailed with Paul. Paul's calm assurance that things would happen just as he told them certainly must have been reassuring to everyone else on the ship. The one bit of bad news was that the ship would run aground and be lost.

Shipwrecked on Malta (27:27-44)

The closing verses of this chapter in Acts tell of the harrowing experiences of those on board the ship as they approached land. The successful escape of everyone from the ship certainly established the credibility of Paul. No doubt, on the remainder of the trip to Rome, people were more inclined to listen when he spoke.

274

The Sailors' Attempt to Abandon the Ship (27-32)

For fourteen days, the ship had withstood the battering of the storm, being driven across the Adriatic Sea. This was not the body of water between Italy and the Balkan Peninsula that we now call the Adriatic. It was, instead, that portion of the Mediterranean that lay between Crete and Sicily. The sailors sensed that they were nearing land, perhaps because they could hear breakers in the distance even though in the darkness they could not see the land. The sailors immediately took soundings and found that the water was one hundred twenty feet deep. A short time later, another sounding indicated that the water depth was only ninety feet deep. The sailors knew that the ship was rapidly approaching land and began to fear that the ship would run aground on the rocky shore. To keep the ship from running aground, they dropped four anchors astern. Usually anchors were dropped from the prow of a ship, but with the wind still blowing them, this would have allowed the stern to swing around toward the land. If they did have to beach the ship, it was much better to go in prow first rather than stern first. Then they prayed for daylight.

The cowardly sailors, concerned for their own safety, plotted to escape from the ship in the lifeboat. It mattered not to them in this crisis that they were violating a rule of the sea that the sailors were to see to the safety of the passengers before they looked to their own safety. Luke does not indicate that the captain or the shipowner were involved in this attempt. Since it was undertaken under the cover of darkness, it may well be that the officers of the ship were not involved. When Paul saw what was happening, he alerted Julius. The soldiers leaped into action, cutting away the lines that held the lifeboat, letting it fall into the water. We wonder why they didn't order the sailors to bring the boat back aboard, since it could have been useful when they finally had to abandon the ship. But had the boat been aboard, it would have been a continuing temptation for the sailors to try to escape again. Both Paul and the centurion knew that the sailors' skilled hands were needed if the passengers were to reach land safely.

Paul's Words of Hope (33-38)

The wait through the long night must have been an agonizing one for those on board the ship. Though they knew that they were close to land, they had no idea what daylight might bring. At this point, Paul once more offered sound advice. By this time when

Paul spoke, most of the passengers would listen to him. His personal courage and his words of hope had won him the respect of both the soldiers and the sailors. Since they had eaten very little for the past two weeks, he urged them to eat. They would need the extra energy the food would supply. If they followed his advice, they would not lose a single hair from their heads, a proverbial expression that was sometimes used in the Scriptures (1 Samuel 14:45; Luke 21:18).

Then Paul set an example for these that none would misunderstand. Taking some bread, he gave thanks to God for it, broke it, and began to eat. In this simple action, Paul preached an eloquent sermon. With exception of Paul and his traveling companions, everyone else on board was a pagan. We have no doubt that during the storm, they had prayed to their pagan gods, but Paul's actions indicated that it was the God he worshiped that had brought them safely through the worst of the storm. With this encouragement, they all began to take food and eat. For the first time, we learn that there were 276 persons aboard (Acts 27:37). Perhaps Luke counted them to make sure that there was food enough for everyone. Some manuscripts indicate that there were only seventy-six persons aboard, but the evidence favors the larger number. This was not an unusually large number of passengers for ships plying those waters. Josephus writes of a ship carrying six hundred passengers that was wrecked in the same general part of the Mediterranean.

Once they had finished their meal, they had another task to complete. They needed to lighten the ship so that they could run the ship aground as close to the shore as possible. To do this, they began to throw the cargo of grain into the sea. It is likely that the ship had taken on water during the storm, and much of the cargo had probably become soaked and thus spoiled. There was certainly no point in trying to save it.

When daylight finally came, they were able to see the land, but no one was able to recognize it. However, they could see an inlet with a sandy beach, which would afford them the best opportunity for beaching the vessel. To prepare for the run to the beach, they cut loose the four anchors that had been dropped from the stern and untied the ropes that held the two paddles, one on each side of the ship, that served as rudders. Then they hoisted the foresail. Apparently the main sail had been lost or thrown overboard earlier. The foresail was used primarily to steer the vessel under normal conditions. However, it could be used to propel the ship forward, but at a slow enough rate of speed as to leave it manageable. The plan was a good one, but as the ship moved toward the beach, it struck a hidden sandbar. The bow of the ship was stuck fast in the mud and sand while the stern was exposed to the pounding of the waves, a precarious position to say the least. Even a modern steel ship would soon suffer severe damage under similar conditions.

The soldiers quickly sized up the situation and proposed to act. They wanted to kill the prisoners lest they escape. The Roman law was quite severe in regard to those in charge of prisoners. If a prisoner escaped, those in charge had to take his place. The actions of the Philippian jailer when he thought the prisoners had escaped illustrated this (Acts 16:27). Since the prisoners other than Paul were probably under the death penalty and were being taken to Rome either to be executed or to appear in the arena, the soldiers were not going to take any chances. It mattered not to them that Paul had not even been convicted of any crime. Just as the sailors earlier had tried to save their own lives by escaping in the lifeboat, so the soldiers now acted out of their own selfish concern. But the centurion took charge and immediately put a hold to their plan. It is obvious that he had grown to respect Paul very greatly and realized that the lives of everyone on board had been spared because of Paul.

He then ordered the passengers to use an orderly procedure in evacuating the ship. Those who could swim were to jump overboard first and swim to the shore. The others who could not swim were to float in to the shore on planks and other pieces of the ship, which was already breaking apart. As a result, everyone reached land safely.

JOURNEY TO ROME

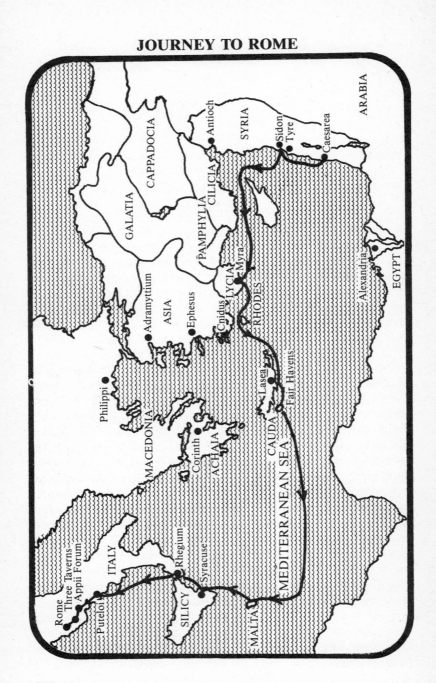

CHAPTER TWENTY-EIGHT

Rome at Last

Acts 28

Hospitality of the Maltese (28:1-10)

God's providential care for Paul and those who traveled with him did not end when they reached land. As a result of the rain and cold, the survivors still faced a difficult time. Exhausted as they were and exposed to the raw elements, they might very well have succumbed to shock or hypothermia. But God had already made provisions for their needs, using the friendly Maltese to minister to them.

Paul Bitten by a Snake (1-6)

Not until the party had struggled safely ashore did they realize that they had landed on the island of Malta. The sailors may have finally recognized the terrain or they may have gained this information from the islanders themselves. Malta, located about sixty miles south of Sicily, has an area of about ninety-five square miles. It was settled by the Phoenicians, probably between 1000 and 800 B.C. The British seized the island from Napoleon in 1800 and controlled it until 1960, when it was granted independence. Its strategic position made it a vital British base in World War II. The traditional place of Paul's landing bears the name of Saint Paul's Bay, and from the description we have from Acts, there is no good reason to doubt that the landing occurred in this area.

Luke comments favorably on the "unusual kindness" of the islanders (Acts 28:2). The King James Version calls these people "barbarous," which might lead us to believe that they were some kind of uneducated savages. But the Greek term is one used for anyone who did not speak Greek or some other widely-spoken language. The Maltese language retained many elements of the ancient Phoenician language. Even to this day, their vernacular reflects their ancient origins. The kind reception they gave the survivors indicates that they were not savages. It is likely that some of them sighted the ship in distress and alerted others to prepare for the survivors who were struggling to get safely ashore. They quickly built a large fire to help dry out the survivors. Since it was raining, the fire must have been built in some kind of a shelter, although finding a shelter large enough to accommodate 276 persons may not have been easy. The survivors must have assisted the natives in gathering fuel for the fire. Paul did not use either his age or his position to exempt himself from this menial task. During his whole career, Paul had never been reluctant to engage in physical labor, an example that we might very well follow today. But as Paul gathered a bundle of sticks and placed them on the fire, a snake, aroused from its torpor, struck him on his hand and, with its fangs penetrating deeply into his flesh, clung to him. The word *viper* (Acts 28:3) indicates that it was a poisonous snake. The response of the natives indicated that they thought it was a deadly snake, for they expected Paul to drop dead, or at least for his hand to swell up (Acts 28:4, 6). Today, there are no poisonous snakes on Malta, but the dense population has, no doubt, led to their extinction.

The islanders had a ready response to the snakebite. It seemed obvious to them that Paul was some kind of a vicious murderer, who, although he had escaped from the sea, was not to escape justice. Many ancients believed that a person who had committed a particularly heinous crime would be pursued and punished by the Goddess Nike, who was the personification of justice. Thus the translators have capitalized the word *Justice* in Acts 28:4. When Paul didn't show any ill effects from the snakebite, the people quickly changed their mind about the situation. If Paul was not a criminal, then he most certainly was some kind of a god. In Lystra, Paul had just the opposite experience. At first, he and Barnabas were acclaimed as gods, but before long, his teaching aroused so much opposition that he was stoned and left for dead (Acts 14:11-19).

Many Healed Through Paul (7-10)

We are not told the details about how the islanders provided for the survivors. It must have placed no small burden upon them to care for nearly three hundred unannounced visitors for a period of several weeks. Luke does mention the hospitality that was extended to Paul and his party by Publius, the chief official of the island. The father of Publius was seriously ill, suffering from fever and dysentery. Some think that the man may have been suffering from Malta fever, which we now recognize as a form of brucellosis or undulant fever. Through the centuries, many people on the island have suffered from it. It is contracted through drinking unpasteurized milk or improperly cooked meat products from goats and cows. Paul visited the man, placed his hands upon him, and prayed. Instantly, the man was healed.

The word of this healing spread rapidly across the small island, and soon others were brought to Paul for healing. Luke does not mention Paul's doing any teaching or preaching during his stay on Malta, but it is hard to imagine Paul's conducting all these healings without mentioning the name of Jesus. There is a tradition that Publius later became the first bishop of the church on Malta, but there is no historical evidence for this.

Paul and his party were honored in many ways. Some of these honors were verbal, but Luke also indicates that the people honored them with material things. They took care of their needs during their stay on the island, and when they were ready to sail to Rome, the islanders provided them the supplies they needed for their journey. When the survivors of the shipwreck had suddenly arrived on the island, the islanders had graciously cared for them. Their kindness had been repaid with many healings and with the opportunity to hear the gospel. Now, out of their gratitude, they once more showered their gifts upon Paul and his party. Kindness begets kindness, and blessings bring renewed blessings, an ancient truth that still applies today.

On to Rome (Acts 28:11-29)

God seems never to be in a hurry to accomplish His purposes. The shipwreck and three-month delay did not alter God's plan to see Paul in Rome; it only changed the schedule a bit. Though Paul kept busy on Malta healing, teaching, and preaching, he must have had some thoughts about what the future held for him. He was eager to see Rome, but at the same time, he must have felt a bit of anxiety about what would happen when he stood in Caesar's court.

Arrival at Rome (11-16)

Paul and his party remained on Malta for three months, the winter months that were not considered safe for sailing. The

281

shipping season in that part of the Mediterranean usually began late in February or early in March. Ships sailing close to the coast might begin even earlier. Another grain ship from Alexandria had spent the winter there, perhaps seeking shelter from the same storm that had left Paul's ship wrecked. Since this was another grain ship in the service of the Roman government, the centurion would be able to take passage on it for his soldiers and his prisoners. In an interesting aside, Luke informs us that the ship bore the figurehead of the twins, Castor and Pollux. These gods were the patrons of sailors. Luke's mention of them reminds us that in the pagan world of the first century, Christians were surrounded on every side by emblems of pagan faiths.

Sailing north, the ship stopped at Syracuse on the eastern end of Sicily. After spending three days there, probably waiting for favorable winds, they sailed on northward, stopping at Rhegium, a port located on the toe of the Italian boot. Some translations indicate that on the voyage from Syracuse to Rhegium, unfavorable winds forced them to take a rather circuitous route. Such unfavorable winds made it quite dangerous to try to navigate the narrow Strait of Messina. They put in at Rhegium to await better sailing conditions, but their stay was short. The very next day, a south wind sprang up, which made for easy sailing up the Italian coast. On the following day, they reached Puteoli, located on the bay of Naples. Although Puteoli was several miles from Rome, its deep harbor made it a favorite port for the heavy-laden Alexandrian grain ships. As they sailed into the bay, they would have a view of Mount Vesuvius. Little did they know that within two decades, it would violently erupt, spewing death and destruction down its slopes.

At Puteoli, they found some brethren. This should not come as a surprise. Puteoli was a port city with a cosmopolitan population. Many travelers from the East would pass through the city on their way to Rome. Some of these may have been Christian businessmen who carried their faith as well as their business wherever they went. Luke does not tell us why they were able to visit with the brethren for a week. It is not likely that the centurion would have been willing to delay his trip on to Rome just to allow Paul the opportunity for this visit. After the seven days, they resumed their travel toward Rome, going afoot this time.

The delay at Puteoli had allowed Christians there to send word on ahead to Rome about Paul's anticipated arrival there. But the brethren in Rome were not content to await his arrival. Instead, they set out from Rome to meet him. One group met him at the Forum of Appius, about forty-three miles from Rome. The other party met him at Three Taverns, about thirty-three miles from Rome. Paul may have been a bit apprehensive about how the church in Rome would receive him. He had been a center of controversy for years and was now arriving in their city in chains. But any doubts he might have had were quickly dispelled by this show of respect and affection. As a result, Paul thanked God and took courage.

Rome at last! Luke states it very simply, not even trying to tell us all of the emotions that Paul must have experienced upon his arrival. At Rome, he would meet friends he had known across the years, friends who had been mentioned in his epistle to the Roman church. At Rome, he would have the opportunity to proclaim the gospel in the very heart of the Roman Empire, something he had longed to do for years. We assume that once he arrived in Rome, Paul was turned over to the proper officials. But he was not confined to prison. Instead, he was allowed to live in his own rented quarters. He was under house arrest with a soldier to guard him at all times. While he was restricted in his movements, he could have visitors and could teach any who came to visit him.

Paul Preaches to the Jews (17-29)

Paul had already met many of the leaders of the church at Rome as they traveled the Appian Way with him. It may also be that during the three days mentioned in Acts 28:17, Paul met with the church, visiting and teaching. Then he turned to the leaders of the Jews. In so doing, Paul carried out his long-standing practice of going to the Jews before he turned to the Gentiles. Paul felt it necessary to explain to the Jewish leaders why he was in chains. He insisted he had done nothing contrary to Jewish law or customs; yet he had been seized and turned over to the Romans. He avoided being critical of the Jews in Jerusalem; so he did not mention that they tried to lynch him. He explained that the Romans had examined him and had found him guilty of no crime worthy of death. He indicated that the Romans had even sought to release him, perhaps referring to the statement of Festus, who clearly did not believe that Paul was guilty of any crime.

However, the Jews had made it plain to the Romans that they did not want Paul released. They wanted to bring him from

Caesarea to Jerusalem for trial. Some even hoped that along the way they might find a way to assassinate him. It would seem that Paul was trying to avoid offending the Roman Jews; so he did not mention their assassination plot. To avoid having to go to Jerusalem, Paul had appealed to Caesar. Once Paul had informed the Roman Jews about the reason for his being in Rome in chains, he went on to point out he was being persecuted because he had faithfully held to the true hope of Israel. That true hope was the promised Messiah fulfilled in Jesus of Nazareth.

But the Jews in Rome had heard nothing from Judea about Paul. That really should not have been surprising. Anyone coming from Judea to Rome and leaving after Paul would have been caught in the same storm and would have had to winter over in some port before reaching Rome. Even though Paul and his party had spent some time along the way between Puteoli and Rome, it is not likely that someone from Judea would have overtaken them. Further, it does not seem that the Jews even tried to send any official communications to Rome about Paul. They had failed before two Roman governors to get him convicted. The likelihood of getting a conviction at the hands of a court in Rome was quite remote.

They had heard nothing bad about Paul and were willing to hear his views. They were familiar with Christianity, which they identified as a "sect" everywhere spoken against (Acts 28:22). It is quite likely that they also knew about the Christians in Rome.

A date was set when they would gather to hear Paul. Since he was under house arrest, they had to come to his house. The terms of his arrest did not prevent him from having visitors, even in large numbers. On this occasion, Paul did not preach a twenty-minute sermonette. From morning until evening, Paul opened the Scriptures to them, explaining to them the kingdom of God. The response to Paul's teaching was similar to the response he had received so many times before when he had taught in the synagogues. Some were convinced and others remained unpersuaded. Apparently, there was considerable discussion back and forth among themselves. Paul's parting words, drawn from Isaiah 6:9, 10, were aimed at those who had closed their minds to the truth. Jesus had quoted this same passage from Isaiah as a reason for His speaking in parables (Matthew 13:13-15). These were the words that God had spoken to Isaiah after the prophet's vision in the temple when he had been cleansed and then sent to preach to his people. The people of ancient Israel had hardened their hearts against God's truth, and some of the Jews to whom Paul was speaking were doing the same thing.

Throughout his ministry, Paul had brought the gospel to the Jews first. When they had rejected it, then he had turned to the Gentiles. Since many of the Roman Jews had rejected the good news, Paul then was free to go to the Gentiles. As the Jews closed the door to the message of salvation, they were opening it to the Gentiles. Since some of the Jews gave Paul a favorable hearing, we would like to believe that he had other opportunities to preach to them, but Luke leaves us in the dark about this matter.

Conclusion of Acts (28:30, 31)

Luke summarizes the two years of Paul's first Roman imprisonment in two brief verses. But the brevity of Luke's account should not lead one to suppose that these were years of inactivity. During this two-year period, Paul was allowed to live in his own rented house, which was more likely an apartment than a house. A soldier would be guarding him all this time. Why Luke ended his narrative after two years had passed without telling us the outcome of Paul's imprisonment we do not know, but several reasons have been suggested. One suggestion was that Paul's accusers had two years during which they might press charges. But since no charges were presented, he was automatically freed at the end of the two years. Another possibility is that Luke completed his treatise to Theophilus before a final disposition had been made of Paul's case. Still another suggestion, but a rather unlikely one, is that Paul was martyred at the end of the two years, but Luke could not bring himself to write about it.

Even though Paul could not go to the synagogue or the church for worship or any other public place, for that matter, he did not allow these restrictions to keep him from preaching and teaching. Paul both preached—that is, proclaimed the good news of God's salvation through Christ—and taught—leading Christians to a more mature life in Him. A steady stream of visitors frequented his apartment. The change of guards each day brought Paul further opportunities for witnessing, opportunities that may have infected the Praetorian Guard with the faith (Philippians 1:13).

Nor was Paul's witnessing confined just to the spoken word. His pen was as busy as his tongue. During this first Roman imprisonment, Paul wrote the so-called prison epistles: Ephesians,

Philippians, Colossians, and Philemon. Many of his friends and co-workers are mentioned in these letters, indicating that they had visited him during this period: Luke (Colossians 4:14), Timothy (Philippians 1:1; Colossians 1:1; Philemon 1:1), Mark (Colossians 4:10), and several others. It was also during this period that Paul met the runaway slave Onesimus and sent him back to his master Philemon.

The closing verse, "Boldly and without hindrance he preached the kingdom of God and taught about the Lord Jesus Christ," would have made a most appropriate epitaph if a headstone had been erected over Paul's grave. For that matter, these words should be a description of every Christian's life.